SUPER
STOCKS

SUPER STOCKS

Kenneth L. Fisher

IRWIN
Professional Publishing®
Chicago • London • Singapore

Library of Congress Cataloging-in-Publication Data

Fisher, Kenneth L.
    Super stocks/Kenneth L. Fisher.— Burr Ridge, Illinois:
IRWIN Professional Publishing, c1984.
    xviii, 248 p. : ill. ; 24 cm.
    Includes index.
    ISBN 0–87094–552–1   ISBN 1–55623–384–1 (pb)

    1. Stocks   2. Corporations—Valuation.   3. Investment analysis.
    I. Title.
HG4661.F48   1984   332.63′22—dc19   84–70258
                                         AACR 2   MARC
    Library of Congress

Printed in the United States of America

    7 8 9 0 MP 7 6 5

To my Mother and Father, who in
so many ways stimulated the events
which made this book possible.
Thanks.

Preface

This book contains powerful new ideas—coupled with variations on some old ones. Over the years they have given me tremendous faith in the investment path I follow. With them you too may develop greater faith in your investment path. Faith is a tremendous power because, among other things, it allows you to act when others are frozen. It is essential to investment success.

Most investment books rehash the same old stuff. Why is this book different from the rest?

This Book Offers Concepts Never Before Presented

Among these concepts are easily implemented yet sophisticated and powerful *new methods* for valuing stocks. They will help you avoid investment mistakes and seek opportunities for spectacular profits. They are tailored for the professional or interested (even if relatively inexperienced) amateur. These new methods are demonstrated within the context of their use in the pursuit of "Super Stocks." A Super Stock is defined to be both:

> A stock which increases 3 to 10 times in value in three to five years from its initial purchase.

>The stock of a Super Company bought at a price appropriate to an inferior company.

A Super Stock generates long-term rates of return between 25 and 100 percent per year. Few stocks perform this well for long. Those that do have certain traits in common. This book covers those traits and how to identify them. To invest in Super Stocks successfully, you need to understand four distinct subjects:

>A phenomenon I call the "glitch."

>New and powerful (yet easily used) methods to determine how much to pay for a stock.

>What distinguishes a Super Company from more common businesses.

>A process of "dynamics" that allows you to identify and act on these opportunities in the day-to-day world.

Anyone can sidestep pitfalls that regularly befoul most professional investors. Avoiding mistakes is just a start. By learning a few principles, you will understand the steps to a staircase of investment success. These principles provide a simple discipline enabling you to outperform most professionals. They can provide professionals a rigorous basis upon which to operate.

Can it really be done? Is it hard? Successful implementation does not require exceptional intelligence or access to inside tips. Anyone can employ these principles successfully at least on a limited scale. Is it worth it?

Consider the results. In early 1981, I purchased for my clients and myself approximately 1.5 percent of the total common shares of Verbatim Corporation, a producer of flexible diskettes used in small computer systems. At the time, virtually everyone I could find on Wall Street thought I had absolutely lost my mind. If one were to invest in diskettes, they all said, invest in Dysan Corporation. Dysan was supposed to have the best technology and management.

The word was Verbatim had bad management, bad technology, and bad products. The popular consensus held it was financially unstable and had a very hard road to hoe ahead of it. Some even implied it might not survive.

Two years later Verbatim stock was up over 15 times my original cost. Verbatim became popular, at higher prices, with everyone from *Value Line* to many major brokerage firms and banks.

What happened to make Verbatim—of whom so many thought so little—increase in value so much?[1] Providing the answer is ex-

---

[1] See the full case history of Verbatim in Chapter 14.

actly what this book is about—how to recognize a Super Stock that is currently perceived by Wall Street as a real turkey.

Why Bother To Share These Concepts with You?

It takes a lot of effort to write a book. Before embarking on this project, I pondered considerably. I reviewed a number of the books on my shelf. My own thoughts were stated perfectly in the words of an author wiser than I. It was in the preface to *Common Stocks and Uncommon Profits* (Harper & Row, 1958):

> Over the years I have found myself explaining in great detail to the owners of the funds I manage the principles behind one or another action I have taken. Only in this way would they have enough understanding of why I was acquiring some, to them, totally unknown security so that there would be no impulse to dispose of it before enough time had elapsed for the purchase to begin justifying itself in market quotations.
>
> Gradually the desire arose to compile these investment principles and have a printed record to which I could point. This resulted in the first groping toward organizing this book. Then I began thinking of the many people, most of them owners of smaller funds than those belonging to the handful of individuals it is my business to serve, who have come to me over the years and asked how they as small investors could get started off on the right path.
>
> I thought of the difficulties of the army of small investors who have unintentionally picked up all sorts of ideas and investment notions that can prove expensive over a period of years, possibly because they have never been exposed to the challenge of more fundamental concepts. Finally I thought of the many discussions I have had with another group also vitally interested in these matters, although from a different standpoint. These are the corporate presidents, financial vice presidents, and treasurers of publicly owned companies, many of whom show a deep interest in learning as much as possible about these matters.
>
> I concluded there was a need for a book of this sort. I decided such a book would have an informal presentation in which I would try to address you, the reader, in the first person. I would use much the same language and many of the same examples and analogies that I have employed in presenting the same concepts to those whose funds I manage. I hope my frankness, at times my bluntness, will not cause offense. I particularly hope that you will conclude the merit of the ideas I present may outweigh my defects as a writer.

I couldn't say it any better myself.

Kenneth L. Fisher

Acknowledgments— How This Book Came to Pass

This book made me appreciate the hackneyed but correct saying, "Books aren't written; they are rewritten." The creation of personal computers allowed many more rewrites than my short fuse otherwise could have tolerated. As the drafts rolled on, a lot of folks made significant contributions.

Jim Michaels, editor of *Forbes*, provided a spark resulting in Chapters 6 and 7. I think of those chapters as his. Jim had read earlier drafts when we met for lunch in Manhattan. He suggested my pricing concepts would be more compelling if I could demonstrate their validity on a broader universe than I had covered to that point. Jim suggested going way back in time and also covering different types of stocks. "Could you do it?" he asked. "Would I do it?" was the real question. It would be theoretically simple—a great idea—but what a lot of work.

Fortunately great sparks can provide their own momentum at times. Jeff Silk, who works with me, was eager and able to devote much of the next three months to the project. I feel the results are among *Super Stocks* highlights, and I am deeply indebted to Jim for the idea and to Jeff for his effort. Jeff is one of those bright young people whose talents I can use only because he is too young for the world yet to have offered him his real opportunities.

Significant statistical assistance also came from Tom Ulrich, a former Fisher Investments employee who has gone on to bigger and better things. Tom provided much of the number crunching behind Chapters 3 and 4.

Early on, Jack McDonald, of the Stanford Graduate School of Business, counseled me in ways that took out much of the glib side of my writing. He made me see the degree to which this could be a serious book. His inspiration shows most heavily in Chapters 8 through 11.

Stanley Kroll helped ease my early strident criticisms of the investment community with less-emotional conclusions. John Train, of Train, Smith Counsel, an outstanding writer and successful investment pro, offered direction in seeking a publisher and in giving me a basic lesson in writing by introducing me to Strunk and White's *The Elements of Style,* which should be required reading for all prospective writers.

Also early on, Harriet Rubin at Harper & Row rejected the concept of the book for her company's use but shared meaningful criticisms in terms of structure and form which were incorporated in the first full draft. I regret that the benefit flowed only one way. Dr. Frank Bruni proofread my preliminary first chapter (later dropped). In the process, Frank showed me how very far I had yet to go, thereby injecting my first sense of realism into this project. Tony Spare of the Bank of California encouraged me to focus the level of technical jargon toward whom it was I wanted the audience to be.

My father, Phil Fisher, has always been my harshest critic and staunchest supporter. Knowing me longer than anyone, and being both an eminently successful investor and writer, he was uniquely qualified to critique my work. His great patience, reading poorly conceived and written early scribblings of what was to later become this book, allowed for a great flow of comments. He pulled no punches in showing me why he felt certain parts needed improvement.

Sam Aronson, Al Haft, and Monte Stern took great pains to read the manuscript from an investor's standpoint. Struggling with each paragraph, they showed me the areas that struck a positive chord and others that put them to sleep at night.

Others, including Dr. Ronald Bean, Bill Gorman, and Bob McAllen, contributed the same level of effort on some portion of the manuscript. Gorman's comments, along with Harriet Rubin's, helped me restructure the first portion of the book. McAllen urged me to keep going when I felt discouraged by the initial responses to Chapters 3 and 4. Ron Bean encouraged me to seek editorial assistance, indicating I had something that needed to be said—but said better. This led me to Barbara Noble.

Knowing I needed help, my wife, Sherri, began searching for someone with editing experience. Things began to happen quickly when she introduced me to Barbara Noble. Not only did Barbara provide two complete passes as an ad hoc editor, she also taught me to write to the extent I am able. At first she wanted to oversee and edit everything I wrote, knowing that I needed it. Then, as she built my facilities like a mother bird pushing her baby from the nest, Barbara declined to work where she was sure I could push myself to handle things on my own. It is a great way to learn. To the extent *Super Stocks* is readable, it is largely due to her effort. Her enthusiasm and patience were unending. I am indebted.

Likewise, without Janet Thurston, it would never have happened. Janet is my right hand at Fisher Investments as chief operating officer. When I want something done, whatever it is, I turn to her, knowing she is one of the few people in life where I never have to worry about the outcome. She does it right the first time. She proofread. She oversaw the production of the manuscript and took more and more of the load off my back whenever I started to stumble.

As the manuscript approached completion, I needed reviewers with fresh insights who weren't swayed by their own prior readings. At this point many of the same people read parts they had not seen before. Others saw my material for the first time. Annie Brody, Ken Koskella (who also introduced me to Annie through Roberta Sheldon), Jack Euphrat, Wally Hagglund, Jim Palmer, Henry Roberts, Steve Walske, and others too numerous to list here provided fresh comments, reinforcement, and final fine tuning prior to pouring the concrete.

Others contributed at various stages in other ways. Fred Krup, for instance, who owns The Book Store in San Mateo and whom I've known since I was a child, took the time to show me how a book like this could fit into the world of the retail book store. Fred and Dick Newhouse introduced me to book sellers like Bruce Degarmeaux, Jack O'Leary, and Tom Turbin, who were generous with their time. Tom Faherty was particularly helpful in showing me where *Super Stocks* could fit into the publisher's world.

With an offer in hand, Annie Brody began negotiating the contract as my agent, doing a creditable job while holding my hand via long distance. I had been talking with Annie, along with other agents, for some time while considering how to locate a publisher. But Annie did more. Her comments led me to delete certain parts of the manuscript, better forgotten. Jeff Shurtleff of Central Park Books let us use his shelves for test photographing several design ideas for the cover.

Special appreciation is due the publisher for allowing me to add Appendix Six at the last minute. Its far reaching implications, by itself, may be as significant as anything else in this book.

Time and space does not allow me to mention everyone who helped along the way. I apologize to those not mentioned through lack of space or oversight. I cannot escape without one additional set of thanks.

While many authors use the acknowledgment section to pay homage to their family, in my case there is a more fundamental reason for the debt. My wife, Sherri, made a very real effort to the book. Not only did she pull a major coup by locating Barbara Noble, mentioned above, but she also spent a good deal of time facilitating for me, both on her own and with Janet Thurston. She set aside her art career, spending endless time working on things like the tractor feed and printer, photocopying the early drafts, and playing the part of gofer to help keep things running smoothly. It was about the only chance she had to see me for much of 1983. Likewise I owe a year to my three sons, Clayton, Nathan, and Jess, who good-naturedly put up with a lack of "dad" on evenings, weekends, and holidays, while I was glued to the computer in the laundry room with the door shut.

To all of you, thanks for helping me say my piece and giving me an experience which I won't need to repeat but which I never want to forget.

K. L. F.

Contents

Part Three   Fundamental Analysis

Appendixes

Part
One

The Anatomy of a
Super Stock

Chapter 1

Get Rich with the "Glitch"

Analyzing Super Stocks—In Search of "The Perfect Glitch"

The most profitable common stock investments come in the form of young, rapidly growing companies that are currently *out of favor* with Wall Street. The stock becomes worth more because the company becomes bigger and the financial community finally comes to appreciate its true value and, along the way, bids up its price.

Young, rapidly growing companies usually grow in cycles. These cycles are tied to a number of causes. The most important is the "product life cycle." Usually young and unseasoned, the managements of these companies can make severe mistakes, which can cause losses and may even threaten the survival of the firm. The best young companies learn from their mistakes. They evolve from there to a better future.

Making mistakes is less a sign of weakness than a sign of evolution. Few companies grow at rapid rates year after year without suffering some irregularity or "glitch" resulting in unfavorable earnings or even losses. Time and time again, a company will be highly revered by the financial community. It will be vividly described by almost everyone as having a rosy future that deserves a high valuation. They may say it has a "better than great—a *superb* management. It's going to gain market share. It's going to get into new markets with existing technology. It's developing new technologies that will open up whole new horizons."

There is a yearly crop of these companies in Silicon Valley. The specific names change slightly over time. These are THE companies people think of as "growth companies." They may be large or small. At the large end, Hewlett Packard has been one for decades. At the small end are companies like Seagate, Masstor, the very tiny Collagen, and the like. There is more than a shred of truth to the myths that develop about them. There may be a few "flies" on some of them that people don't see. When the flies are finally found, the stocks suffer. They may drop so severely that it takes months or even years to recover fully to their prior levels.

Some never do recover in a meaningful way. The flies start to show up, and—for the first time—earnings decline or fail to materialize on schedule. The financial community batters the stock, which can drop as much as 80 percent over a few months. The "experts" then decide that management isn't very good after all—that management probably has been misleading investors. They decide the markets have less potential than management had led them to believe. They decide the technology is weak.

The company is not apt to be as bad as they think. Nor was it apt to be as good as they had previously thought The latter is probably less true than the former. The company was probably a very good company. The problem is simply that expectations, and the stock price, were just too high early on.

Cycles start with a creative product idea and initial market research. The firm goes through an engineering cycle where a lot of money is spent and initial low-yield production begins. This is followed by initial heavy marketing expense. Up to this point, the new product—which at best is a project—has done nothing but drain money.

Initial orders come in early, causing a great deal of optimism. Initial shipments are apt to be behind schedule in order to assure quality that will protect the product's reputation. Finally shipments of the product begin. Sales start to build. Eventually enough volume is secured to generate an operating profit. On a graph it would look about like Illustration 1–1.

Then the product starts to mature. Perhaps new competitors appear. The market starts to become saturated. Sales flatten out. (See Illustration 1–2.)

Years later, product sales finally start to decline. (See Illustration 1–3.) The product has matured. Perhaps it is replaced by new technology. Margins fade and finally disappear. In time the product line may be sold off to someone who takes it on at a lower capital cost. Perhaps it is discontinued altogether. Eventually it is almost certainly phased out. This is a complete product life cycle. A graph of the company's sales of the product throughout the product life cycle might look like Illustration 1–4.

ILLUSTRATION 1–1

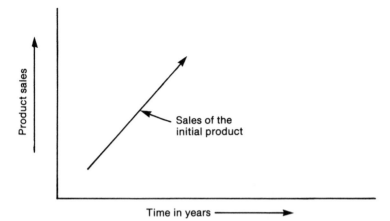

Product sales

Sales of the
initial product

Time in years ⟶

ILLUSTRATION 1–2

Product sales

Product sales as
growth slows

Sales of the
initial product

Time in years ⟶

ILLUSTRATION 1–3

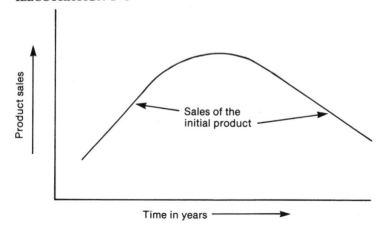

Product sales

Sales of the
initial product

Time in years ⟶

ILLUSTRATION 1–4

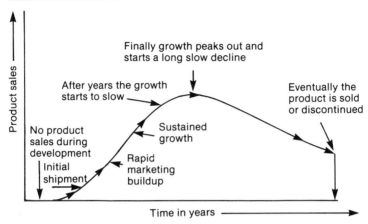

The period from when the product had sustained growth until the sales have been gradually declining for several years could be thought of as "the prime years" of a product's life—when most of the profit is made. It is comparable to the middle of an adult's life. It is when disappointments are least liable to occur. The earlier years—when a product is viewed as speculative in nature—have the most excitement, tension, and risk.

The declining years are disconcerting but usually expected. This is a little like a great athlete in his last years—Muhammed Ali, Archie Moore, or Joe Lewis in their last few fights: hollow shells of their former greatness.

Usually, long before its peak, management knows the product is about to run out of steam. They typically have planned ahead to identify and develop new products so as to maintain growth. If management does it right, total sales keep growing. (See Illustration 1–5).

Over the years they repeat this process with new products. (See Illustration 1–6.)

Management proved its ability to introduce and manage a single product. Now it is managing products in different stages of development. Managements of these companies are usually young and learn as they go—"on-the-job training." Along the way—and particularly at this stage—they are liable to make some mistakes. Sometimes they don't anticipate their first product running out of steam as soon as it does. Or they may take longer to develop additional products than anticipated. Perhaps the product doesn't work quite right initially. Market reception may be slower than anticipated. There could be many other problems. In any case, the result is a glitch. (See Illustration 1–7.)

ILLUSTRATION 1–5

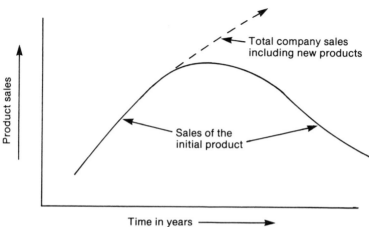

ILLUSTRATION 1–6

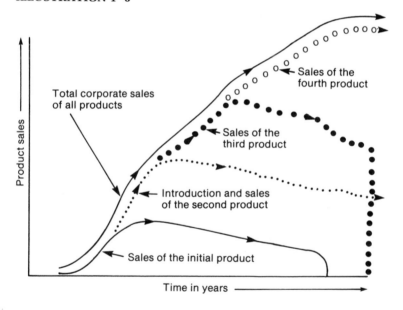

Let us go back to the first illustration. In the early stages of the product cycle, the company grows quickly—not only in sales but also in profits. Profit growth is likely to increase faster than sales for a while as the company gets over its early start-up costs. Superimposed on the first illustration, profits now show as on Illustration 1–8.

ILLUSTRATION 1–7

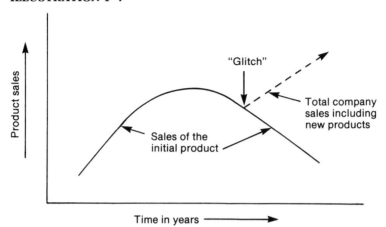

ILLUSTRATION 1–8

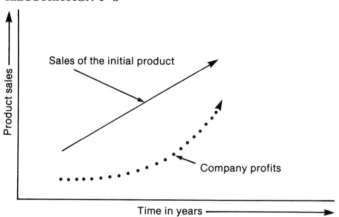

ILLUSTRATION 1–9

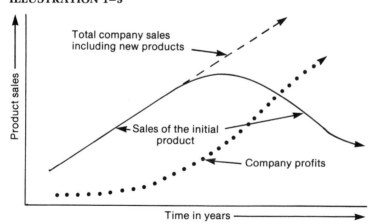

As the product starts to run out of steam, profits start to decrease. If the company correctly introduces additional products on time, profits continue to rise without significant interruption. (See Illustration 1–9.) But if the company suffers a glitch, the result will be quite different. Profits decline. The trend is apt to change very quickly from having increasing quarterly profits to losses. Why?

The next illustration shows the typical pattern in a glitch. As sales flatten out temporarily, profits decline. Losses may even occur. Profits decline without a significant decline in sales because:

1. All costs previously had risen month to month in anticipation of ever greater sales volume to cover those costs. Companies spend money in anticipation of future growth. They build overhead, marketing capability, and a production force before they are needed. They do this so people and facilities will be in place and ready when needed. This ties in to the hackneyed saying, "You have to spend money to make money." It will take management some months to get a rein on costs and to cut them back to levels consistent with lowered expectations for the short-term future.

2. More unanticipated money must be spent to overcome the problems. Whatever caused the problems in the first place will need to be solved. This is bound to cost. If customers expect delivery, they will need to be placated. More money will likely be spent in these months on marketing to keep customers from defecting to other suppliers.

3. Assets may need to be written down (or off the books of the company). If the problems were tied into processes or procurement that yielded bad inventory or equipment, it will be worth less than indicated on the books. The auditors will want prompt adjustment.

Soon profits may turn into losses. Later, as problems are ironed out, revenues start to grow again. Losses then start to decline. In a short time, profitability resumes, followed by steadily increasing profits. The whole process looks as shown in Illustration 1–10.

Young companies frequently suffer glitches as they mature. The best young managements improve with their mistakes. Some years later, these exciting little companies are likely to be much, much larger than at the time of their first troubles. Looking back years later, this whole cycle would look about like Illustration 1–11.

Sometimes, in the development of a company, several glitches occur years apart, caused by different factors. The first glitch may be just as described. The second may be due to the arrival of significant competition or by a first experience with a strong economic decline

ILLUSTRATION 1–10

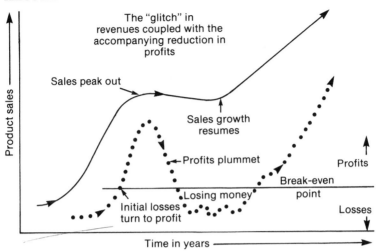

ILLUSTRATION 1–11

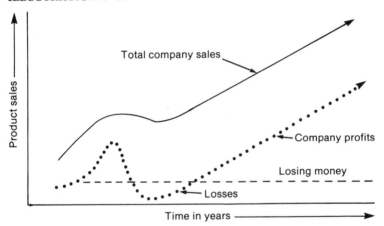

such as those of 1974–75 or 1981–82. There can be many reasons. One glitch may be much more significant than another. An example might look like Illustration 1–12.

What happens to the stock during a normal growth cycle? Its price typically fluctuates even more violently than profits. In the early stages of the product cycle, as sales and profits soar, the previously unknown company gains a reputation for an outstanding product, technology, and far-sighted marketing. The stock rises more rapidly than profits or sales. (See Illustration 1–13.)

ILLUSTRATION 1–12

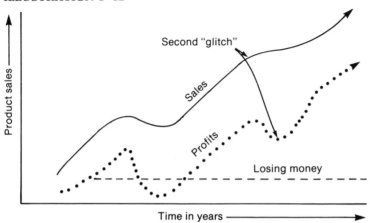

ILLUSTRATION 1–13

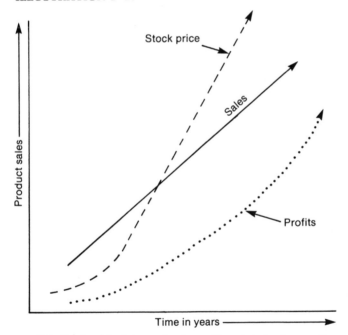

Note: Relationship of changes in sales, profits, and stock prices over time is shown by using a different scale for each. This graph is not meant to reflect any absolute relationship between them.

If the company successfully introduces new products on time, the stock price may continue to grow for years at about the rate of sales and profit growth. If the company suffers a glitch—which most companies do at some time, the stock price is apt to plummet. Most of those who previously thought the company so wonderful now become disenchanted with management and their apparent lack of ability to foresee and act on the future.

Instead of appreciating a normal sign of evolution, many investors condemn a company that fails to live up to their expectations. Disappointed, Wall Street finds it easier to blame management ineptitude than to see its own prior excesses. As disenchantment with the stock becomes more pervasive, its price tumbles further and further. Thirty percent of a stock's value can vanish in a few days. Eighty percent or more can disappear over a period of months. Time and again, stocks are bid up to unrealistic levels as investors set their sights on excessively high expectations. As the company encounters a glitch in its growth, the stock comes crashing back down. (See Illustration 1–14.)

Very few investors have a rational basis for valuing growth stocks in the face of a lack of earnings. The stock loses supporters

ILLUSTRATION 1–14

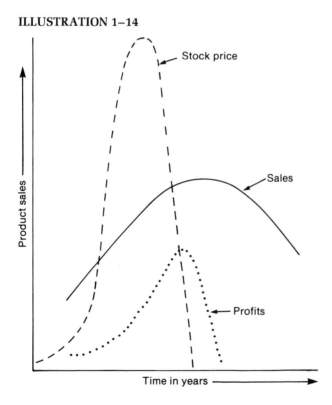

and falls, in time, much too far. The best managements react to difficulties and overcome them. In time, sales pick up. Later, profits begin to pick up. Simultaneously with the profit resurgence, the stock price begins to rebound. (See Illustration 1–15.)

ILLUSTRATION 1–15

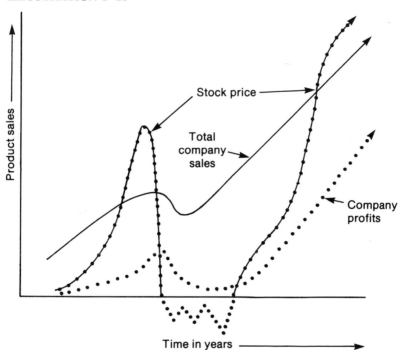

Several years later, the company reaches new highs in sales and profits. Its stock is very much higher than during the glitch. Holding the stock throughout its entire life offered shareholders a satisfactory return with a few frightening moments along the way. Buying the stock right after the glitch—but before the recovery—would have resulted in a phenomenal return.

The stock of a company that grows at above-average rates is a Super Stock when bought right after a glitch. The glitch phenomenon pushes the stock price down. It is this depressed price which allows for the abnormal returns of a Super Stock.

Over the years, the company evolves into a true giant. As it gets bigger, its growth rate and profit margins are likely to become smaller. The market is less likely to value the company so highly. The stock price increases, but probably at a much slower rate than when the company was smaller and faster growing. Looking back 30 years later, the glitch is hardly visible in the sales line but makes up a significant amount of the variation in the stock price. This might look as shown on Illustration 1–16.

We have seen a pattern—the glitch, which occurs to most young, rapidly growing companies at some time in their evolution. This

ILLUSTRATION 1–16

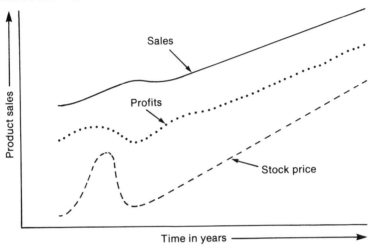

process accounts for a much larger percentage of the stock's fluctuation than the fluctuation of sales or earnings. By learning to take advantage of this phenomenon, it is possible to benefit from it—to reap the profits from most of the stock price fluctuation without having to wait for all of the growth. It is the glitch that makes Super Stocks out of Super Companies. If you learn how to price these correctly, you can reap the profits of a Super Stock—and get rich with the glitch.

What Makes the Glitch Twitch?

Tough Times Separate the Men from the Boys

It is natural for a rapidly growing young company to make some mistakes while maturing. There are sound reasons why mistakes are almost bound to occur. There are also sound reasons why Wall Street has emotional difficulty dealing with these problems. Understanding what makes the glitch twitch is essential to profit from it. Consider the glitch in more detail. Follow a Super Company on its path from early spectacular success, through a glitch, and on to recovery and further growth.

A Warning First

Remember this description pertains only to Super Companies. (See Chapters 8, 9, 10, and 11 for details of what distinguishes a Super Company.) Many companies will have a spectacular record for a period of time, perhaps years, and then suffer reversals from which they never recover. Some of these go on to bankruptcy. Others remain among the "living dead" forever. Finally, some recover to an extent but evolve into nothing more than perpetual mediocrity. These companies don't have managements with the inherent ability to recognize their own mistakes, correct them, and evolve further. While it may be possible to profit from correctly timing turn-arounds in mediocre companies, this is unlikely to yield exceptional profits for most investors.

Rapid growth has within it the seeds of instability. A rapidly growing company continually changes. As this happens, the environment changes. If a company grows at 35 percent per year, with normal employee turnover, about half of the employees have been there a year or less. A few experienced personnel are managing an ever-larger body of newcomers who haven't yet learned what the company is all about. They are likely to have some significant effect on the way the company evolves, for better or for worse. The corporate culture is forged by their interplay.

In this unstable environment, problems germinate easily. Problems frequently remain unnoticed until they later have substantial impact on the business. They are most apt to make their presence felt as the normal product life cycle starts to take its toll on the growth and profitability of older products.

The company's next generation of products may not live up to performance expectations created by its prior products. Alternately, management may overestimate the life cycle of its existing product(s). They may fail to invest in equipment and processes to keep production costs falling. This is shortsighted. It is liable to generate short-term cash at the expense of long-term product viability. This is sometimes called turning the product into a "cash cow"—treating a product like a "cow" which is "milked" for all the short-term cash you can get.

Failure to introduce new products in a timely fashion can lead to a glitch. Cash cowing and product-introduction timing problems are two quite common mistakes. Mistakes may crop up almost any place and in any way. They may include bad quality control and bad inventory management, which can result in old inventory needing to be written off as product specs change. Just as bad, it can mean bad yields by a production crew inexperienced in problem solving. Usually, by the time these problems are recognized, it is too late to avoid serious financial repercussions.

Consider the path of a Super Company as it first encounters a glitch in its growth. The company has been doing well for several years. Orders, shipments, and profits have been rising steadily. The first sign of trouble is apt to be a flattening of the order rate. Management hopes this is just temporary. With only a few weeks of data, it may be just an aberration. Perhaps they fear the economy is turning weak. Orders continue to be scarce. The company is now shipping more products on a monthly basis than its incoming order rate. Its backlog of unfilled orders falls.

As the problems are felt, management of a Super Company scrambles to find and correct them. After a quick-and-dirty period of self-analysis, the company assesses the extent of the previously unforeseen damage. At this time, it can't be sure of the exact nature or magnitude of the difficulties. Earnings disappointments and, perhaps, a net loss are announced to the world. Efforts are focused internally. Management tends to isolate themselves from the outside world. They refuse most calls from interviewers and newspaper reporters. (It is hard to face the outside world when you aren't sure of the cause or even the magnitude of your problems.)

They give up most of whatever time they may have previously devoted to the investment community. This isn't apt to help the stock price in the short term as investors begin to become skeptical. If the company has had a full-time investor relations person, they may send him out of town, so he won't have to face the people who are used to asking questions. "Mr. Johnson is out of town for the next three weeks. May I take a message?"

The problem is that, for the time being, the company doesn't have many answers. It is prone to cancel any scheduled informational meetings for groups of institutional investors. Partly, management is embarrassed and would just as soon not see all those faces that were counting on them so much. (It's like a boxer after a losing fight—he simply doesn't feel like seeing anyone. His pride is hurt.)

Legal counsel also advises of risks associated with misleading investors. "Keep quiet until you are sure the problem is well understood and can be explained correctly." The biggest reason for self-isolation is that management just plain needs the time—time to determine the exact nature of the problems and take remedial action. These are the times that separate the men from the boys.

Top management resumes looking at who has done what, and why. Why have orders slipped? Why are costs higher than anticipated? Why are customers returning products? Is there a quality control problem? They go through this more critically than they've done in months—maybe years—maybe ever. Heads may roll. Innocently enough, some managers may have contributed to the creation of the problems through inexperience or incompetence.

Top management will react to the way these people participate in the search for solutions. Some may not wholeheartedly support what they perceive to be a "witch hunt" by top officers of the company. Others will be more positive toward what top management is trying to do. Managers uncooperative to this process of critical self-analysis are likely to be terminated.

Whether or not heads roll if progress isn't made, one head should—the president's. If he doesn't make something happen or demonstrate that he is correcting the deficiencies within, the board will often intervene. It may step in to conduct its own analysis of why the chief executive is not more forcefully coming to grips with the problems. As the board presses the man responsible for performance, he will either:

 1. Perform.
 2. Resign.
 3. Be fired.
 4. Convince the board to ignore its otherwise normal duty (if so, it just lost Super Company status).

Management will look to see if there are any assets of questionable value on the books. They will focus particularly on areas where problems have occurred. After all, personnel who create problems in operations also are liable to have mismanaged assets.

While taking their lumps, it is easier for management to take them all at once. Management may look beyond the immediate difficulties, searching out areas of potential future problems. They will blame anything possible on the mistakes and personnel of the past. This implies to all interested parties the promise that similar mistakes will not recur in the future. They won't want new problems to materialize soon, so they develop an attitude of "biting the bullet."

If assets can be written off the books, they will be. "Get your problems behind you" becomes management's slogan. They will not want future embarrassments. More losses are announced. Again, none of this helps the stock price in the short term. By now, the financial community has battered down the stock price by 30 to 50 percent. Possibly another 20 percent drop is still in store for the stock in the slow months of rebuilding immediately ahead ("Squeeze those last turkeys out before the stock takes off and up").

The company enters a phase where it slowly starts to rebuild, without much immediate visible progress. Over the months that follow, the company lowers its overhead. It may drop developmental programs that never should have been started. It may initiate others. Whole product lines may be dropped.

Proven winners within management may be given additional areas of responsibility that need extra attention. Lesser performers may be reassigned to areas appropriate to their capabilities. New people are likely brought in from senior positions in other firms. Some people are promoted within the firm. These people are needed to fill:

 1. Functional slots that had not been filled before because a need for them had not been perceived prior to the problems.
 2. The slots of people who have been terminated for reasons of incompetence or poor mental attitude.

More senior managers are likely to be brought in from outside than are promoted from within. This occurs because the company suffers from the rapid buildup of inexperienced and inappropriate people that accompanies rapid growth. When you fire a person for incompetence or attitude, it takes exceptional skill and soul-searching to know if that person's subordinates were part of the problem or the solution.

Top management doesn't want to take chances promoting people who may not be fully up to higher levels of responsibility. Instead, the company is more apt to turn to senior personnel from outside. These new people are usually older, proven performers in their area of expertise. Most importantly, they are carefully chosen for their personality. They are deemed to fit into the "culture" top management is trying to create within the company. Some members of the old management team are apt to be transferred to new capacities.

For months, the reconfigured management team struggles with problems. The stock is apt to continue to perform poorly. Efforts of management are remedial. Deficiencies are corrected. In time, management actions start to pay off. Initial signs of recovery come as either the introduction of new products or a pickup in the order rate for existing products.

They'll Bitch at the Glitch

The financial community by now has built up such a sense of skepticism about the company that it will ignore the early signs of vitality. "A recovery at XYZ, you say? We've heard that before. So what? Even if they do recover, they have poor growth prospects."

More than 95 percent of all professional investors do not personally visit the companies they invest in on a regular basis—if at all. Instead, they rely on an intermediary layer of security analysts who pass on information and conclusions to final decision makers.

Security analysts are compensated directly (or through brokerage commissions) by the decision makers who buy stocks. This separation of the investor from the company tends to cultivate little or no sense of long-term ownership in the investors' minds. Buyers who once considered themselves long-term holders may now be concerned chiefly with the short-term outlook.

Security analysts know on which side their bread is buttered. When a company has suffered a glitch, many analysts naturally tend to portray problems with the company rather than problems with their prior analysis of the situation. This is only human nature. They are apt to perceive the management as inept. They may even perceive management as slightly, if not significantly, deceitful. They are very likely to envision management as much too optimistic.

Regardless of what the financial community wants to perceive, the company is making progress. Its turn-around is real. The stock is as low as it can get. In the months ahead, as the recovery builds steam, order rates pick up. Then revenues start to rise rapidly. Profits start to come slowly at first. Then over a period of 18 to 24 months, profit margins come to exceed 5 percent and higher.

At first, from its low, the stock may double quickly with relatively little appearance of business progress. This is because the financial community pessimism had been carried too far to the extreme. The stock was down much too low and had no where to go but up. At this stage, brokerage-firm comments are likely to encourage investors to stay away from the stock until "greater earnings visibility is present."

After the first double in price, the stock responds to the business fundamentals. As earnings materialize, the stock responds. In several years, the company develops a new record of success, and new groups of institutional investors (other than the ones who got hurt before) "discover" the stock. These new devotees will develop the same kind of overoptimism that we saw when we first started the story.

In a period of three to five years, the stock has risen more than 3 to 10 times in value from its low. The rise came in three parts. The first part was because the financial community was too bearish on the stock, and it had no where to go but up. The second part can be attributed to simple business fundamentals as the company became larger and earned more money. The last leg of the rise came from a new crowd of institutional investors becoming much too optimistic about the company. They bid the stock up into never-never land.

"Success Has a Thousand Fathers, but Failure Is a Bastard"

We've seen that even outstanding managements make mistakes. We've seen why and what happens when they do. We've seen that it is perfectly normal and can even be anticipated as a sign of evolutionary progress in management. The fundamental problem is that investors develop expectations for companies which originally may be much too high.

It is rare for a management to deceive a professional investor. It is almost always the investors who deceive themselves. Suppose a portfolio manager or analyst has owned or recommended a high-priced stock which gets into trouble and drops precipitously. Most will usually sell out the stock at a loss. Disgusted with the management that "misled" them, they seldom buy the stock back later. Later is a very good time to buy. It may be the best time.

When a stock goes up, individual investors claim credit for being smart enough to have bought low. When a stock goes down, few holders advertise their mistake. This is only human nature.

An older gentleman I know at Paine Webber in Boston used to comment on this phenomenon by saying, "Success has a thousand fathers, but failure is a bastard." Very few people volunteer their failures. Individuals who have lost money in a stock are more apt to look for someone else to blame.

We've seen that investors can have expectations for a company which are much too high. Likewise, we've seen that a growth glitch can cause too low an estimation of the future of a company. Obviously, neither view is completely correct. Is there no happy medium? Was the original financial community view of the company as a wonderful business more or less correct than their later view of the company as a bad business? There are no hard-and-fast rules. This is the heart of the investment problem.

We are discussing Super Companies. If truly a Super Company, the original perception, when the financial community thought it was a Super Company, is more correct than the later more-dismal view. Management, having learned from its mistakes, becomes unlikely to make others nearly so significant for years to come. The company is apt to continue rapid growth for a very long time.

With many of these stocks, the best thing to do is to hold them close to forever. First, one must buy them correctly. That requires taking advantage of the recurring cycle of financial community condemnation of a company suffering a glitch.

Some Companies Make It—Some Don't

Again, it is unwise to buy a stock on the assumption that all companies can recover from their problems. Some never do. They may be a little like bad boxers. Business and investing have a lot in common with boxing. Lots of boxers can look good for a few rounds and then later get tagged and be on the ropes. The key to survival as a boxer is instinctively to react in times of trouble. Some do. Some don't. Some fighters will get tagged in the third round and go down for the count. Others recover, make it through the round, and then drag themselves through the rest of the fight. They may be on their feet but without much real life left in them. They aren't knocked out, but they lose the fight anyway.

A select few are of championship caliber. They may get tagged at times. After all, they are taking risks. When they do, they instinctively react by covering, getting their head clear, and attacking to rebuke the thrusts of their opponents. Their spirit rises to the occasion. It isn't that one boxer necessarily trains harder than the other, although that is frequently the case. Championship quality resides in the head and the heart as much as or more than in the body. The body follows the heart and soul.

The key to investing, as much as anything else, is to be able to determine which are the ones going down for the 10 count, which are the hangers-on, and which are the ones of championship quality. Concentrate all focus on the winners.

In the early days of transistors, Texas Instruments and Transitron became darlings of Wall Street. Both were accorded high values and had devoted followings. Both companies suffered glitches. Texas Instruments, as a Super Company, evolved through the process, developed itself, and went on to decades of new glories.

Transitron, on the other hand, never got off the ropes. For over 20 years, Transitron muddled in bankruptcy, periodic losses, and a weak balance sheet. It suffered from a management unable to take advantage of the truly phenomenal growth that transistors and their offspring, integrated circuits, have enjoyed. Investing in Texas Instruments could have made someone a small fortune. Investing in Transitron could have lost a large one.

Throughout this book, you will see numerous examples of wild swings in financial-community expectations providing opportunities and losses for investors. Consider one brief sketch now—Measurex.

Measurex produces digital process control electronics for producers of sheet-like products such as paper, steel, and plastics. Coming public at $20 per share in 1971, the stock quickly rose into the mid-30s. It was fascinating to see Wall Street's assessment of this little company. Year after year, it was the favorite pick of the Western security Analysts' Association as the stock most likely to do well in the 12 months ahead. Dave Bossen, Measurex's president, was widely regarded as one of the best managers ever. Measurex had approximately $9 million per year in sales then. Analysts commonly forecasted Measurex would be a $250–$500 million sales company in 5 to 10 years. (See Illustration 2–1.)

Unfortunately, the stock didn't perform well. In fact, it went down. This went on for years. Between 1974 and 1976, the stock bounced mainly between 10 and 20. By this time, analysts were becoming disgusted. Fewer and fewer even bothered to keep abreast of the company.

The company grew rapidly, but not rapidly enough to keep up with expectations. By 1977, it was a $60 million company. But by then, there were few believers. The stock promptly increased fourfold in value in the ensuing couple of years. From a low of 10½ in 1977, it increased to a high of 48½ in 1979.

As the stock rose—phoenixlike from the ashes—so did financial-community interest. Between 1977 and 1980, Measurex really coined money. It grew to $120 million in revenue and averaged profit margins in excess of 7 percent.

ILLUSTRATION 2–1

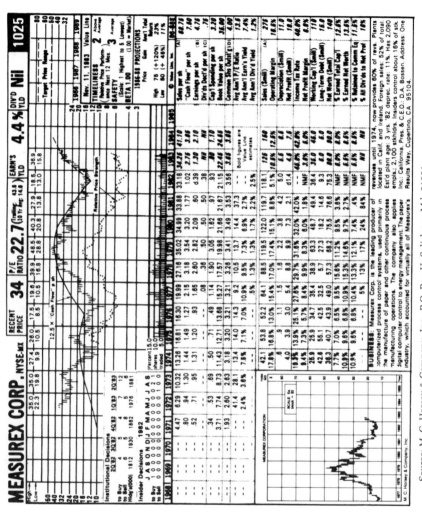

Source: M. C. Horsey & Company, Inc., P.O. Box H, Salisbury, Md. 21801.
Source: *Value Line Ratings & Reports.* Reprinted by permission of the publisher. Copyright, Value Line Inc.

As a supplier of expensive pieces of capital equipment, when the 1979 to 1983 recession unfolded, Measurex was particularly hard hit. The stock dropped back down below its original public offering price. In 1982, it wallowed at levels of between $13 and $15 per share. Measurex was a $120 million revenue company, with a book value in excess of $20 dollars per share. It had a strong balance sheet and a truly experienced management. It now possessed better technology than ever before. Yet if you asked most people in the financial community in 1982 and 1983, they would have told you it was a dog of a company with a bad management.

Why? They would likely recite an event from 1973. It wasn't because the company hadn't grown. It was essentially because it hadn't lived up to the extraordinarily high expectations the financial community had set for it. Between 1972 and 1982, Measurex had grown from $8 million to $118 million in revenues—a compound growth rate of 31 percent, which isn't too bad. But it wasn't the magic Wall Street wanted.

By 1982–83, the expectations for Measurex were certainly too low. It is common for financial people to claim disregard for Measurex on the basis that Dave Bossen "misled" them about the size of the markets available to Measurex. "If you can't trust a CEO, you shouldn't own his company." I agree with the sentiment, but I was there. I remember. These are professional investors who are supposed to dig into things and independently verify facts. Bossen was certainly very optimistic and upbeat. He had to be optimistic—this was his life. He made some strong and optimistic statements. What he did was no more than most chief executives do when their stock is the darling of Wall Street.

If Bossen's statements could mislead these "professional" investors, they must have done precious little independent verification. (I know a man who would love to help them own some more substantial assets—perhaps a piece of the Brooklyn Bridge.)

Measurex's stock had gone from 20 to the mid-30s, back down below 10, back up over 45, then back down below 15. It has since recovered back into the low 30s. On such a roller coaster ride, it is important to maintain objectivity. If your view of a company is cluttered with past resentments toward management, you can't see objectively. If you buy high and sell low and feel bitter along the way, you are just the battered boxer on the ropes who needs to clear his head.

If you listen to or are influenced by people who spend their lives on the ropes, you are liable to stay out of the ring. Clear your head. Learn to forgive management its failures to live up to expectations. See management for what it is—people doing a job—people who, along the way, can present you with some real opportunities.

In an example such as Measurex, the key is knowing when it is cheap and when it is not. What makes cheapness? Why would it rise from its lows and fall from its highs?

The key to pricing—the essence of a Super Stock—is to buy a Super Company at the time the financial community believes it is a real dog. This means buying after management has made mistakes severe enough to disenchant most of Wall Street. It means learning to forgive management their mistakes (a matter of the heart as much as of the head). It means objectively pricing something that is out of favor. The next five chapters discuss pricing and the keys to doing just that.

Part Two

Valuation Analysis

Chapter 3

Conventional Approaches to Stock Valuation— The Riddle: Ten Times Earnings Is Too High and a Thousand Times Is Too Low

The Problem: If Left Field and Right Field Don't Work, Get out of the Stadium

The biggest problem anyone faces in the market is knowing how to value stocks. While pricing can't be done perfectly, it is simple. It can be done well enough that perfection isn't necessary. The beauty is that a good pricing policy is so easy. The irony is that so few people have an appropriate concept for pricing.

The most popular ways to value stocks are by using conventional yardsticks of earnings or asset values—often the wrong ways. (In fact, *any* way most of the financial community views anything is apt to be wrong.) Some use these one way—others use them another.

While there is nothing inherently wrong with earnings or assets, they are the *results* of other things. Profits are a result, not a cause. Stocks move off the same causes that cause the earnings. Stocks move because of something. Earnings and assets fluctuate because of something. The emphasis should be on the *cause* in *because*. Most notions suggest investors should adapt these techniques slightly differently—relocate within the outfield to play ball—while the investor really needs to get to a whole different stadium. This chapter explores conventional stock valuation methods and their weaknesses. (Chapters 4 through 7 describe new and radically different valuation methods.)

Earnings-Based Methods

Valuing a company on the basis of future earnings growth became popular during the 1950s. In the 1960s and early 1970s, people reaped excellent profits from growth-stock investing. This worked well initially because so few did it. Therefore, there was only a small premium being paid for the truly outstanding company with a dramatic potential for future growth. Devotion to so-called growth stocks became a financial fad. Things got way out of hand. In the 1960s, early 1970s, and again in the early 1980s, the market valued numerous little "growth" stocks at 40 to 100 times earnings and more.

Take the typical stock recommended by a typical brokerage firm. The recommendation suggests a stock should rise because the price-earnings ratio (P/E) is such and such. Or the "earnings will increase" to such and such. Or the P/E ratio is "too low" because of such and such. Maybe the P/E is "low in relation to its historical range." Or the stock is selling at a "low multiple" in relation to the Standard and Poor's 500.

Earnings forecasts have become the most common form of stock valuation, but few successfully employ them. Why? Specific and precise earnings-per-share forecasts don't work. Financial life is too illusory. Consider the two basic approaches.

The "Underpriced, Low P/E" School

The "Low P/E" school says the current low price-earnings ratio of the stock is supported by earnings that will not go down significantly. The low price of the stock in relation to earnings seems to indicate Wall Street thinks the earnings will fall. The low P/E school believes that in time Wall Street will realize the earnings won't fall. At that time, they expect the stock to rise.

The limitation here is threefold. First, forecasting specific earnings per share is extraordinarily difficult to do for any period. Contrary to popular belief, lots of stocks sold at low price-earnings ratios in 1929. Then the earnings vanished. Caterpillar Tractor, for instance, sold at eight times earnings in 1929. Three years later, at a fraction of the price, it had an infinite price-earnings ratio—it *had* no earnings. (See Chapter 7 on IBM and other stocks in the 1920s and 1930s.)

Second, numerous arbitrary factors are involved in how earnings are calculated. Some of these are merely accounting variables which may change over time. In Accounting 1, everyone learns the only real figure on a balance sheet that doesn't involve lots of assumptions is "Cash." The rest are all based on assumptions which, quarter-to-quarter, management and/or the accounting industry may be changing.

Every time an accounting principle is changed—which is very regularly, management and auditors need to interpret how that change need be applied to them. Every time conditions change in the company—which is almost daily, management and its auditors need to figure out how those changes should be interpreted in an accounting sense.

Third, even if you do a perfect job of forecasting earnings—which no one does, you are likely to make only a small amount on your money with this approach. Successfully applied, it can make 100 percent on your money, but it won't make 10 times your money. It just won't work. The markets may not be efficient, but they aren't so inefficient as to allow for that kind of variation between consensus opinion on earnings, reality, and stock prices.

The Growth Stock School of Thought

The "Growth Stock" school of thought believes that as a company grows, the stock responds—perhaps irregularly—to rising earnings that accompany growth. Given enough growth, this school envisions a rising price for the stock virtually regardless of the price initially paid. The growing earnings make the P/E ratio become lower and lower until eventually the stock just has to respond—as if a coiled spring were released. At its worst, this school of thought was represented by those who bought and held the large-capitalization, well-known growth stocks of the late 1960s and early 1970s. When growth in earnings didn't materialize fast enough to meet expectations, the stocks fell.

This philosophy suffers from two limitations. The first is the same as with the low P/E school—it's just very hard to forecast earnings, even one or two quarters in advance. Analysts frequently suffer embarrassment as events unfold in a different manner than they had predicted.

The second limitation to this school of thought—and one that is less well understood—is that, again, even if your earnings estimates are right, the stock may not perform well. Why? The stock market discounts the future. The price is likely to already have compensated for future growth. This ties into the old saying, "The market knows"—which is particularly true if the stock is widely perceived as a growth stock.

A correct forecast for next year's rising earnings likely will not be accompanied by a rising price if, a year or two later, the company runs into problems. "The market knows." This is the magic of the market at its best. Stocks more often than not hit their peak long before their earnings do. Consider the earnings of two hypothetical companies, along with their stock prices for the same periods:

				Quarter			
	1	2	3	4	5	6	7
Company A:							
Earnings/share	.20	.25	.37	.40	.45	.55	.60
Stock price	12	15	22	24	27	33	36
Company B:							
Earnings/share	.20	.25	.37	.40	.45	.55	.09
Stock price	12	15	22	22	16	12	8

Company A shows steadily rising quarterly earnings at an irregular rate and a stock price that is exactly 60 times quarterly earnings. (Of course, the world never works this precisely, but it helps the illustration.) Company B shows the same earnings numbers until the last quarter, but its stock peaks out a full year before the earnings decline commences. The inefficient market is efficient enough to allow for the future in rough form even if we can't rationalize it. This principle is well understood in academic circles and led to the formalization of the "Random Walk" school of thought.[1]

Still, successful earnings forecasts, whether employed in a low P/E or rising-earnings mode, can allow the user some degree of success. If there weren't some utility to them, they would have been widely discredited after all these years.

But the plain truth is they don't do an outstanding job. Almost everyone is using them, and precious few get exceptional results. Earnings-based methods are extremely unlikely to point out a Super Stock. To meet the minimal requirements of capital appreciation as a

---

[1] The "Random Walk" school of thought seems to have built a perfect rationalization for giving up. If you have given up, might I suggest joining them, closing the book, and turning out the lights.

Super Stock requires increases in value of at least three times cost in five years.[2] This means rising earnings of at least 25 percent per year with no decrease throughout the period in price-earnings ratio. While not inconceivable, it leaves little room for error.

At the other end of the spectrum, a Super Stock needs to have the potential to increase as much as 10 times in three years. Such an increase would require a compound three-year earnings growth rate of over 115 percent per year, which is hard to conceive.

The weakness of earnings-based valuation techniques becomes all the more obvious by considering what happens if you don't allow for their use. If you take away earnings, how do you value a company? If you take away the earnings, most of the financial community loses its ability to value a stock. ASK A STOCKBROKER HOW HE VALUES A COMPANY IF HE CAN'T USE EARNINGS AS HIS BASIS. You're apt to get some very interesting answers.

The Ben Graham Approach—"Remarkable but Not Enough"

Ben Graham wrote, taught, and lectured widely. He is frequently referred to as the "Father of Security Analysis." His book by that title, *Security Analysis,* has been THE basic textbook in the field for nearly 50 years.[3] Another, *The Intelligent Investor,* is widely regarded as a classic for eager novice investors.[4] Here is what John Train says about Graham in *The Money Masters:*[5]

> Benjamin Graham ranks as this century's (and perhaps history's) most important thinker on applied portfolio investment, taking it from an art, based on impressions, inside information, and flair to a proto-science, an orderly discipline.

To a generation of investors, Graham's concepts have come to be known as the "value approach to investing." Graham bought stocks on a formulated basis, using low price-earnings ratios and, particularly, balance-sheet criteria. He bought productive assets that would eventually produce earnings, and he bought them as cheaply as possible. He looked for large dividend yields backed by strong balance sheets. He would identify "cheap" companies, buy them, and hold them for two years or until they appreciated 50 percent—whichever came first. It works well but has limited upside. Using this approach

---

[2] See the original definition of a Super Stock in the introduction.

[3] Benjamin Graham, *Security Analysis* (New York: McGraw-Hill, 1934).

[4] Benjamin Graham, *The Intelligent Investor* (New York: Harper & Row, 1947).

[5] John Train, *The Money Masters* (New York: Harper & Row, 1980), p. 83.

makes money but doesn't get people into the early stages of an IBM or Xerox. It also tends to generate a high percentage of its return in short-term income rather than tax-advantaged, long-term capital gains.

Did you ever try to value technology stocks on the basis of assets? It is usually a bizarre attempt. Most of the Super Stocks of our time, those in which you could have made 5, 10, or 20 times or more on your money, could never have been bought on the basis of asset value.

Warren Buffett built a fortune of several hundred million dollars, applying his own variation of Ben Graham's concepts. Few have ever done nearly as well. Of the nine legendary investors chronicled in *The Money Masters,* John Train called Buffett "the investor's investor."[6] He was independent and self-disciplined. He bought large and, at times, nonliquid positions in bargain companies that others avoided. He did so with uncommon accuracy. For 13 years, from 1956 to 1969, he compounded money at a 30 percent average annual rate without a single "down" year. Very few ever do nearly this well. But there are few Warren Buffetts—to date, perhaps just one. Buffett had the added advantage of learning while he worked for Graham. Others worked for Graham, but few did so well. Most are said to have achieved quite reasonable results. But what if you want more than just reasonable results?

The Solution

If buying a stock based on earnings is "left field" and buying a stock based on asset value is "right field," then it is better to get into a whole different stadium. Don't think in terms of buying stock— forget the stock aspect. (After all, isn't the so-called per-share thing just another result?) The more fundamental notion should be that you are buying a business. What would someone pay to buy the whole business—lock, stock, and barrel? If investors would always ask themselves this simple question before buying stock, it would save a lot of money. What would someone pay to buy this whole business?

Most investors don't even stop to consider how much business a company does. All they look at are earnings per share and net assets per share. Serious academic books on investment ratio analysis rarely mention the top half of an income statement. They rarely ask the question, "Just how much business does this business do?"

---

[6] Ibid., p. 1.

One leading book in the field has entire chapters devoted to:

P/E ratios.

Earnings growth rates (one-year and four-year).

The Ben Graham approach.

Dividends, changes in dividends, and payout ratios.

Rates of return on total investment.

Debt/capital ratios.

Total invested capital.

But not a word is mentioned of sales, cost of goods sold, or gross profit margins.[7] We want to get our focus off of earnings and asset-based valuations methods. Instead, we want to focus on:

How much business a company does.

The basic cost structure associated with that business.

The way in which a private owner would think about the business.

It may sound preposterous, but 10 times earnings can be way too high a price to pay for a company—while 1,000 times earnings may be too low a price to pay for *exactly the same* company. I like the concept of multiples. (When I was in the fourth grade, 11 × 8 was 88. In spite of wars, hippies, calculators, the new math, Richard Pryor, and Apple Computers, it still is 88. So I like multiples.) I just don't like price-earnings multiples. I prefer other multiples—particularly sales multiples. I choose to value stocks in terms of Price Sales Ratios (PSRs), actual and potential profit margins, and Price Research Ratios (PRRs). These concepts of pricing are primarily what this book is all about.

To make uncommon profits, it only makes sense to avoid conventional approaches to valuation. Most of the best buys I've made occurred when I invested in a company either losing money or making so little that the price-earnings ratio was meaningless or, more appropriately, seemingly infinite. I've made lots of money buying stocks at a thousand times earnings or more, but very little buying stocks at 10 times earnings or less. How would a private buyer value the potential acquisition of an entire company that was either losing money or just barely breaking even? With that riddle solved, it becomes a low-risk, high-reward proposition to buy stocks.

---

[7] Donald M. Peterson, *Financial Ratios and Investment Results* (Lexington, Mass.: Lexington Books, 1974).

Pricing Is Everything—
Use Price Sales Ratios

Bulls, Bears, and Turkeys

People forget. In their careless abandon of fundamentals, they ignore any sense of long-term value. Still, the bird comes home to roost. Usually it's a turkey.

On my conference table, when I'm in an optimistic mood, I keep a large plastic bull with huge horns on its head and testicles hanging between it's legs. It's impressive by most standards. Just barely visible, sitting under its testicles, I keep a tiny multicolored plastic turkey.

Usually people never notice the turkey. If they do, they seem hesitant to acknowledge it. Occasionally, someone asks what the turkey is for. I explain that everyone knows what a Bull Market is, but most don't see the perfectly obvious—right under the sexiest part of the bull sits a real turkey.

People forget. Just as the market reaches high levels, people forget that stocks go down. Based on hopes and dreams, they pay prices that have little resemblance to what a private buyer would pay for the whole business. A stock can rise 70 percent from an already high level in a Bull Market but fall just as much, or more, in a Bear Market. (Under the sexiest part of the bull sits a real turkey.) Most people think there are Bull Markets and Bear Markets. There are, but there are also Turkey Markets. Super Stocks largely defy Turkey Markets. A perfect Super Stock is the stock of a business which:

- Can generate internally funded future long-term average growth of approximately 15 to 20 percent.

- Will generate future long-term average after-tax profit margins above 5 percent.
- Is bought at a price sales ratio of 0.75 or less.

Understanding Price Sales Ratios (PSRs)

Price Sales Ratios (PSRs) are the most powerful single valuation method with which I am familiar. They are not well known, less well understood, and seldom used within Wall Street. They work much, much better than price-earnings ratios. They are an almost perfect measure of popularity. This chapter is about how and why. (Using PSRs optimally leans on an understanding of profit margin analysis—covered in Chapters 10 and 11.)

The price sales ratio is just like a price-earnings ratio that uses corporate sales instead of corporate earnings. It is the total market value of a company divided by the last 12 months' corporate sales. To calculate the market value, multiply the stock price by the total number of shares of stock in existence.[1] If a stock is $15 per share and there are 4 million shares outstanding, the market value is $60 million ($15 × 4 = $60). If the company's corporate sales last year were $80 million, then the price sales ratio is 0.75 ($60/$80 = 0.75). If, instead, its sales were only $20 million, then its PSR is 3.0.

Illustration 4–1 is *Value Line* data for Applied Magnetics. Line 4 shows the total number of shares of stock. (Line numbers are on the right-hand side of the page.) At the top of the page, lines 1 and 2 show the high and low stock price for each year. (Don't get confused here. Take it slowly—it gets clearer very soon.) Multiplying line 1 by line 4 gives the high market value for the year. Line 2 times line 4 gives the low market value for the year. Dividing the market values by line 5 gives the PSR.

Applied Magnetic's 1980 high market value was $118.6 million ($24.3 × 4.88 million = $118.6 million). The low market value was $48.3 million ($9.9 × 4.88 million = $48.3 million). This gets a little tricky. Remember that whenever we look at a stock price, we only have historical data to go on. So we have to use the prior year's data. Applied Magnetic's sales in 1979, as per line 5, were $90.4 million. Its high PSR for 1980 was then 1.31 ($118.6 million divided by $90.4 million = 1.31). Its low PSR for 1980 was 0.53 ($48.3 million divided by $90.4 million = 0.53).

---

[1] The most correct total number of shares is the "fully diluted shares outstanding." This refers to existing shares plus exercisable options outstanding. Fully diluted shares are displayed prominently in annual reports. Reference is commonly made to "primary shares outstanding." This refers to the number of shares before calculation for "full dilution."

ILLUSTRATION 4–1

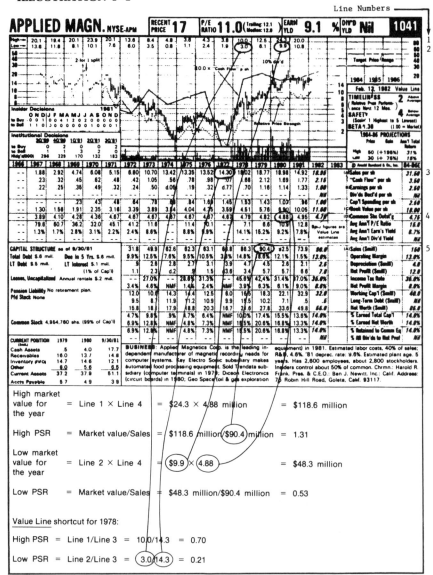

The following figures and calculations appear in the illustration:

High market
value for = Line 1 × Line 4 = $24.3 × 4.88 million = $118.6 million
the year

High PSR = Market value/Sales = $118.6 million/$90.4 million = 1.31

Low market
value for = Line 2 × Line 4 = $9.9 × 4.88 = $48.3 million
the year

Low PSR = Market value/Sales = $48.3 million/$90.4 million = 0.53

Value Line shortcut for 1978:

High PSR = Line 1/Line 3 = 10.0/14.3 = 0.70

Low PSR = Line 2/Line 3 = 3.0/14.3 = 0.21

Source: *Value Line Ratings & Reports*. Reprinted by permission of the publisher. Copyright, Value Line Inc.

There is a short cut when using *Value Line* data. Line 3 shows sales per share. Dividing line 1 or 2 by line 3 will give you PSRs directly.[2] (Line 1—the high PSR; line 2—the low.)

---

[2] The short-cut method for PSR calculation with *Value Line* numbers sometimes results in slight rounding errors. Ignore rounding errors—they aren't significant when using PSRs.

You can waste lots of time and effort on whether to use the bid price for the stock, the offering price, the last, or whatever. Most of this is just splitting hairs. It's not too significant. Likewise, lots of hairs can be split on exactly how many shares are outstanding. How many options should be included in the figure? Don't waste your time.

Price Sales Ratios vary from numbers lower than .05 all the way up to numbers well over 20. They vary according to all kinds of things. Some companies should have substantially different PSRs than others. But why should one consider Price Sales Ratios at all? Because they measure popularity relative to business size.

Price Sales Ratios are of value because the sales portion of the relationship is inherently more stable than most other variables in the corporate world. If you've done your homework on the fundamentals of a company's business, it is possible to find companies where earnings have shifted from extreme profitability to losing small (or even large) amounts of money, while sales have temporarily flattened after years of rapid growth.

It is rare to see a Super Company have a truly substantial sales decline. It is quite common to see one suffer from severe earnings reversals. (See the "glitch" described in Chapters 1 and 2.) A 5 to 10 percent decline in sales followed by a couple of flat years is about the worst one might expect from a Super Company. The increased relative stability of sales, in relation to other financial yardsticks, allows you to use sales as an anchor to windward in the process of securities valuation.

What Does the Relationship between Price and Sales Mean?

By itself, a PSR shows how much the stock market is willing to pay for a dollar of a company's sales—what the financial community, de facto, thinks of the company—its popularity. A company's worth to a private buyer should be a function of the volume of future sales and average future profit margins—how much future business it will have and how much money it will make doing that business. Think what this implies.

A company with $100 million in annual sales and also $100 million in market value obviously has a PSR of 1.0. Suppose, by chance, it earned a 10 percent after-tax profit margin (10 percent of $100 million sales = Earnings of $10 million).[3] Then it follows that

---

[3] Profit margins will be covered in great detail in Chapters 10 and 11. For now suffice it to say that the profit margin is net after-tax profits divided by sales. If sales were $100 million and profits were $3 million, the profit margin would be 3 percent ($3/$100 = .03 = 3 percent).

the company has a price-earnings ratio of 10 ($100 market value ÷ $10 earnings = A 10.0 price-earnings ratio). If, instead, it earned a 5 percent after-tax profit margin, then it would have a price-earnings ratio of 20 (Profit = 5 percent of $100 million sales = $5 million. $100 ÷ $5 = 20).

Table 4–1 shows price-earnings ratios reflecting what a company's PSR would be assuming varying levels of future profitability.

TABLE 4–1
Implied Price-Earnings Ratios under Varying Levels of Profit Margins and PSRs

	Profit Margins (percent)					
PSRs	12	10	7.5	5	2	1
.12	1.00	1.20	1.60	2.40	6.00	12.00
.25	2.08	2.50	3.33	5.00	12.50	25.00
.50	4.17	5.00	6.67	10.00	25.00	50.00
.75	6.25	7.50	10.00	15.00	37.50	75.00
1.00	8.33	10.00	13.33	20.00	50.00	100.00
1.50	12.50	15.00	20.00	30.00	75.00	150.00
2.00	16.70	20.00	26.67	40.00	100.00	200.00
3.00	25.00	30.00	40.00	60.00	150.00	300.00
4.00	33.33	40.00	53.33	80.00	200.00	400.00
5.00	41.67	50.00	66.67	100.00	250.00	500.00
6.00	50.00	60.00	80.00	120.00	300.00	600.00
10.00	83.33	100.00	133.33	200.00	500.00	1,000.00

This table represents what price-earnings ratios various Price Sales Ratios and profit margins equate at. For instance, when a company sells at 1.0 times sales and earns 7.5 percent after tax, it is the equivalent to a price-earnings ratio of 13.33. This is useful in comparing what a current PSR is equivalent to in terms of future price-earnings ratios under varying levels of profitability. Keep this handy for further use.

Study this table. Understanding it can save you more than you could imagine. The first example just cited (10 percent margins) is represented by the intersection of the fifth row and the second column. When the example is modified (5 percent margins), it is represented by the fifth row and fourth column.

Table 4–1 shows the relationship between profit margins, price-earnings ratios, and PSRs. Once comfortable with Table 4–1, use it to consider companies with varying levels of profitability and financial community valuation.

What is the bottom line? To buy stocks successfully, you need to price them based on causes, not results. The causes are business conditions—products with a cost structure allowing for sales. The results flow from there—profits, profit margins, and finally earnings per share. Note that to this point, nothing has been said about anything on a per-share basis. Avoiding per-share concepts forces one to continue to focus on the overall business, including its size, which (as shall be explained shortly) is critical to the successful implementation of PSRs.

A Case in Point: The Datapoint

An example will clarify the use of PSRs as an analytical valuation tool. Illustration 4–2 is from an article appearing in "Heard on the

ILLUSTRATION 4–2

Datapoint Is Riding Wave of New Popularity As Investors Bid Up Price in Heavy Trading

By R. FOSTER WINANS

Datapoint got more "Dear John" letters last year than a boatload of sailors. But now the San Antonio, Texas-based maker of computer systems is starting to receive Valentines.

The company saw 30% of its market value, or about $800 million, evaporate in a matter of a few months early in 1982 after it disclosed that its orders and earnings projections had been overstated. Datapoint shares fell to a meager 10⅞ from 51⅞ as earnings fell 95% for the year ended July 31.

The stock struggled back and finished the year near 18. But the Valentines really have started arriving in the past two weeks. The shares have jumped 22% in the last nine trading days to close yesterday at 25⅛, unchanged. A big chunk of the gain came Friday, when Datapoint surged 12% on heavy volume. In the past two days, about 5.5% of the company's

21 million shares outstanding have changed hands.

Traders say the buying binge has come from several brokerage houses. That kind of action suggests that rumors of a takeover bid, which have been linked to the stock for almost a year, are ill-founded. Instead, analysts say, the stock may be playing catch-up with the rest of the technology issues, and buyers may be betting on a turn-around in the company's fortunes, bolstered by an expected economic recovery.

Although some investors still are skeptical about the company's future, and have dumped the stock recently, at least two analysts have been giving Datapoint favorable reviews lately.

Peter T.T. Lieu, technology analyst at Furman Seiz Mager Dietz & Birney, says Datapoint "is a whale of a buy." Mr. Lieu's estimate for Datapoint's fiscal 1983 earnings is the highest on Wall Street, $1 a share. That gives the stock a current price-to-earnings ratio of about 25 rich even compared with some of the most attractive players in the technology game, such as IBM, at 13, and Control Data at 11.

ILLUSTRATION 4–2 (*concluded*)

Mr. Lieu likes the company "for its qualitative aspects," meaning, he says, that Datapoint's cash position has improved substantially to a projected $109 million by July, from about $50 million on hand at the end of fiscal 1983.

"That's an amazing balance-sheet improvement for a company that looked like it was going bankrupt last year," he asserts.

He says the company has a solid, sophisticated customer base, including 13 of 14 major New York City banks and the lion's share of the market for systems that allow minicomputers to talk to one another.

Because of its strong customer base, Mr. Lieu concludes the company could enjoy a surge in sales and earnings when the economy begins to show meaningful improvement.

Lawrence W. Roberts, an analyst at Hambrecht Quist, San Francisco, is less optimistic about Datapoint's earnings recovery this year. He forecasts 30 cents to 50 cents a share for fiscal 1983. But he agrees that, in a good economy, the company has the potential to earn at least $2 a share in fiscal 1984.

One of the biggest valentines the company received arrived January 20, the day Trust Co. of the West filed with the Securities and Exchange Commission in a purchase of 5.7% of Datapoint's shares outstanding.

That investment has helped offset major selling by big institutions. For example, T. Rowe Price and BEA Associates between them, have flushed out of their portfolios a total of about 2 million shares.

Many analysts seem to agree that the stock remains a sell.

"For short-term investors, now is probably a good time to step out of the stock," says Frederick D. Ziegel, an analyst at Salomon Brothers. Mr. Ziegel also is forecasting another year of depressed earnings for fiscal 1983, about 50 cents a share, and a modest recovery for fiscal 1984, to about $1.50 a share. The numbers, he says, are "fluid; when you get down to these low levels, it's tough to put confidence in our estimates. The estimates may be low."

For long-term investors to be buying the stock now, he says, "you have to believe that the company will be able to bring new systems into a highly competitive and changing marketplace. I'm not sure one could comfortably make that statement."

Datapoint already may be meeting obstacles. In April 1981, the company announced an electronic switching device, called ISX, that it said "should make a substantial contribution to our growth and profits over the next two years and beyond."

Now, almost two years later, a Datapoint spokesman says, "We've had some difficulty with ISX, particularly in software, and haven't shipped any lately. To date, it has been somewhat of a disappointment." He adds that ISX has generated "virtually no revenue."

The company doesn't comment on the Street's earnings estimates, saying only that it is "optimistic" that it will benefit in an economic recovery.

Street" in *The Wall Street Journal* (February 15, 1983). It covers the roller coaster ride Datapoint had recently provided investors. Read the first three paragraphs. Datapoint shares had dropped rapidly in value from 51⅞ to a low of 10⅞. They then rebounded to 25. In the process, as is explained, a lot of people got Excedrin headaches. But what really happened? The article says a lot, but it doesn't give a good answer. Wall Street loves mystery.

Datapoint's 1981 high had been 67½. For illustration purposes, it is sufficient that on April Fools' Day 1981 it was 58. At 58, the company had a market value just under 1.25 billion dollars ($1,183,000,000). In the prior 12 months, the company had racked up sales of about $363 million. The PSR was exactly 3.25. As *The Wall Street Journal* article points out, the stock then fell to a low of 10⅞. Its market value was then $222 million. It had lost more than 80 percent of its April Fools' Day value.

Its sales hadn't declined measurably: Its PSR, therefore, was reduced from 3.25 to 0.61. The earnings had disappeared. It was a typical growth glitch. Datapoint's sales actually grew over time fairly rapidly. By the time *The Wall Street Journal* article appeared, Datapoint's annual sales had climbed to a level of about $514 million. Profitability had begun to return (like the glitch described in Chapter 1). By then, of course, the stock had more than doubled from its low. But what really happened?

Originally, Wall Street placed much too high a valuation on Datapoint (a PSR of 3.25). No company of Datapoint's size should ever be valued at a PSR of 3.25 if investors want a prayer of making significant long-term profits. Later, Datapoint fell too low (a PSR of 0.61). Patiently holding any Super Company with a PSR below 0.75 results in good to spectacular profits.

A Super Stock Is a Super Company Bought at a Low PSR Relative to the Company's Size

PSR Rules for making 3 to 10 times your money in three to five years with super stocks:

RULE 1: Avoid stocks with PSRs greater than 1.5. Never ever buy any stock with a PSR greater than 3. A stock selling at a PSR this high can increase rapidly, but only based on "hype." Stay away—unless you want small short-term profits at the risk of large long-term losses. I can't reemphasize this enough to small investors.

RULE 2: Aggressively seek Super Companies at PSRs of 0.75 or less. There are always some around. There is no shortage. Hold them for a long time—make some money.

RULE 3: Sell stock in any Super Company when the PSR rises to between 3.0 and 6.0. If you don't want to take much risk—sell at 3.0. If you are willing to take slightly more risk—hoping excessive optimism will continue to sweep the stock price up, hang on hoping for 6.0—maybe higher if you like gambling.

Companies selling at high PSRs already have high expectations in Wall Street's eyes. Super Companies selling at low PSRs are ones with which the financial community has become discouraged and about which they are overly skeptical.

What Is a Low PSR, What Is a High PSR, and Why?

Go back to the Datapoint example for a moment. Investors who purchased the stock at a PSR of 3.25 got clobbered. Those who bought at a PSR of 0.6 made out like bandits. At a PSR of 0.6, Datapoint was selling at a market value equal to only about six times 1982 earnings and about five times analysts' later estimates for 1984 earnings (read on in *The Wall Street Journal* article—Illustration 4–2). Is it any wonder that a Super Company selling at five times next year's earnings should have an increasing stock price? In this one case, a PSR of 3.25 was too high, and a PSR of 0.6 was quite attractive. Is that always the case?

Studying the Solution

Other things being equal, PSRs decline as companies get bigger. At Fisher Investments, we've tracked the PSRs of an objective universe of 62 technology companies over a five-year period. During the period, PSRs expanded substantially—particularly for smaller companies. Yet throughout the study, several things remained constant.

- Big companies tended to have lower PSRs than did smaller companies.
- The bulk of the pleasant surprises came from stocks starting at PSRs less than one.
- Most disappointments came from stocks sporting the highest PSRs just prior to the poor results.

We used a data universe picked for its objectivity—the monthly statistical summary from the San Francisco investment banking firm of Hambrecht & Quist. For years, Hambrecht & Quist has been a leading specialty boutique in the field of technology investing and underwriting. Their *Monthly Statistical Summary* gives statistical data about the companies they follow. By using their data universe, we weren't picking the stocks to be followed. They did it for us.

Nearly all these companies are technology concerns.[4] Starting with the 1978 summaries, we tracked the stocks on a quarterly basis. Over time, some stocks dropped off the list, either through acquisition, bankruptcy, or simple loss of interest on the part of Hambrecht & Quist.

When a company left the list because it was acquired by another company, we valued it out of the list at date and price of acquisition. When a company dropped off the list through Hambrecht & Quist's loss of interest, we gathered the necessary information to continue the study with that stock included (as if it continued on the list uninterrupted). In one instance, a company left the list through bankruptcy. (We continued it on the list until the price fell to a level reflecting bankruptcy and then withdrew it.) The data universe conveniently broke down into three categories by size of companies.

1. Thirty-eight companies with less than $100 million of sales.
2. Fifteen companies with sales between $100 and $600 million.

(Then there was a gap. No companies in the data universe had sales between $600 million and $1 billion.)

3. Nine companies had sales over $1 billion.[5]

The first point of interest is how low the PSRs were for the entire list of the smaller companies. As will be shown later, in 1982 and 1983, numerous companies of this size range had PSRs of 3 through 10—all the way to 30. But in early 1978, the highest PSR on the list was 2.53 for Waters Associates. The average of the 38 companies was a PSR of only 0.80. The lowest on the list was Infomag, with a PSR of 0.24. Table 4–2 shows the names and rankings of the 10 highest PSR stocks on the list of small companies. These were among the most highly valued companies in the world in 1978.

---

[4] Hambrecht & Quist did have some nontechnology stocks in their universe. Conveniently, they kept these together in two subsections. We could discard the nontechnology stocks and focus completely on technology issues. One of the subsections, entitled "Special Situations," included both technology and nontechnology companies. We included the technology companies—like MSI Data, and Amicon. We excluded the nontechnology companies such as Mervyn's. The only stock we debated whether or not to include was Itel, which started out with an above-average PSR. We decided not to include Itel, choosing to view it essentially as a financial company rather than a technology company. As it turns out, had we included Itel, it would have reinforced the study's conclusions.

[5] These sizes reflect sales at the beginning of the time period. By the end of the five years, most of the companies were much larger.

TABLE 4–2
The 10 Highest PSR Companies on the January 31, 1978,
Hambrecht & Quist Statistical Summary, Each Having a
PSR over 0.90

Rank	Name	PSR	12 Months' Revenue	Market Value
1	Waters Associates	2.53	$34 million	$86 million
2	Manufacturing Data Systems	1.46	24	35
3	Tesdata	1.38	13	18
4	Plantronics	1.19	54	64
5	Four Phase System	1.13	80	90
6	MCI Communications	1.13	72	81
7	Tymshare	1.00	92	92
8	Sycor	0.99	72	71
9	Advanced Micro Devices	0.93	82	76
10	Computer Automation	0.92	52	48

Consider how they performed in the period thereafter. There were three spectacular successes. They were: Manufacturing Data Systems, number 2 on the list; MCI Communications, number 6 on the list; and Advanced Micro Devices, number 9 on the list. People who held these stocks made plenty of money.

From a market value of $35 million, Manufacturing Data Systems left our list when it was acquired by Schlumberger in early 1981 at a market value of $212 million. At the time, it had a PSR of 3.8. In a most exceptional performance, MCI increased in value from $81 million to close out our study in early 1983 at $4.9 billion (repeat, BILLION dollars). That gave MCI a closing PSR of 4.9—far and away the highest value of any company of its size range. MCI is the highest-valued company, on a PSR basis for its size range, in the world. Finally, Advanced Micro Devices increased in value from $76 million to $986 million and a PSR of 2.9 in early 1983.

By contrast, some stocks were noted disappointments. Tesdata was number 3 on the list in 1978, with a market value of $18 million. By early 1983, the value had dropped to $10 million, reaching a low of $4 million in 1982. Computer Automation began the study with a market value of $48 million and ended the study with a market value of $29 million. The highest PSR stock, Waters Associates, while not a disaster, was certainly a big disappointment. In 1978, it had a market value of $86 million and a PSR of 2.53—clearly the fair-haired darling of the crowd. It dropped off the list when it was acquired by Millipore in the second quarter of 1980 for only $91 million.

Others in the so-called top 10 were in one way or another rather ho-hum performers. Sycor, for instance, was bought out for just 8 percent more than its starting value. Tymshare started the study with a market value of $92 million and rose to a temporary high of $622— at which point it had a PSR of 2.6, later falling to a market value of only $204 million and a PSR of 0.67.[6]

To understand how badly 7 out of 10 of these high price sales ratio companies acted, it is necessary to understand that these were very unusual years for technology stocks as a whole—a period of almost unprecedented rise. During this period, the Hambrecht & Quist index of technology stocks rose more than 5 times in value, or a compound average growth rate of approximately 40 percent. With this background condition, the poor action of 7 out of 10 of the highest PSR stocks becomes rather significant.

Examining the low PSR stocks provides a startling contrast. At the bottom of the list, Infomag, with a lowly PSR of 0.24 and a market value of only $8 million, concluded the study under a name change to Computer & Communications Technology. It had a market value of over $150 million and a PSR of over 2.0. Granger Associates started with a market value of only $9 million and a PSR of 0.50. It concluded the period with a market value in excess of $250 million and a PSR over 5.0. Granger's PSR multiple increased more than tenfold in the five-year period.

Some of the low PSR stocks had small multiple increases, yet performed quite well regardless. Finnigan Corporation, for instance, began the study with a PSR of 0.43 and a market value of only $9 million. It ended the study with a PSR of 1.20 but a market value of $66 million—more than seven times higher than in the beginning. California Microwave (see case history in Chapter 15) started the study at a value of $19 million and a PSR of 0.63. In early 1983, it had a market value in excess of $150 million and a PSR of 1.50. Rolm (a true Super Stock throughout the period) started with an almost exactly average PSR for the group at 0.81 and a market value of $29 million. It ended the period with a market value of over $1.1 billion and a PSR of over 2.5.

A significant part of the appreciation of these stocks was due to the powerful Bull Market that evolved in technology stocks as they became ever more popular. (More recently, technology stocks became overpriced on a PSR basis. It's been a strong Bull Market.) By November 1982, 27 stocks on Hambrecht & Quist's list had PSRs over 3.0. Of these, eight had PSRs over 6.0. After that, the rate of increase accelerated. By May 1983, 54 stocks on the list had PSRs over 3.0, and 27 had PSRs over 6.0. (Remember that in early 1978, the highest PSR on the list was only 2.54.)

---

[6] This gave Tymshare a compound rate of growth of less than 15 percent, which isn't bad but hardly justifies ranking among the world's top-valued companies.

Note how low PSRs were in 1978 compared to 1983. By comparing PSRs over the entire last half-century (Chapters 6 and 7), it becomes clear that PSRs of so-called technology stocks were low in 1978 and high in 1983. (Don't buy stocks simply because they have low PSRs: You need quality as well.)[7]

Without exception, all of the stocks on the list increasing 500 to 1,000 percent started the study at PSRs of less than 1.5. Only two such Super Stocks had PSRs over 1.0. The relative performance provides some insights. The third of the list with lowest PSRs consistently outperformed the high PSR third (quarter by quarter). If you take MCI and Advanced Micro Devices out of the group, the comparison becomes more dramatic. (Of course MCI and AMD are worth a lot by themselves.)[8] The interesting thing is that out of a universe of objectively selected but homogeneous stocks—each chosen for quality, the low PSR stocks provided more potential for profit and less potential for risk than did the high PSR stocks (quarter by quarter and for the whole period). Avoid high PSR stocks on that basis alone.

Getting the Right Slant on Stocks

Table 4–3 shows the number of companies by size and level of PSR on the Hambrecht & Quist list of November 1982. For example, in the first column, second row, there were four companies which were between $100 and $200 million in sales and had PSRs between zero and 1.0. Likewise, in the fourth column, row four, there was only one company in the $300 to $400 million sales range with a PSR between 3.0 and 4.0.

A diagonal line on Table 4–3 sloping upward to the right from the bottom left demarcates what I call never-never land. The region to the right of this slanted line represents combinations of PSRs and sizes which either no companies have attained or were attained by only a few of Wall Street's "sacred cows." The names of the few companies which are on or to the right of the line are indicated. These few were the most richly priced companies on the list for their size on a PSR basis. Each of them is a standout in some way. They include AMD, Apple Computer, Intel, MCI, Prime Computer, Tandem Computer, Tandon, and Wang. The highest PSR on the Novem-

---

[7] In fact, the very worst companies of the world, on their way to bankruptcy, sell at very low PSRs just prior to giving up the ghost.

[8] One conclusion reached from studying these changes is that Hambrecht & Quist did an outstanding job selecting a list of stocks with such winners—with losers relatively few, losses relatively small, and average gains so spectacular. Their continual weeding out and adding other companies to the list over the five-year period tended to weed out future losers and add back stocks which, in the interim, would perform better than the stocks they had replaced.

TABLE 4-3
Relationships between Price Sales Ratios and Size of Companies Covered in the H&Q Statistical Summary of November 1982

Last 12 Months' Annual Revenue	Number of Companies with Price Sales Ratios between:							Total
	0–1	1–2	2–3	3–4	4–5	5–6	6+	
$0–100 million	8	17	16	3	2	5	8	59
$100–200	4	7	2	3	2	1*	0	19
$200–300	2	2	1	0	0	0	0	5
$300–400	1	2	2	1†	1‡	0	0	7
$400–800	2	4	2§	0	1‖	0	0	9
$800+	11#	5	2**	0	0	0	0	18
Total	28	37	25	7	6	6	8	117

* Tandon
† AMD
‡ Tandem
§ Apple and Prime Computer
‖ MCI
Includes such legendary greats of yesteryear as Data General, Motorola, National Semiconductor, Northern Telecom Storage Technology, Texas Instruments, and Tektronix.
** Wang and Intel

ber 1982 list was Intecom, with a PSR of 18¾. It had only $18 million in revenues. The eight highest are shown on the following list:

Company	$Millions of Annual Revenue	$Millions of Market Value	PSR
Intecom	18	338	18.78
Collagen	9	120	13.33
Home Health Care	22	217	9.86
Genentech	26	251	9.65
Convergent Tech	63	568	9.02
Seagate	44	316	7.18
Tera Corp	32	221	6.91
Evans & Sutherland	48	326	6.79

It's not that these stocks can't rise. They did rise from these levels in the strong market of November to May 1983. But the potential reward is not worth the risk. Remember Datapoint. In fact, while rising in value from November to May, the group did not do as well as the low PSR stocks on the list. (The high PSR groupings consistently underperform the low PSR groupings over the medium to long term.)

Several individual stocks have stood out as exceptions to this rule, but the number of exceptions is small enough to be of little investment consequence. MCI, for example, had a PSR that rose from an already-high level to an extraordinarily high level as it grew to be a large company. It stood out as a unique exception. Looking at Table 4–3 again, it's off by itself to the right of the diagonal line. But there were few such exceptions. (MCI later tumbled.)

Swimming Upstream as You Grow

Another interesting outcome of the study was a consistent trend for PSRs to be lower for extremely large companies than for comparable smaller ones. This was less pronounced at the beginning of the study than at the end (but was true throughout). The very highest PSRs were always among the smaller companies. Of the nine companies on the list with sales over $1 billion, the average PSR in early 1978 was only 0.63. Hewlett Packard and DEC are among a very small but elite group of the most highly valued of all companies for their size. Eliminating these two brings the average PSR for this group to only 0.41.

As a company increases in size, it can look forward to the eventuality of its PSR being no higher than the highest PSRs for other

companies of its future size. THIS IS AMONG THE MOST IMPOR-
TANT CONCLUSIONS OF THIS STUDY. (I can't emphasize its importance enough.)

The portion of Table 4–3 on the largest companies indicates the
relative degree to which PSRs decrease as company size increases.
The 11 companies with sales over $800 million and PSRs less than
one are not companies with poor images. They are companies which
were greatly revered over the decades, including Texas Instruments,
Storage Technology, Data General, and the like.[9]

The five with sales over $800 million and PSRs between 1.0 and
2.0 are interesting because three of them were just barely billion-
dollar companies. In fact, only two multibillion-dollar companies on
the list, HP and DEC, had PSRs greater than one. These few companies were distinguished by their high PSRs in relation to the size
they have attained. They were, by comparison, almost as richly
priced as many of the small companies selling at much higher PSRs.
(DEC later tumbled.) The bulk of the rest of the huge legendary
technology companies of modern times, the ones so strongly held by
the institutional portfolios, had PSRs less than one.

A Fear of Heights

High PSRs can be dangerous. We know that as a company grows and
in time becomes huge, its PSR tends to compress. As companies
grow beyond the billion-dollar sales size, their PSRs tend to fall
below one. Few escape that fate. Those that do escape don't have
PSRs much higher. Since PSRs decline with size, if a company is too
big for its PSR (if there are few companies its size with such high
PSRs), it is vulnerable and yet has poor appreciation potential.

Consider an example. Verbatim Corporation is discussed as a
case history in Chapter 14. Looking ahead from 1983, it doesn't
appear cheap. In midsummer 1983, the stock was in the low 50s, and
Verbatim had a market value of over $610 million with annual sales
of $120 million—a PSR of 5.1. I think Verbatim is a great company. It
should have a spectacular future in floppy disks. Yet the nature of a

---

[9] This list is dated more than six months before Texas Instrument's personal
computer problems began to surface. At the time, TI was viewed as a "safe" personal
computer "play." It had a high PSR (just under 1.0) for a huge company but a low PSR
compared to smaller companies. By the time of this writing, the tables had turned. TI
lost its luster, announcing major writedowns and losses. Its PSR had fallen to 0.67 in
midsummer 1983—neither high nor low for a company its size.

To demonstrate the degree to which these low PSR companies were once revered, one need only look at past PSRs. In 1973, Data General had a PSR of 12.59 and a
price of $49. In 1983, the stock was in the mid-60s with a PSR of 1.03. Storage
Technology had a PSR of 4.3 in 1973 with the stock at $7. After hitting a peak at $40¾,
the stock traded around $16 in 1983 with a PSR of 0.60. Along the way, Storage
Technology had grown from $26 million to a $1 billion in sales. Texas Instruments
had a peak PSR in 1973 of 3.26. It was less than a quarter of its current size then.

company its size with a PSR as high as this is scary. Unless the whole market rises (so that all multiples rise in a dramatic way), it becomes unlikely Verbatim will have a market value significantly greater than a billion dollars when it gets to be about a billion dollars in sales.

The Threshold of Never-Never Land

Verbatim will have to grow 10 times in sales to get an approximate doubling of the stock price.[10] What is the probability it will grow 10 times in sales in a time period short enough for a substantial return on a single doubling of the price? Not too likely. (To meet our minimum Super Stock requirement, it would have to do this in only three years.) More likely, in striving for rapid growth, they will need cash and sell more stock, increasing the amount of stock outstanding—increasing the market value and the PSR without increasing the value of the existing owners. (The compression of PSRs as companies grow occurs in parallel with the dilution from stock offerings aimed at funding the growth.)

I'm not saying that Verbatim can't go up in value. It can. What I'm saying is that for the stock to go up, it has to swim upstream against rough water. The more it swims upstream in 1983, the more people will be hurt—or at least sadly disappointed—later on. (Verbatim later tumbled.) Referring again to Table 4–3, let me point out that when I originally purchased Verbatim, it was in column 1, row 1 of the comparable January 1981 list. By the time I finished selling the stock in 1983, it had moved to column 6, row 2, which is the threshold of never-never land.

The Economics of Going Public

Many initial public offerings were completed in 1982 and 1983 at PSRs that can only cause later grief. Investors are extraordinarily liable to lose substantial amounts of money on many, if not most of them. When a company goes public at 10 times sales, it is the same as 100 times earnings for a company earning 10 percent after-tax profits (consult Table 4–1). Few companies earn 10 percent margins for long. Most of these high PSR public offerings will result in long-term losses rather than the gains investors expect.

Investors seem to pay little attention to the degree to which these companies are truly outstanding industrial concerns. Greed-crazed

---

[10] Suppose Verbatim grows tenfold from $120 million in sales to $1.2 billion. If it then has a PSR of 1.0—a reasonably prosperous assumption, it will have a market value of $1.2 billion. This is exactly twice its current market value of $610 million.

"investors" phone their brokers, frothing at the mouth to get 300 shares of his new offering—XYZ. Then when told that it isn't XYZ after all—but instead ZXY, they want it just as much. After all, it is the "new deal." In these kinds of frothy markets, people are convinced stocks will go up. They pay very little attention to fundamentals.

Even so, paying attention to fundamentals is relatively pointless if a stock is priced at the lofty PSRs of the 1982–83 new-issue market. Among the biggest losers when this Bull Market ends will be purchasers of extremely high PSR stocks which subsequently fail to live up to expectations.

Another big group of losers is apt to be among those who buy the few extremely high PSR stocks which DO live up to expectations (for the same reason Verbatim is too high). If you run through what is required to generate a payback on a stock selling at 10 times sales, you will be running a long time. Better to buy a municipal bond. When this kind of crazy market action gets started, there almost always follows a period of retribution when many suffer. This time is apt to be no different. The Turkey Market gives money to those with excesses of skill and experience—and experience to those with excesses of money and greed. Long after the bulls and bears have retired from the field, the turkeys are still out there gobbling.

Even so, some stocks can be cheap, even at the highs of a Bull Market. When a company falls from favor, it can plummet far and fast as in the Datapoint example. This can be as true in a Bull Market as in a Bear Market. My successful investment in Verbatim, for example, was purchased at the very top of the 1981 Bull Market. Once the process of disenchantment starts, it is prone to the extreme. Likewise, when too optimistic, the process swings to the other extreme. Buying a Super Company at a PSR of 0.75 or less is a no-lose situation. Why?

It's a no-lose situation because it will soon sell at some very low price-earnings ratio and grow rapidly from there.[11] A PSR of 0.75 means the relationship between market value and sales is 0.75 to 1.0. Yet soon its sales will increase 20 to 40 percent, so that it's future PSR based on its present price will be 0.6 or less (0.75/1.20 = 0.62— 0.75/1.40 = 0.54). A 0.6 PSR is theoretically equivalent to 12 times earnings for a business that will soon earn 5 percent after-tax margins (extrapolate from Table 4–1). It's only eight times earnings for a company that will earn 7.5 percent after-tax margins (also Table 4–1).

---

[11] *Some* implies that you can't tell what the future price-earnings ratio will be. You can't. As stated in Chapter 3, specific earnings forecasts don't work. The whole concept of the PSR is aimed at buying stocks at prices where your vision of the future earnings numbers doesn't have to be precise.

We have seen that a Super Stock is the stock of a Super Company which has been purchased at a Price Sales Ratio of 0.75 or less. We have also seen that using PSRs allows investors a clearer and more stable vantage point from which to view stock valuation than any other single tool. It may be used either with companies earning money or losing it. It may be used when short-term profit margins are either extremely high or low. It may be used to assess what value a private buyer might pay to acquire an entire company. It may be used as a warning sign to indicate potential future danger in a stock's price.

Yet by itself, the PSR is still a limited single tool—a powerful one to be sure, but still limited. No single tool allows enough cross-check capability to ensure results. Life just isn't that easy. When considering technology stocks, a valuable cross-check to the PSR is the Price Research Ratio (PRR)—considered in Chapter 5.

Price Research Ratios—
The Cost of a Good
Set of Brains

The Problem—Landing a Whale

If you want to land a whale, it's a little silly to try to bring it in with only one line. Get as many harpoons in that whale as possible. Secure it from all sides. If you want to land a Super Stock, it helps to have several different lines into the valuation process. This helps insure you're getting a Super Stock and not just a Super Company (at too high a price). Price Research Ratios (PRRs) can help point out blind spots in the use of Price Sales Ratios (or any other valuation method).

This chapter pertains only to technology companies. Price Research Ratios provide an analysis of the value of research. Technology companies make up a significant portion of the universe of Super Companies. Therefore, PRRs play an important role in the analysis of Super Stocks.

PRRs help avoid mistakes in two ways:

> They help avoid buying companies which are cheap on a Price Sales Ratio basis and are thought to be Super Companies but in reality aren't.

> They give a clue when a Super Company with a seemingly high Price Sales Ratio is in reality quite cheap.

For reasons explained later, the PRR is not as powerful as the PSR. Nevertheless, it is a valuable cross-check to see if the PSR is misleading in some respect.

What Is the Price Research Ratio?

The Price Research Ratio (PRR) is the market value of the company divided by the corporate research expenses for the last 12 months.[1] The PRR is a simple arithmetic relationship between the stock price and the research budget of the company. Note that it is not a relationship between the stock price and the productivity or output of research.

To understand the value of the PRR, it is necessary to understand the research function and what makes it tick—a concept too few understand. There is a lot of jargon floating in the press these days about research. If you listen to what newspapers, Wall Street, or successful technology companies may say regarding R&D, you can become confused. Research, R&D, product development, commercial development, engineering—or whatever else you want to call it—stems from the same source at most businesses. It is nothing more than a functional tool used in the process of satisfying customer needs. There is no magic to it.

Research Is Just a Commodity

At most businesses, research is commoditylike in that there is nothing particularly unique in the process. Unique research does exist, to be sure, but only in a relatively few large institutions—like Bell Labs, Hewlett Packard, IBM, Texas Instruments, government labs, and universities: These are the places unique primary or fundamental research is done. What is done by everyone else is more aptly termed *commercial or applied development.* Commercial development, as its name implies, is eminently more useful than fundamental research. (It may not be quite as titillating to some.)

The notion of research as a commoditylike function is not popular. People want to believe that very complicated things in research are as unique as they are complicated. Some managements would have you believe they have a truly unique technology and engineering group. They want you to believe this creates great difficulty for their competitors. Many companies with high stock market valuations push this point *ad nauseum.*

Many brokerage firms touting technology firms make a similar point. It's almost never (spelled n-e-v-e-r) true. Usually, at best, such companies have a time lead over competition in the marketplace.

Research is a relative commodity. Research is managed—at times—with some difficulty. It is a relative commodity, neverthe-

---

[1] The market value of the company is simply the fully diluted number of shares of stock outstanding multiplied by the stock price.

less. Some firms do a better job of managing the commodity than others, but the differences are fairly small. They just don't seem small because the results that come out of research can vary widely firm to firm.

How can the research be commoditylike, yet the results of research be unique or noncommoditylike? Why does one firm seem to have exceptionally productive research while another has unproductive research? How can this be if, in fact, research is a relative commodity? What significant difference is there between research at various firms? The answer can be expressed in one word—*marketing*.

Market Research Wags Technical Research

Market research, in its most fundamental form, determines the nature and success of the product produced. Thereby it determines the relative success of research. One firm can have better research than another—it happens all the time. It is largely because the company with the better research had earlier done a better marketing job. It understood what technology would be needed to exploit a market opportunity. (Exceptions occur when companies with poor marketing get lucky—the right technology and product, by chance, at the right time.)

Adam Osborne saw a hole you could drive a truck through in the personal computer market. In four months, the Osborne 1 was designed, developed, and ready to go. It sold hundreds of millions of dollars and set a whole trend others would have to follow in personal computing—portability. Osborne didn't have better research. (Research and product development was quite simple—it took four months.) What Osborne had was a deadly accurate (and perhaps lucky) perception of future market needs that served the company well in its first two years.

Osborne failed to develop substantial management around him. As the market matured and he relied on his entrepreneurial market sense, he failed to perceive correctly the next evolutionary stage in personal computers—IBM compatibility. That single marketing error made the research on his next two computers, the Vixen (never released—project terminated by IBM PC introduction) and the Executive 1, virtually worthless. It also made the company virtually worthless. In September 1983, Osborne was forced to let all its production workers go, shrinking employment from a peak of 1,000 employees down to only 80. The survival of Osborne Computer Corporation was at stake. Osborne's only hope was in designing an IBM-compatible machine which could catch up to the rapidly changing market. An accurate perception of the market made Osborne. An inaccurate market perception killed it. Understanding the markets is more important in technical products than the technology itself.[2]

Frequently, a company spends years in the development of a product but is forced, shortly after introduction, to write it off or sell out to someone else. The financial loss can be quite severe. Years of research expense are wasted. The money spent on research obviously wasn't worth much. Why? Because the company had not correctly understood the market.

In early 1983, I visited Lynch Communications Systems in Reno, Nevada. They had just written off a new product called ATLAS, a next-generation product for answering-service bureaus. Annual reports indicated the bulk of recent research efforts went into ATLAS. But the product was being written off—at a cost of $5 million. They weren't getting much for their money.

When queried, management proudly pointed out the product's excellent state-of-the-art technology. They wrote it off because it couldn't be sold. Customers (who wanted the system) were in sufficiently poor financial condition that they couldn't arrange to have the purchases financed. No financing, no purchases—the Lynch research was just money down the drain.

Management did not perceive this as a basic flaw in marketing. Lynch didn't even have a corporate marketing manager. Dick Dertinger, the chief executive officer, spent a large part of his time as a traveling salesman for their overseas business. He is quite good at it. But who was responsible for the broader realm of marketing? With poor marketing, the result is valueless research.

Companies with poor marketing seldom see their problem. They go from one mistake to another. They should bite the bullet and bring in top-flight marketing people and then turn new-product decisions over to them. Instead, they keep stumbling around repeating their mistakes. This is the way legends are built—sad legends. If a company isn't good at marketing, it isn't good. A technology company that isn't good at marketing, isn't good at technology. A Super Company is competent (not necessarily perfect) at marketing.

Companies with a strong sense of the market and strong overall management (Super Companies) efficiently build a research organization to achieve their purposes. This is, after all, what a company does when it first gets started. Someone has an idea for a product. Then they hire the people necessary to make it happen. (This is what happened with the earlier-mentioned Osborne Computer example.)

Most venture capitalists say they would much rather back a company led by a strong marketer who is weak in technology than a strong technologist who is weak in marketing. The research organi-

---

[2] *The Wall Street Journal*, September 12, 1983, p. 31.

zation can be built. No one researcher is all that unique once a company gets rolling. Managements sometimes think someone is particularly unique, but it isn't often true.

Suppose we're running a small but significant company—say $50 million per year in sales. To build a research organization to address a new market, we do a little research of our own—most likely with our existing vice president of engineering. We identify the leading people in the field. The VP of engineering hires and manages them in a rather conventional fashion. It isn't terribly hard to do.[3]

Isn't there still a big difference among R&D efforts? Not so much. Most of the variance in results boils down to finding what to develop in the first place. What should the product be like? How should it perform? Why will the customer prefer it over other alternatives? What is the motivation that generates the sale? These kinds of marketing factors determine up to 80 percent of the effectiveness of research.

The other 20 percent varies with the capability of management. Within this 20 percent, long-term results will vary from company to company. Again the Super Company gets the better long-term results. Better results are not easy to achieve. They require:

Just plain better management.

A willingness to hire the best.

A charisma that encourages, and requires, the best efforts of each employee.

An exquisite sense of time management.

Devotion to the unique characteristics of (at times) eccentric geniuses in engineering—seeing them as people.

A steadfast "eye on the ball."

These skills are somewhat rare. They make the difference between Vince Lombardi and Vinnie the plumber.

The Solution

What does all this have to do with the valuation of stocks? Simply *don't pay too much for research.* To buy a Super Stock, you need to buy a Super Company at a low price. Avoid the lure of supposed research magic. There's no magic in engineering. The real key to

---

[3] Books exist on research management. I'm not going to delve into this matter further since it is largely outside this book's scope. Interested readers might start with *Principles of R&D Management* by Philip H. Francis (New York: AMACOM, 1977). Those wanting more can source from his annotated bibliography. My own personal experiences are contained in appendix four.

what a company will get out of its research lies in marketing. Once you determine marketing capability, valuing research becomes a relatively easy thing to do. (A few problems are probed later.)

Rules for Using PRRs

Using PRRs can help you stay out of trouble. To buy a Super Stock, consider these rules:

RULE 1: Don't ever buy a Super Company selling at a PRR greater than 15. There are always plenty that can be bought at lower valuations.
RULE 2: Find Super Companies with a PRR of 5 to 10. You are unlikely to find them at PRRs much below 5. (Some other company already may have acquired them at these low levels.)

PRRs indicate how much the market values a company's R&D. Since we know there isn't any real magic in engineering and most research success is really just a function of good marketing, it becomes obviously silly to pay too much for research. Most initial public equity offerings of the early 1980s were at 15 times research or more—often much more. The really hot ones were at 50 to 200 times research. With these, the PRR and the PSR are exactly what they should be—they are relatively perfect reflections of each other. They indicate the stock is way too high. Perhaps money can be made in these stocks But they don't qualify as Super Stocks because, starting at these prices, people aren't likely to make 3 to 10 times their money in three to five years. People are more apt to lose money buying these high-PRR initial offerings.

Looking beyond initial offerings, the same rules apply. In Chapter 3, Verbatim is shown having a high Price Sales Ratio. It also had a very high PRR in 1983 at just over 100. This is scary. First, the market places a very high value on sales. Then, if research is low relative to the market value, from where are enough new products to come to make sales grow enough to push up the stock? Avoid these high-priced companies. (If other people make money on them, who are you to begrudge them that? At least make sure that you won't be losing money. Be sure that you are making it instead.)

If the PRR is a reflection of the PSR, why bother with it? Because the two are not always reflections of each other. In the instances where they are not, some interesting questions need to be answered before money is invested. They are perfect reflections of each other if the PSR and PRR for that company are either both low or both high.

But what if the PSR is low while the PRR is high? What if the PSR is high while the PRR is low? Consider some cases.

The PRR helps when a Super Company seems high priced (based on PSRs) but is really rather cheap. Consider a Super Company with a marginally high PSR like 1.0. Suppose it has a very low PRR like 5.0. The implication is that current research expenditures, on perceived market opportunities, will soon give birth to a new set of products (or even product lines) which will boost sales and profits. Check it out (spelled m-a-r-k-e-t-i-n-g). If true, this Super Company may be worth the marginally high PSR because of the events that caused the very low PRR. If it's not true, it is probably because marketing is bad. Then the research expense won't bear fruit so that it isn't really a Super Company.

Using PRRs in conjunction with PSRs may force serious consideration of a Super Stock that you otherwise would overlook. The PRR helps an investor find opportunities that otherwise might be missed.

Recently, I bought stock in Finnigan Corporation (San Jose, California). It is the world's leading producer of mass spectrometers, a sophisticated form of analytical instruments. The stock seemed somewhat high for me on a PSR basis at 1.0. Yet on a PRR basis, it seemed inexpensive. This prompted me to look further, where—sure enough—a lot of new-product development that could have significant future benefit was brewing. Time will tell if this investment will be successful. But without the PRR, I would have shied away from the PSR and missed what may be an exciting opportunity, worthy of time and effort.

Consider a company portrayed by others as a Super Stock (a rather bad sign if people are touting it). Suppose it is selling at a PSR of only 0.75. On a price sales basis, it seems to meet our requirements. (Notice that absolutely no mention whatsoever is made here of earnings.) But suppose the PRR is 25. This is too high. It implies that the company isn't spending what it should to maximize its future. Research is being conducted at a low level. Apparently, marketing is not making the effort or else just not finding opportunities.

Since there isn't any magic, the company's research efforts may produce results but not at a level from which dramatic sales improvements are likely to flow—hence the low PSR. Perhaps the company is making acquisitions because it can't find enough internal opportunities. Management may understand its market perfectly. Seeing low potential for growth, it has chosen this low R&D/high-acquisition effort.

Using PRRs in conjunction with PSRs in this case resulted in avoiding an investment which, on the surface, appears to be a Super Stock but certainly isn't. It isn't even a Super Company. The low PSR was just bad bait. The PRR in this case helped avoid buying a probable loser.

Problems with PRRs

It is a mistake to be too precise with PRRs. They should be used as a broad gauge of value. Don't try to fine tune them. Instead, use the PRR to point out the rare instance where the Price Sales Ratio fails to give an accurate interpretation of value. Think first in terms of Price Sales Ratios. You wouldn't buy one stock because its PRR was 10.4 and not buy another because its was 11.8. That kind of precision will only cause grief. There are many other more-important swing factors.

PRRs shouldn't be used as a sharpshooter's gun. One company may show slightly more of its expenses as R&D than another would. Remember—the true efficiency of one research organization can be up to 20 percent more than another. It is silly to use PRRs with the intent of greater accuracy than 20 percent. It is an absolute mistake to buy a stock singularly because the PRR is low. A lot of R&D can be totally worthless. A low PRR by itself can be just bad bait. Avoid trying to be too cute—use PRRs only as a broad gauge cross-check. The highest value of the PRR is not in seeking out cheap stocks but in helping avoid mistakes.

The PRR is a new idea. Financial people aren't used to it. It is neither widely understood nor accepted. Any new idea meets some resistance. Various criticisms have surfaced. Some are valid. Most are not. By exploring them you will have a better idea of where the use of the PRR fits in and where it doesn't.

CRITICISM 1: "Different firms account for things differently. What one firm counts as R&D, another doesn't. Since the figures aren't comparable, making comparisons based thereon is obviously silly."

This may be correct in a few instances but not often. To a growing degree, firms are accounting for R&D more uniformly. Most publicly held corporations tend to overstate, or at least fully state, their research efforts. Research has become fashionable. If a company isn't doing much research, many are convinced the company just doesn't have a future.

R&D first became a byword with politicians in the 1970s as California's former Governor Edmund G. (Moonbeam) Brown became the country's first significant elected technology advocate. Now even the president makes public overtures to R&D. All politicians are for it—none against. Committees meet regularly in Congress to consider ways to promote venture capital for technology companies.

Silicon Valley has its own congressman advocate in Ed Zschau. Congressman Zschau gets strong press as the founder/chief executive of a successful technology company turned public servant.

The result of all this enthusiasm is tremendous tax advantages for research expenses incurred. Auditors march to their clients, drumming the theme of Congress. They show clients how they can save present and future tax dollars by declaring otherwise marginal items as research. Whatever can possibly be considered research these days, is. So research, if not overstated, is usually as fully stated as possible. (Still, some companies may display a bit more as R&D than others, as is pointed out by the next criticism.)

CRITICISM 2: "Government-funded R&D may not be included. It still can teach a company valuable skills that can later be applied to commercial products."

While government-funded R&D may not translate directly into commercial products, employees pick up skills. At another time— perhaps immediately or years later, something they learned can help develop a commercial product.

I agree. In fact, PRRs should cover the total engineering effort of a company, including not only government-funded R&D but also any form of third-party-sponsored research or engineering (such as commercial third-party sponsorship). Some companies don't show third-party-sponsored research in their annual reports, but the information is still readily available—usually detailed in their SEC Form 10-K, which is available from the company upon written request.

Third-party-sponsored R&D may not only contribute directly to the technical effort but may also contribute indirectly to its marketing input. California Microwave has an interesting viewpoint on the subject. Dave Leeson, the founder, chairman, and CEO, explains that if they can't persuade a customer to front at least some money for R&D, the customer isn't terribly anxious to get the product. When this happens, Cal Microwave has to focus long and hard on whether the market really is there.

Accordingly, Cal Microwave gets commercial third-party-sponsored R&D funding for a high percentage of its activities. A higher percentage of employees than normal work in engineering; a lower percentage, in marketing. In a sense, the engineers are doing the marketing. Perhaps this works for Leeson because his firm deals in large average prices for its contracts. One to $15 million contracts are common. (It would be tougher to obtain significant third-party R&D funding selling jelly beans.)

What about the rare instance where third-party-sponsored R&D funding is not detailed in the company's SEC Form 10-K? An approximation of research activities *can* still be obtained. It is easy to ask for the number of engineers who work directly on a company's engineering effort (usually but not always in the 10-K). It is also in industry trade association directories.[4] What percentage of a company's total labor force is devoted to engineering? As a general rule, you can estimate that two thirds of this percentage rate about equals R&D expenses as a percentage of sales. This will be off the mark a bit, but not by much.

Suppose, as an example, a company has 12 percent of its total labor force devoted to engineering, including both company-sponsored and third-party-sponsored R&D. It is likely that the company's R&D expense, as a percentage of sales would be about 8 percent (12 percent $\times$ 2/3 = 8 percent). Using this basis, even if a company does not break out third-party-sponsored R&D, an estimate of R&D expense is possible.

CRITICISM 3: "Companies that spend R&D dollars on defensive activities aimed at maintaining their markets should be valued at a lower basis than companies that spend R&D dollars on aggressively expanding into new and growing markets. The PRRs shouldn't be comparable."

This argument is not valid. Defensively oriented firms should have lower PRRs. The numbers are comparable. This is one of the best arguments for confining investments to Super Companies. A Super Company won't spend excessively on defensive projects—it won't have to. This argument won't pertain to Super Companies. Therefore it won't pertain to Super Stocks.

---

[4] Ask your reference librarian for help in locating these sources. A typical source, for example, in the laser industry would be the *Laser Focus Buyer's Guide*. It is published yearly (by Advanced Technology Publications, Inc., 1001 Watertown St., Newton, MA 02165) and shows the number of employees by area. This type of publication also shows much more—product types and families, detailed product specs, services available, general technical information, vendors, industry companies by functional area, and definitions of terms. (What exactly is an *etalon* or an *autocollimator*? Do they suffer from *attenuation*?)

CRITICISM 4: "Industries exist where there is such demand that it doesn't take much R&D to fuel a lot of growth. Again, the PRRs of these companies will not be comparable."

I agree. It sounds like superior marketing got them there in the first place. Marketing research leads technical research. Super Stock PRRs tend to fall within the ranges of 5 to 15. There are few exceptions where a good product design costs so little that it allows for high PRRs and a stock price compressed like a coiled spring waiting to burst forth. Besides, common sense says that if a product can be designed for "peanuts," technology probably wasn't very critical.

CRITICISM 5: "Since marketing is so important in determining the profitability of R&D, why place emphasis on the PRR?"

This is the beauty of it—also where people have trouble accepting the notion. Research, being commidity-like, can be quantitatively analyzed quite quickly. The PRR is a quantitative method *to measure something that can be quantified* to help determine appropriate value. The magic is in marketing. Marketing, therefore, can't be quantitatively analyzed. Marketing must be qualitatively analyzed. Place your qualitative analysis primarily on marketing. From that determine if it is a Super Company.

CRITICISM 6: "Bigger companies will have lower PRRs because they can spread the same R&D effort over more units. Look at IBM versus its plug-compatible follower Amdahl."

Yes, bigger companies are likely to have lower PRRs. There is method to the madness. Since PSRs and PRRs tend to parallel each other, and since bigger companies tend to have lower PSRs, it follows that bigger companies will tend to have lower PRRs. Amdahl has usually had a higher PSR and PRR than IBM. I don't know enough about Amdahl to know if it is a Super Company or not. I do know enough about IBM to know that it is a Super Competitor. I would prefer not to compete with IBM if possible. The real issue is to look at Amdahl and try to decide whether or not it is a Super Company. If not, don't buy it. If it is, use the PSR and PRR together to figure out if it is a Super Stock.

Granted other criticisms can be leveled at the concept of PRRs. Many come from people who think there is something quite magical about R&D. There isn't. It is because it isn't magical that the PRR has quantitative validity. The Price Research Ratio is just one simple way to see how much the financial community is paying for a good set of brains. A good investor needs to know what a good set of brains is worth.

Chapter 6

Applying Price Sales Ratios to Nonsuper Stocks

PSRs, the Broader Concept

So what happens to stocks that don't qualify as Super Stocks? You inherited some stock from Uncle Morris? Perhaps you work for a company. Or your next-door neighbor does. Maybe you like huge companies. Maybe you hate huge companies. Perhaps you are interested in certain industries. You want to study each company in those fields. Most companies are not Super Companies—therefore most stocks are not Super Stocks. How do you apply PSRs to stocks of special interest to you?

The history of PSRs (back through the 1920s) shows their validity as an analytical tool. PSRs won't tell you what stocks to buy—they tell you what stocks to avoid. They point to areas of interest. Only minor modifications to the definitions of "high" or "low" PSRs (in Chapter 4) are necessary.

This chapter looks at a little theory and a lot of history. It examines:

PSRs, the broader concept.

Lessons of the past—PSRs in the Bull Market of the 1960s and early 1970s.

PSRs and the Great American Smokestack Stock.

PSRs as a stock market timing device.

PSRs in the "garbage dump" of the stock market.

The next chapter will look at PSRs in the historical perspective of the 1930s. PSRs have value in the analysis of most stocks. The basic theme is similar to the application of PSRs to Super Companies:

1. Avoid buying any stock at a high PSR.
2. Seek opportunities among stocks with low PSRs.

History reveals the power of Price Sales Ratio analysis. Buying stocks at high PSRs either results in:

• Substantial losses.
• Comparatively small profits.

The largest profits regularly result from buying stocks at low PSRs. Nonsuper companies must be bought at lower PSRs than Super Companies. This makes common sense. We will see how and why this works.

As a general rule, buy stocks of huge companies at PSRs of 0.4 or less. In even the strongest of Bull Markets, most should be sold at 2.0 or less. Even the greatest should be sold as their PSR approaches 3.0. So-called smokestack stocks should be sold as their PSRs approach 0.80—if not lower—depending on future profit-margin potential.

Small, obscure companies with low historical profit margins may sell at PSRs as low as .05. Purchase of these small companies requires the utmost attention to future margin analysis (see Chapters 10 and 11). They should be sold when their PSR is high relative to their future margin potential.

Lessons of the Past—PSRs in the Bull Market of the 1960s and Early 1970s

The 1960s through 1973 represent a set of Bull Markets that have seen few peers. Optimism was rampant. New issues came public at a tremendous rate and at very steep prices. People talked of a new era in stocks. Many big companies sold at 30 to 60 times earnings and smaller ones at 100 times earnings and more.

In the 1960s, smaller companies caught the headlines. In the early 1970s, people began to talk of the "Two-Tier Market" as larger companies led the market. As always, the excessive optimism ended with a period of retribution. The nine years after 1973 were difficult for stocks as a whole. Prices plummeted and later failed to recover to new highs. (Both 1974 and 1982 saw stock prices so low that the typical stock could have been bought substantially below liquidation value.)

Certain sectors did better. Technology stocks started a Bull Market in 1978 that was sustained through the period. Oil stocks had a strong period in which they set new highs. But most stocks languished below their 1968 or 1972 highs.

Throughout the 1960s and 1970s, PSRs pointed out opportunities and potential problems. In both the 1960s and the "Two-Tier Market" of the early 1970s, stocks sold at outrageous PSRs. The simple act of selling stocks—because the PSRs were too high— would have saved investors a great deal of money.

Investors should sell even the greatest of large companies when their PSRs approach 4.0. Consider some examples:

Illustration 6–1 is a graph of the stock of Control Data. At its peak in 1968, it had a PSR of 4.4. This is a very high PSR for a company that was roughly equivalent—adjusting for inflation—to a billion-dollar company today. Its stock price was $80 per share. By 1975, the price had fallen to under $6—a loss of more than 90 percent. At that low level, its PSR was only 0.18.

By 1981, the stock was still only half its 1968 level despite Control Data being seven times larger than it had been in 1968. Had the stock been purchased when its PSR first broke 0.4 in 1974, losses would have been confined to less than a year. The stock went on to more than triple in the next six years. Buying it on the basis of a low PSR could have offered a nice return. Holding Control Data after it had a high PSR was a disaster.

DEC is an example of a different kind of failure. The stock has risen over the years—just not enough to be impressive in light of the company's growth. DEC as a business performed beautifully. It grew from about $135 million in sales in 1970 to over $3 billion in 1981— a compound growth rate greater than 30 percent per year. Still the stock offered a relatively poor overall return because the PSR originally was so high. Less than a third of its growth translated into higher stock prices. It had a peak of $42 per share in early 1970. In 1981, it hit a brief peak of $113—a compound rate of return of only 9.1 percent. That would be fine had it not been among the all-time growth companies. At its 1970 peak, DEC's PSR was 9.0.

Stocks at such high PSRs should be sold. DEC's high initial valuation promoted poor performance considering its growth. By 1981, DEC's highest PSR was down to 1.9. Its growth had been absorbed by the falling PSR rather than translating itself into rapidly rising stock prices. DEC is one of the few companies to have grown fast enough to offer *any* return starting from a high PSR. From another angle, holding the stock from early 1970 to 1975 would have shown losses in spite of tremendous growth. At its worst, the losses would have come to 62 percent of the original price. By 1975 at its low, DEC's PSR had fallen to 1.4. Even the greatest of growth rates does not offer

ILLUSTRATION 6–1

The PSR is:

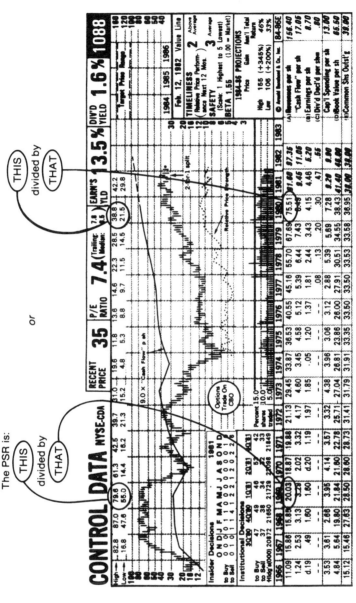

Source: *Value Line Ratings & Reports*. Reprinted by permission of the publisher. Copyright, Value Line Inc.

a superior stock return when coupled with a high initial PSR. By the early 1980s, having grown into a huge company, its PSR was still among the highest for companies of its size, suggesting a rather poor future performance. (DEC tumbled in late 1983.)

Eastman Kodak (EK) is an outstanding company, acknowledged as such for decades. In the 1960s, investors came to believe in it more and more. By 1973, it hit peaks of $150 for the stock and a 7.0 PSR. Dismal results were a certainty. It should have been sold when the PSR broke 3.0. Ten years later the company was vastly larger, yet the stock never recovered. Along the way, the stock was less than half its highest level. From the mid-1960s, when its PSR hit 4.0, it would have been easy to generate a higher future rate of return doing almost anything other than holding EK. Selling when the PSR was at 3.0 wouldn't have hit the absolute peak—but would have avoided the future losses. (See Illustration 6–2.)

Johnson & Johnson was another great growth company which failed to live up to expectations because the expectations were originally too high. As a company with more than $1.5 billion in sales in 1973, it basked in the financial community's limelight. Its PSR was 5.4 at the time. During most of the next 10 years, the stock could easily have been purchased for less than three fourths of its 1973 value—in spite of the company growing almost fivefold in size. (See Illustration 6–3.)

Compare the results we have been looking at to Motorola. It never had an outrageously high PSR. Its moderate growth fueled a rising stock price. In 1968, it had a PSR of only 1.1. In 1972–1973, it had a PSR of only 1.5. From its peak in 1973, it fell 50 percent in 1974–75—but stayed down only briefly. Its moderate growth brought back most of the earlier peak price by 1976. By 1981, Motorola hit new highs. While not dramatic, its moderate PSR allowed for results that were better than those achieved by the overall market.

In 1968, Polaroid had a PSR of 8.3 and a price of $140. In 1973, its PSR was 6.7 and the stock price was unchanged. From 1974 to 1983, it would fail to ever exceed $60. Most of the time it sold for less than $40. From its peak to its bottom, it lost more than 87 percent of its market value. "Losing" could have been avoided by selling the stock merely because the PSR was too high. It would have been better to ignore the predictions of how much the stock would grow and how much it would earn. Forget about everything other than that the stock is too high. (See Illustration 6–4.)

I could go on with examples from the great growth stocks of the 1960s: Avon, Bausch & Lomb, 3M, Black & Decker, IBM, Schering-Plough, Watkins-Johnson. They all fit. AM International and Xerox were absolute screamers. These so-called growth stocks couldn't grow fast enough to justify their excessively high early valuations. If

ILLUSTRATION 6-2

EASTMAN KODAK NYSE-EK

RECENT PRICE	P/E RATIO	EARN'S YLD	DIV'D YLD	
68	**13.6** (Trailing: 11.7 Median: 16.0)	**7.4 %**	**5.2 %**	**157**

Target Price Range
1986 1987 1988 1989

TIMELINESS (Relative Price Performance Next 12 Mos.) **5** Lowest

SAFETY (Scale: 1 Highest to 5 Lowest) **1** Highest

BETA .90 (1.00 = Market)

1986-88 PROJECTIONS		
	Price	Gain	Ann'l Total Return
High 165	(+145%)	26%
Low 130	(+ 90%)	21%

© Value Line, Inc.

	1968	1969	1970	1971	1972	1973	1974	1975	1976	1977	1978	1979	1980	1981	1982	1983	1984	1985	1986-88E
Sales per sh	16.40	17.01	17.24	18.42	21.52	24.98	28.37	30.69	33.65	36.97	43.45	49.74	60.31	63.61	65.33	62.15	68.45		(A) 97.45
"Cash Flow" per sh	2.99	3.29	3.39	4.49	5.23	5.19	5.24	5.83	5.99	7.71	8.44	9.62	10.42	10.49	8.60	11.00		15.60
Earnings per sh	2.33	2.49	2.50	2.60	3.39	4.05	3.90	4.03	3.99	5.59	6.20	7.15	7.66	7.12	4.20	6.50		(B) 10.70
Div'ds Decl'd per sh	1.14	1.25	1.32	1.34	1.39	1.99	2.06	2.07	2.10	2.33	2.90	3.20	3.50	3.55	3.55	3.65		(C) 4.00
Cap'l Spending per sh	1.73	1.75	1.92	1.82	1.56	2.22	3.42	3.53	3.08	2.64	2.74	3.74	5.59	7.32	9.06	8.20	7.25		8.25
Book Value per sh	11.39	12.60	13.78	15.04	17.05	19.30	21.21	22.95	24.92	26.84	30.10	33.40	37.35	41.66	45.56	46.25	49.20		64.90
Common Shs Outst'g	161.21	161.55	161.55	161.58	161.58	161.58	161.59	161.59	161.59	161.38	161.40	161.41	161.41	182.50	165.75	165.75	165.00		169.30
Avg Ann'l P/E Ratio	32.7	30.1	28.0	31.6	32.8	23.1	25.1	24.6	15.7	9.9	9.2	8.1	9.4	11.0	Bold figures are		14.0
Relative P/E Ratio	3.1%	3.3%	3.6%	3.2%	2.7%	3.1%	4.3%	4.1%	6.4%	10.1%	10.9%	12.4%	10.6%	9.1%	Value Line		7.1%
Avg Ann'l Div'd Yield	1.5%	1.7%	1.9%	1.6%	1.1%	1.4%	2.2%	2.2%	2.1%	3.4%	4.2%	5.1%	5.5%	4.8%	4.6%	estimates		3.2%

CAPITAL STRUCTURE as of 6/12/83

Total Debt $850.4 mill. Due in 5 Yrs $362.0 mill.
LT Debt $590.4 mill. LT Interest $39.0 mill.
Incl. foreign subsidiaries debt $66 mill. 4⅛% debs. ('88) each conv. into 10.42 common shs. at $96. Incl. $275 mill. 8¼% debs. ('07) callable after 12/14/84 at 107.43; conv. into 9.78 com. shs. at $102.25.   (6% of Cap'l)

Leases, Uncapitalized Annual rentals $32 mill.

Pension Liability None in '82 vs. None in '81

Pfd Stock None

Common Stock 165,700,000 shs. (94% of Cap'l)

	1974	1975	1976	1977	1978	1979	1980	1981	1982	1983	1984	1985	1986-88E
Sales ($mill)	4583.2	4958.5	5438.2	5967.0	7012.9	8028.2	9734.3	10337	10815	10300	11350		(A) 16500
Operating Margin	28.7%	26.6%	26.1%	25.3%	28.3%	25.0%	23.6%	24.3%	22.5%	18.0%	22.5%		23.5%
Depreciation ($mill)	209.5	232.6	291.9	322.7	342.2	361.3	399.2	454.0	575.0	710	750		830
Net Profit ($mill)	629.5	613.7	650.6	643.5	902.3	1000.8	1153.6	1239.0	1162.0	898	1077		1810
Income Tax Rate	45.5%	44.6%	44.3%	46.4%	46.3%	41.4%	41.2%	43.2%	37.9%	40.0%	41.0%		41.0%
Net Profit Margin	13.7%	12.4%	12.0%	10.8%	12.9%	12.5%	11.9%	12.0%	10.7%	8.8%	9.5%		11.0%
Working Cap'l ($mill)	1551.8	1543.0	1697.6	1953.3	2436.9	2781.1	2998.2	2944.0	3143.0	2945	3225		5060
Long-Term Debt ($mill)	124.6	127.7	139.1	154.4	163.2	178.3	207.9	208.0	489.0	600	650		600
Net Worth ($mill)	1837.3	1843.2	1968.9	2113.4	2316.9	2622.3	2928.3	3257.3		7665	8155		10985
% Earned Total Cap'l	17.8%	16.1%	15.7%	14.5%	15.7%	18.1%	18.6%	18.5%	14.6%	8.5%	12.5%		16.0%
% Earned Net Worth	18.4%	16.6%	16.2%	14.9%	18.6%	18.6%	19.1%	18.3%	15.4%	9.0%	13.0%		16.5%
% Retained to Comm Eq	9.0%	7.6%	7.9%	7.0%	10.8%	9.9%	10.6%	9.9%	7.7%	1.5%	6.0%		9.0%
% All Div'ds to Net Prof	51%	54%	51%	53%	42%	47%	45%	46%	50%	85%	55%		45%

Institutional Decisions

	2Q'82	3Q'82	4Q'82	1Q'83	2Q'83
to Buy	159	177	164	167	148
to Sell	174	165	163	165	203
Hld'g(000)	87373	89985	90347	89240	81492

Insider Decisions

	M	J	J	A	S	O	N	D	J	F	M	A	M	J	J
to Buy	0	0	0	0	0	0	0	0	1	7	5	3	0	0	0
to Sell	0	1	0	1	0	0	1	0	0	2	2	1	2	1	2

20.0 X "Cash Flow" p sh

Options Trade On CBO

Relative Price Strength

Percent shares traded: 6.0 / 4.0 / 2.0

| High | 83.4 | 84.6 | 100.0 | 149.8 | 151.8 | 117.5 | 110.0 | 120.8 | 86.8 | 68.1 | 66.9 | 74.8 | 85.4 | 98.1 | 91.8 | | | |
| Low | 68.6 | 52.6 | 72.0 | 93.3 | 103.5 | 57.6 | 63.0 | 81.5 | 48.8 | 41.1 | 47.8 | 42.9 | 60.6 | 65.4 | 64.1 | | | |

Value Line

Sept. 30, 1983

ILLUSTRATION 6–3

JOHNSON & J'SON. NYSE-JNJ

RECENT PRICE	P/E RATIO	EARN'S YLD	DIV'D YLD	
44	14.7 (Trailing: 16.7 Median: 18.0)	6.8%	2.7%	233

	1968	1969	1970	1971	1972	1973	1974	1975	1976	1977	1978	1979	1980	1981	1982	1983
High	20.1	20.1	33.3	44.3	44.1	39.8	33.3	32.2	26.0	29.7	26.8	33.8	39.4	51.3	51.5	
Low	11.2	12.4	18.9	31.4	33.8	24.4	24.1	23.8	20.7	21.8	21.6	22.0	28.3	32.5	40.1	

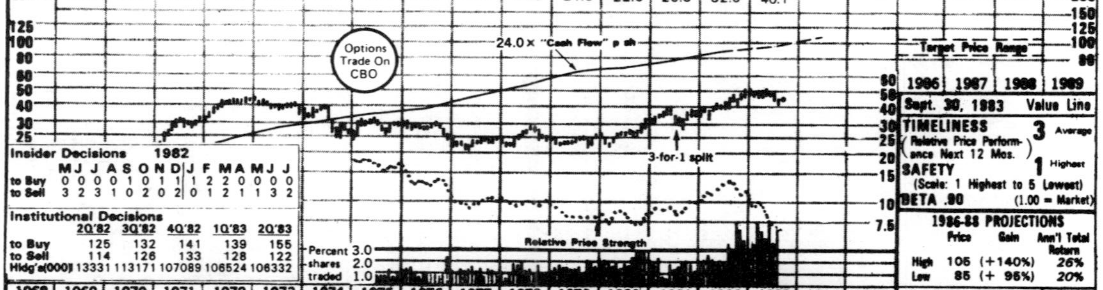

Insider Decisions 1982

	M	J	J	A	S	O	N	D	J	F	M	A	M	J	J
to Buy	0	0	0	0	1	0	1	1	1	2	2	0	0	0	0
to Sell	3	2	3	1	0	2	0	2	0	1	2	1	1	3	2

Institutional Decisions

	2Q'82	3Q'82	4Q'82	1Q'83	2Q'83
to Buy	125	132	141	139	155
to Sell	114	126	133	128	122
Hldg's(000)	13331	113171	107089	106524	106332

Sept. 30, 1983 Value Line

TIMELINESS 3 Average
(Relative Price Performance Next 12 Mos.)
SAFETY 1 Highest
(Scale: 1 Highest to 5 Lowest)
BETA .90 (1.00 = Market)

1986-88 PROJECTIONS

	Price	Gain	Ann'l Total Return
High	105	(+140%)	26%
Low	85	(+ 95%)	20%

1968	1969	1970	1971	1972	1973	1974	1975	1976	1977	1978	1979	1980	1981	1982	1983	1984	1985	© Value Line, Inc.	86-88E
3.63	4.00	5.99	6.78	7.79	9.34	11.18	12.78	14.43	16.60	19.48	22.93	26.09	28.86	30.46	**32.45**	**37.25**		Sales per sh (A)	**52.00**
.42	.48	.69	.82	.96	1.14	1.28	1.45	1.62	1.90	2.24	2.58	2.91	3.31	3.70	**3.85**	**4.60**		"Cash Flow" per sh	**6.50**
.30	.36	.50	.61	.72	.86	.93	1.06	1.18	1.41	1.67	1.92	2.17	2.51	2.79	**2.80**	**3.40**		Earnings per sh (B)	**4.75**
.07	.09	.11	.14	.15	.18	.24	.28	.35	.47	.57	.67	.74	.85	.97	**1.06**	**1.20**		Div'ds Decl'd per sh (C)	**1.70**
.18	.24	.32	.40	.45	.59	.91	.78	.68	.98	1.27	1.49	1.96	2.08	2.49	**2.60**	**2.90**		Cap'l Spending per sh	**4.10**
2.06	2.36	3.19	3.70	4.33	5.03	5.77	6.61	7.45	8.43	9.47	10.82	12.24	13.51	14.80	**16.50**	**18.70**		Book Value per sh	**27.00**
163.72	166.03	167.27	168.18	169.26	172.57	173.35	174.10	174.75	175.52	179.56	183.64	185.41	187.06	189.13	**191.00**	**192.00**		Common Shs Outst'g	**198.00**
32.5	40.6	34.0	47.5	55.5	45.7	35.0	28.0	24.5	16.6	15.4	12.5	12.3	13.6	14.6	Bold figures are Value Line estimates			Avg Ann'l P/E Ratio	**20.0**
3.1%	2.5%	2.9%	2.1%	1.8%	2.2%	2.9%	3.6%	4.1%	6.0%	6.5%	8.0%	8.1%	7.4%	6.9%				Avg Ann'l Earn's Yield	**5.0%**
.7%	.7%	.7%	.5%	.4%	.4%	.7%	1.0%	1.2%	2.0%	2.2%	2.8%	2.8%	2.5%	2.4%				Avg Ann'l Div'd Yield	**1.8%**

CAPITAL STRUCTURE as of 1/2/83
Total Debt $356.1 mill. **Due in 5 Yrs** $285.7 mill.
LT Debt $142.2 mill. **LT Interest** $15.0 mill.
(Total interest coverage: 7.0x)
(5% of Cap'l)

Leases, Uncapitalized Annual rentals $40.7 mill.

Pension Liability None in '82 or '81

Pfd Stock None

Common Stock 189,127,000 shs. (95% of Cap'l)

1974	1975	1976	1977	1978	1979	1980	1981	1982	1983	1984	1985		86-88E
1937.2	2224.7	2522.5	2914.1	3497.3	4211.6	4837.4	5399.0	5760.9	**6200**	**7150**		Sales ($mill) (A)	**10200**
16.5%	16.6%	17.0%	17.4%	17.5%	16.8%	15.6%	16.1%	15.2%	**16.0%**	**16.5%**		Operating Margin	**17.0%**
59.9	68.6	77.5	86.5	103.1	121.2	138.7	152.4	176.2	**200**	**230**		Depreciation ($mill) (D)	**330**
161.6	183.8	205.4	247.3	299.1	352.1	400.7	467.6	523.4	**535**	**650**		Net Profit ($mill)	**935**
42.4%	40.7%	43.2%	42.8%	41.8%	40.5%	40.7%	40.4%	33.5%	**39.5%**	**39.5%**		Income Tax Rate	**39.5%**
8.3%	8.3%	8.1%	8.5%	8.6%	8.4%	8.3%	8.7%	9.1%	**8.6%**	**9.1%**		Net Profit Margin	**9.2%**
527.8	630.8	765.5	896.3	1032.8	1089.3	1197.5	1321.0	1352.9	**1450**	**1600**		Working Cap'l ($mill)	**2400**
43.9	39.4	26.7	37.1	52.1	69.6	70.1	91.7	142.2	**130**	**215**		Long-Term Debt ($mill)	**300**
999.4	1150.8	1301.9	1479.1	1700.8	1986.7	2269.1	2527.9	2799.5	**3155**	**3595**		Net Worth ($mill)	**5450**
15.7%	15.6%	15.6%	16.4%	17.2%	17.3%	17.3%	18.1%	18.1%	**16.5%**	**17.5%**		% Earned Total Cap'l	**16.5%**
16.2%	16.0%	15.8%	16.7%	17.6%	17.7%	17.7%	18.5%	18.7%	**17.0%**	**18.0%**		% Earned Net Worth	**17.0%**
12.0%	11.7%	11.1%	11.2%	11.7%	11.6%	11.6%	12.2%	12.2%	**10.5%**	**11.5%**		% Retained to Comm Eq	**11.0%**
26%	27%	30%	33%	34%	35%	34%	34%	35%	**38%**	**35%**		% All Div'ds to Net Prof	**36%**

Source: *Value Line Ratings & Reports.* Reprinted by permission of the publisher. Copyright Value Line Inc.

ILLUSTRATION 6-4

POLAROID CORP. NYSE-PRD

RECENT PRICE	P/E RATIO	(Trailing: 38.3) (Median: 22.0)	EARN'S YLD	DIV'D YIELD
29	18.4		5.4 %	3.4 %

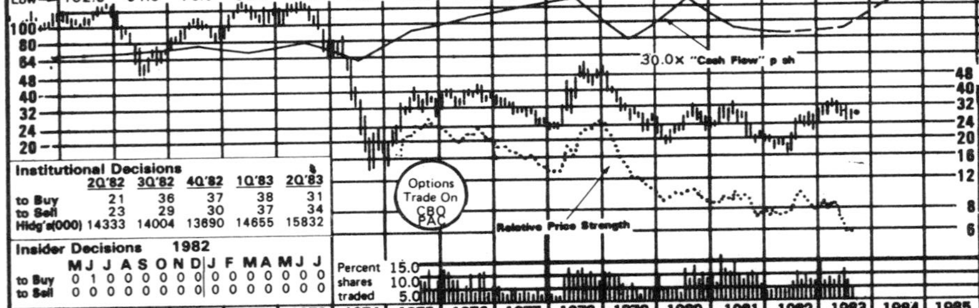

166

TIMELINESS 3 Average
(Relative Price Performance Next 12 Mos.)

SAFETY 3 Average
(Scale: 1 Highest to 5 Lowest)

BETA 1.05 (1.00 = Market)

1986-88 PROJECTIONS

	Price	Gain	Ann'l Total Return
High	90	(+210%)	35%
Low	60	(+105%)	23%

Options Trade On CBO

Relative Price Strength

30.0x "Cash Flow" p sh

Source: *Value Line Ratings & Reports.* Reprinted by permission of the publisher. Copyright, Value Line Inc.

a company was large and had a high PSR, its stock was either a big future disappointment or an outright disaster.

The concept applies equally well to small companies. Lynch Communications Systems was a high-flying, high-PSR stock in the 1960s. Its stock dropped from a peak price of over $40 per share and a PSR of 4.6 to under $4 and a PSR of 0.35. Bought at the bottom, it increased more than fivefold in the next four years—not too bad for a company few would classify as a Super Company. (See Illustration 6–5.)

Applied Magnetics, ADP, Computervision, High Voltage Engineering, International Rectifier, Measurex—are all good examples of the same principles applying to little companies. There are countless others. You can find a few small companies that did grow fast enough to offer a good return on a high PSR.

Intel is one. You could have bought Intel at its 1974 peak of $16. It had a PSR of 8.5. In the next seven years, Intel grew more than 13-fold. Buying the stock at $16 would have allowed you to triple your money in the next six and one half years. This is not quite a Super Stock rate of return. Intel *was* a Super Company. Its stock was too high to allow it to be a Super Stock. If you had wanted to own Intel, you could have done it a better way. You could have bought it in late 1974 or early 1975, at a price of less than $4 with a PSR of 1.1. From these levels, you would have made 10 times your money in the same time period.

Suppose you held Intel from its $16-per-share value for the next seven years for a threefold increase. You could have done as well applying the PSR concept to large diversified "smokestack" stocks.

PPG Industries was a well-diversified $1.7 billion company in 1974. (See Illustration 6–6.) It was number one or number two in each of its four areas of endeavor—glass, chlor-alkali-based chemicals, paints and coatings, and fiberglass. It is a company seldom given credit for its inherent quality, probably because it serves the mundane auto and housing industries. It could have been bought at a PSR of 0.30. In the next seven years, it more than tripled yet never had a PSR greater than 0.60.

Similar results could have been achieved with better-known companies. U. S. Steel is a stock I wouldn't own on a bet. Yet even here—with poor basic operating results in the business, the principles easily would have allowed an investor to almost triple his or her money from 1972 to 1976. It could have been bought nicely at low PSRs in the high stock market of 1972–1973. Starting with a peak PSR of only 0.35, it rose steadily through the 1974–1975 market decline. It hardly felt the overall market crumble.

Look at results from less well known companies. Consider Universal Leaf of Richmond, Virginia, an exporter and importer of to-

ILLUSTRATION 6-5

LYNCH COMMUN. ASE -LYC

RECENT PRICE	P/E RATIO	Trailing: / Median:	NMF	EARN'S YLD	DIV'D YLD
12	15.8	18.1 / 24.9 / 13.5	12.0	6.3	1.0 %

1022

High — 40.5 / 29.0 / 27.1 / 29.5 / 16.4 / 8.3 / 5.4 / 8.4 / 10.0 / 18.1 / 24.9 / 25.8 / 16.0 / 13.4 / 15.0
Low — 26.0 / 11.5.0 / 18.8 / 11.3 / 6.0 / 3.0 / 3.0 / 4.0 / 6.6 / 7.3 / 13.5 / 12.0 / 9.4 / 6.9 / 10.5

20.0 x "Cash Flow" p sh.

Target Price Range
1986 | 1987 | 1988 | 1989

12-2-for-1 split.

TIMELINESS **3** Average
(Relative Price Perform-ance Next 12 Mos.)

SAFETY **4** Below Average
(Scale: 1 Highest to 5 Lowest)

BETA 1.10 (1.00 = Market)

1986-88 PROJECTIONS
	Price	Gain	Ann'l Total Return
High	30	(+160%)	27%
Low	20	(+65%)	15%

Nov. 11, 1983 Value Line

Insider Decisions 1982
J A S O N D J F M A M J J A S
to Buy 0 0 0 0 0 0 0 0 0 0 0 0 0 0 1
to Sell 0 0 0 0 0 0 0 0 0 0 0 0 0 0 0

Institutional Decisions
	2Q'82	3Q'82	4Q'82	1Q'83	2Q'83
to Buy	3	2	4	2	1
to Sell	4	2	2	2	0
Hldg's(000)	138	151	167	169	195

Relative Price Strength

Percent shares traded: 12.0 / 8.0 / 4.0

1968	1969	1970	1971	1972	1973	1974	1975	1976	1977	1978	1979	1980	1981	1982	1983	1984	1985	© Value Line, Inc.	86-88E
7.56	7.97	7.53	7.90	7.61	10.75	11.35	9.43	12.96	13.82	18.05	26.72	20.68	17.03	19.69	20.00	23.80		Sales per sh	30.30
1.17	1.27	1.10	1.12	.63	1.00	.85	.63	1.05	1.16	1.42	1.87	.79	.60	0.06	1.05	1.35		"Cash Flow" per sh	2.10
1.06	1.13	.95	.95	.46	.75	.60	.42	.80	.85	1.10	1.45	d1.36	.25	d.47	.68	.95		Earnings per sh (A)	1.50
.38	.40	.40	.40	.40	.40	.40	.25	.23	.33	.40	.40	.25	.10	.10	.10	.12		Div'ds Decl'd per sh (B)	.25
.35	.17	.32	.19	.24	.06	.26	.20	.33	.50	.61	3.06	1.02	.44	1.13	.90	1.00		Cap'l Spending per sh	1.00
4.12	5.85	6.43	6.47	6.50	6.50	6.15	6.25	6.85	7.37	8.09	9.15	7.61	10.19	9.64	10.00	10.70		Book Value per sh	13.65
1.56	1.63	1.63	2.02	2.04	1.82	1.82	1.83	1.81	1.82	1.87	1.89	1.91	2.78	2.79	2.80	2.80		Common Shs Outst'g (C)	3.30
32.8	16.9	16.9	21.1	23.7	44.3	12.8	8.8	8.6	9.2	11.2	12.0	- -	51.9	- -	Bold figures are Value Line estimates			Avg Ann'l P/E Ratio	16.5
3.1%	3.3%	4.7%	4.2%	2.3%	7.8%	11.4%	9.9%	11.6%	10.9%	8.9%	8.3%	- -	1.9%	- -				Avg Ann'l Earn's Yield	6.1%
1.1%	1.2%	2.0%	1.8%	2.0%	4.2%	7.6%	5.9%	3.3%	4.2%	3.3%	2.3%	1.5%	.8%	1.0%				Avg Ann'l Div'd Yield	1.0%

CAPITAL STRUCTURE as of 6/30/83
Total Debt $13.4 mill. Due in 5 Yrs. $1.8 mill.
LT Debt $13.0 mill. LT Interest $1.1 mill.
Incl. $9.9 mill. 8½% conv. sub. debs. (1999), callable at 108.5-100.0, conv. into 50 com. shs. at $20. Incl. $.4 mill. capitalized leases.
(Interest not covered). (32% of Cap'l)

Pension Liability None vs None in 1981

Pfd Stock None

Common Stock 2,793,052 shs. (68% of Cap'l)

20.6	13.4%	17.2	11.7%	23.5	25.1	33.7	50.4	39.5	47.4	54.9	57.0	67.0		Sales ($mill)	100
14.0%	14.4%	13.7%	13.7%	14.0%	12.0%	NMF	8.3%	6.8%	8.5%	9.5%		Operating Margin	12.0%
.5	.4	.8	.5	.6	.8	1.1	1.1	1.2	1.1	1.2		Depreciation ($mill)	2.0
1.1	.5	1.6	2.1	2.8	d2.6	.5	d13	.5	1.9	2.6		Net Profit ($mill)	5.0
47.9%	44.5%	46.5%	44.9%	45.7%	43.7%	- -	18.5%	- -	44.0%	45.0%		Income Tax Rate	45.0%
5.3%	4.4%	6.2%	6.1%	6.1%	5.5%	NMF	NMF	NMF	3.4%	3.9%		Net Profit Margin	5.0%
10.4	9.2	11.5	14.0	14.1	17.4	26.4	30.7	26.6	25.0	25.0		Working Cap'l ($mill)	45.0
3.5	1.6	2.9	4.5	3.4	10.0	22.5	12.7	13.2	13.0	12.5		Long-Term Debt ($mill)	15.0
11.2	11.4	12.4	13.4	15.1	17.3	14.5	28.3	26.9	28.0	30.0		Net Worth ($mill)	45.0
8.7%	6.5%	10.2%	9.4%	12.3%	11.5%	NMF	4.6%	NMF	6.0%	7.5%		% Earned Total Cap'l	9.5%
9.8%	6.6%	11.8%	11.7%	13.7%	16.1%	NMF	1.9%	NMF	7.0%	8.5%		% Earned Net Worth	11.0%
3.2%	2.5%	8.5%	7.2%	8.8%	11.8%	NMF	1.1%	NMF	6.0%	7.0%		% Retained to Comm Eq	9.5%
67%	61%	28%	38%	36%	27%	NMF	40%	NMF	14%	13%		% All Div'ds to Net Prof	17%

Source: Value Line Ratings & Reports. Reprinted by permission of the publisher. Copyright, Value Line Inc.

ILLUSTRATION 6–6

PPG INDUSTRIES NYSE-PPG

RECENT PRICE	36	P/E RATIO	9.6	(Trailing: 12.1 Median: 7.0)	EARN'S YLD	10.4%	DIV'D YLD	3.6%	887

High	14.0	15.0	16.7	15.7	12.2	19.5	20.0	15.8	17.2	20.4	29.2	26.8	37.3
Low	10.5	10.7	12.0	7.1	8.1	11.7	12.8	11.6	11.9	13.1	17.8	14.5	25.1

Target Price Range
1986 | 1987 | 1988 | 1989

6.5 x "Cash Flow" p sh

2-for-1 split

3-for-2 split

8 2-for-1 split

Options Trade On PHL

Relative Price Strength

TIMELINESS 3 Average
(Relative Price Perform-ance Next 12 Mos.)

SAFETY 2 Above Average
(Scale: 1 Highest to 5 Lowest)

BETA 1.00 (1.00 = Market)

1986-88 PROJECTIONS
	Price	Gain	Ann'l Total Return
High	65	(+55%)	14%
Low	40	(+10%)	7%

Insider Decisions 1982
	J	J	A	S	O	N	D	J	F	M	A	M	J	J	A
to Buy	0	1	0	0	0	1	0	0	0	0	0	0	0	0	0
to Sell	0	1	0	0	1	4	1	3	1	1	4	3	0	0	2

Institutional Decisions
	2Q'82	3Q'82	4Q'82	1Q'83	2Q'83	3Q'83
to Buy	48	44	51	50	62	62
to Sell	47	47	45	45	35	62
Hld's(000)	31150	31994	33336	33179	33170	35439

Percent 6.0
shares 4.0
traded 2.0

1968	1969	1970	1971	1972	1973	1974	1975	1976	1977	1978	1979	1980	1981	1982	1983	1984	1985	© Value Line, Inc.	86-88E
17.00	18.65	17.79	19.97	22.39	24.25	27.96	30.24	36.11	40.03	43.81	47.37	47.30	49.32	47.39	52.15	56.35		Sales per sh	71.60
1.51	1.73	1.40	1.97	2.34	2.51	2.61	2.66	3.81	3.04	3.72	5.17	5.09	5.26	4.63	5.95	6.95		"Cash Flow" per sh	8.90
.79	.88	.50	1.02	1.33	1.49	1.50	1.43	2.43	1.47	2.10	3.39	3.17	3.14	2.26	3.40	4.20		Earnings per sh (A)	5.75
.45	.47	.47	.47	.49	.53	.57	.58	.67	.79	.85	.94	1.06	1.16	1.18	1.23	1.34		Div'ds Decl'd per sh (B)	2.00
1.85	1.84	2.16	1.99	1.48	2.12	3.19	2.74	2.77	3.38	4.10	3.86	6.01	5.53	6.50	5.70	5.65		Cap'l Spending per sh	4.00
10.31	10.72	10.63	10.89	11.73	12.87	13.81	14.60	16.36	16.98	18.15	20.49	22.48	23.95	24.54	26.50	29.00		Book Value per sh	37.50
61.43	61.67	61.49	62.02	62.35	62.37	62.38	62.39	62.45	62.60	63.78	65.26	66.77	67.99	69.54	70.00	71.00		Common Shs Outst'g (C)	74.00
16.5	13.7	19.0	12.3	11.2	7.2	5.4	6.8	6.9	11.5	6.4	4.3	5.2	7.2	8.3	Bold figures are Value Line estimates			Avg Ann'l P/E Ratio	8.0
6.1%	7.3%	5.3%	8.1%	8.9%	13.9%	18.5%	14.7%	14.5%	8.7%	15.6%	23.3%	19.2%	13.9%	12.1%				Avg Ann'l Earn's Yield	12.5%
3.5%	3.9%	4.9%	3.7%	3.3%	4.9%	7.0%	5.9%	4.0%	4.7%	6.3%	6.5%	6.5%	5.1%	6.3%				Avg Ann'l Div'd Yield	4.3%

CAPITAL STRUCTURE as of 6/30/83

Total Debt $622.5 mill. Due in 5 Yrs $245.8 mill.
LT Debt $533.6 mill. LT Interest $48.0 mill.
Incl. $71.7 mill. capitalized leases.
(Total interest coverage: 10.5x) (23% of Cap'l)

Leases, Uncapitalized Annual rentals $25.2 mill.

Pension Liability None in '82 vs. None in '81

Pfd Stock None

Common Stock 69,740,120 shs. (77% of Cap'l)

	1744.0	1886.6	2254.8	2505.8	2794.0	3091.8	3158.4	3353.6	3295.5	3650	4000		Sales ($mill)	5300
	13.0%	13.1%	16.9%	16.4%	16.1%	15.5%	14.7%	13.7%	11.3%	15.5%	17.0%		Operating Margin	18.0%
	69.0	76.8	86.5	98.6	105.1	118.6	130.7	146.7	166.6	180	195		Depreciation ($mill)	2.35
	93.7	89.0	151.5	91.7	132.1	218.9	209.2	211.2	155.1	238	300		Net Profit ($mill)	425
	33.7%	39.4%	43.0%	52.0%	42.9%	41.8%	40.5%	38.0%	23.0%	37.0%	38.0%		Income Tax Rate	40.0%
	5.4%	4.7%	6.7%	3.7%	4.7%	7.1%	6.6%	6.3%	4.7%	6.5%	7.2%		Net Profit Margin	8.0%
	395.4	509.4	564.8	581.7	594.6	707.6	629.8	585.7	511.1	620	600		Working Cap'l ($mill)	1000
	366.9	483.9	468.8	504.3	503.6	517.4	523.7	514.0	550.4	675	635		Long-Term Debt ($mill)	500
	861.1	910.9	1021.6	1063.0	1157.9	1337.5	1501.1	1628.4	1706.9	1855	2060		Net Worth ($mill)	2775
	8.7%	7.7%	11.4%	7.2%	9.1%	13.0%	11.4%	11.0%	8.0%	10.5%	12.5%		% Earned Total Cap'l	13.5%
	10.9%	9.8%	14.8%	8.6%	11.4%	16.4%	13.9%	13.0%	9.1%	13.0%	14.5%		% Earned Net Worth	15.5%
	6.8%	5.8%	10.8%	4.0%	6.8%	9.3%	9.3%	8.2%	4.3%	8.0%	10.0%		% Retained to Comm Eq	10.0%
	38%	40%	27%	53%	40%	28%	33%	37%	52%	36%	32%		% All Div'ds to Net Prof	35%

Nov. 4, 1983 Value Line

Source: *Value Line Ratings & Reports.* Reprinted by permission of the publisher. Copyright, Value Line Inc.

bacco. Between 1972 and 1981, its stock grew, peak to peak, at a
15½ percent annual rate. It did so during a very rough stock market
while its sales grew at only a 7½ percent annual rate and profit
margins averaged only 3 percent. What Universal Leaf had going for
it was a low initial PSR at 0.18. (See Illustration 6–7.)

Or consider Northrop Corp., the Los Angeles jet manufacturer.
Sales from 1972 to 1981 grew at a respectable 14 percent. Profit
margins averaged about 3 percent. But the stock price, starting from a
peak PSR in 1972 of only 0.15, bounded forward at a 23 percent
average annual rate. Raytheon is a similar example. Its sales grew by
16 percent. Margins steadily improved: Its PSR, which had a high in
1972 of 0.51, rose to 0.81 by 1981. Along the way, the stock had risen
at a 23 percent average annual rate. (See Illustration 6–8.)

New York City's Handy & Harman was spectacular. From 1972 to
1981, its stock increased, peak to peak, at a 29 percent annual rate.
The company grew at only a 12 percent rate. Margins bounced
around from 1.3 percent to 3.8 percent back to 2.2 percent and up to
3.8 percent. But the stock started with a PSR of only 0.20. From
there, with only reasonable business results, the stock was a real
winner. (See Illustration 6–9.)

The Japanese camera manufacturer Canon had a peak PSR in
1972 of 0.58. Its stock price increased more than ninefold in the next
nine years. Of course, it had tremendous growth. But so did companies that started out at high PSRs and then had poorly performing
stocks.

We could go on with examples. Through the 1960s and 1970s,
using the principles of PSR analysis would have been valuable. Selling—or not buying high-PSR stocks—would have allowed an investor to avoid most stocks which were long-term disasters. Most of the
best opportunities, whether Super Companies or not, came from the
ranks of low- to medium-PSR stocks An investor could have made a
better-than-average return doing little other than avoiding high PSR
stocks.

Didn't any low PSR stocks go down? Of course they did. In 1974
and 1975, most stocks fell. Low-PSR stocks were no exception. On
average, they fell less and recovered more quickly and farther than
high Price Sales Ratio stocks.

Were there exceptions to the rule? Yes. The principle area of
exception seems to be in natural resource related stocks. Consider
Great Lakes Chemical, for example, which produces bromine. It regularly sold at PSRs exceeding our guidelines. The stock performed
very well, increasing sevenfold from 1972 to 1981. There were a
number of exceptions in the area of oil and gas. Companies like Tom
Brown, Dorchester Gas, Getty Oil, Petro-Lewis, Phillips Petroleum,

ILLUSTRATION 6-7

UNIVERSAL LEAF NYSE-UVV

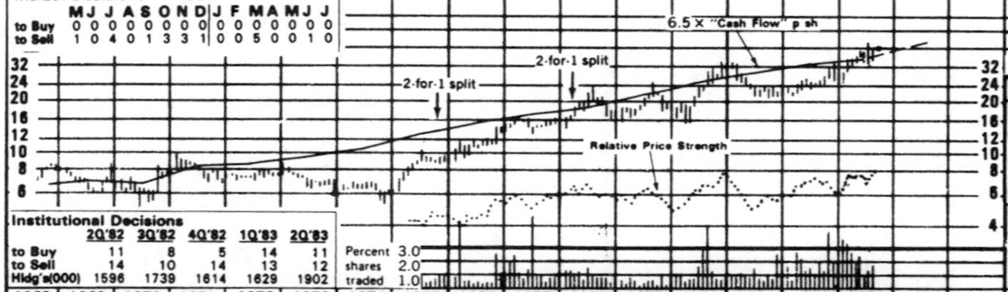

RECENT PRICE	P/E RATIO	(Trailing: 0.5 Median: 0.5)	EARN'S YLD	DIV'D YLD
40	8.6		11.7%	4.6%

338

Source: *Value Line Ratings & Reports*. Reprinted by permission of the publisher. Copyright, Value Line Inc.

ILLUSTRATION 6-8

NORTHROP CORP. NYSE-NOC

RECENT PRICE	P/E RATIO	EARN'S YLD	DIV'D YLD	
82	11.7 (Trailing: 18.3 / Median: 8.0)	8.6%	2.3%	571

Target Price Range: 1986 1987 1988 1989

Value Line — Oct. 21, 1983

TIMELINESS 3 (Relative Price Performance Next 12 Mos.) — Average
SAFETY 3 (Scale: 1 Highest to 5 Lowest) — Average
BETA 1.25 (1.00 = Market)

1986-88 PROJECTIONS

	Price	Gain	Ann'l Total Return
High	230	(+180%)	37%
Low	155	(+90%)	20%

Insider Decisions 1982 / Institutional Decisions

CAPITAL STRUCTURE as of 6/30/83
Total Debt $45.3 mill. Due in 5 Yrs. $42.0 mill.
LT Debt $10.9 mill. LT Interest $1.2 mill.
Incl. $5.3 mill. capitalized leases. (2% of Cap'l)

Pension Liability None in '82 vs. None in '81

Pfd Stock None

Common Stock 15,212,877 shs. (98% of Cap'l) as of 7/31/83

	86-88E
Sales per sh	387.00
"Cash Flow" per sh	27.75
Earnings per sh	16.00
Div'ds Decl'd per sh	4.00
Cap'l Spending per sh	9.70
Book Value per sh	77.50
Common Shs Outst'g	15.60
Avg Ann'l P/E Ratio	12.0
Avg Ann'l Earn's Yield	8.3%
Avg Ann'l Div'd Yield	2.1%
Sales ($mill)	6000
Operating Margin	10.0%
Depreciation ($mill)	180
Net Profit ($mill)	250
Income Tax Rate	42.0%
Net Profit Margin	4.2%
Working Cap'l ($mill)	150
Long-Term Debt ($mill)	15.0
Net Worth ($mill)	1200
% Earned Total Cap'l	21.0%
% Earned Net Worth	21.0%
% Retained to Comm Eq	16.0%
% All Div'ds to Net Prof	25%

© Value Line, Inc.

Source: Value Line Ratings & Reports. Reprinted by permission of the publisher. Copyright, Value Line Inc.

ILLUSTRATION 6-9

HANDY & HARMAN NYSE-HNH | **RECENT PRICE** 19 | **P/E RATIO** 19.4 (Trailing: 34.5, Median: 8.5) | **EARN'S YLD** 5.2% | **DIV'D YLD** 3.2 - % 1.6 | **591**

TIMELINESS 4 (Relative Price Performance Next 12 Mos.) Below Average
SAFETY 4 Below Average
(Scale: 1 Highest to 5 Lowest)
BETA 1.20 (1.00 = Market)

Target Price Range 1986 1987 1988 1989
Oct. 21, 1983 Value Line

Right-hand scale: 80 60 50 40 30 25 20 / 16 12 10 8 6 5 4 3

1986-88 PROJECTIONS

	Price	Gain	Ann'l Total Return
High	35	(+86%)	18%
Low	20	(+5%)	5%

11.0 x "Cash Flow" p sh
Relative Price Strength
© Value Line, Inc.

High / Low prices:
High: 5.8 5.3 4.1 3.3 3.5 | 4.7 5.1 5.3 6.0 9.6 19.4 33.3 34.5 20.4 24.0
Low: 4.5 2.5 2.3 2.4 2.4 | 3.0 3.4 3.6 4.9 5.6 7.8 10.8 17.5 12.3 16.5

Insider Decisions (1982)

	J	J	A	S	O	N	D	J	F	M	A	M	J	J	A
to Buy	0	1	0	0	0	1	1	0	0	0	0	0	0	0	0
to Sell	0	1	0	0	1	1	1	0	1	0	0	0	0	0	0

Institutional Decisions

	2Q82	3Q82	4Q82	1Q83	2Q83
to Buy	6	11	8	8	8
to Sell	4	3	8	3	11
Hldg (000)	4233	4580	4717	4678	4623

Percent shares traded: 6.0 / 4.0 / 2.0

Per-share and valuation data

	1968	1969	1970	1971	1972	1973	1974	1975	1976	1977	1978	1979	1980	1981	1982	1983	1984	86-88E
Sales per sh	16.22	16.07	11.56	12.34	16.87	23.95	28.15	23.84	25.70	28.23	34.53	46.39	55.76	44.39	36.25	42.05	46.75	64.30
"Cash Flow" per sh	.44	.47	.33	.23	.29	.54	1.07	1.10	1.03	1.15	1.32	1.48	2.61	2.34	1.37	1.70	2.34	3.45
Earnings per sh (A)	.33	.36	.20	.09	.12	.37	.88	.90	.75	.82	.96	1.02	2.04	1.71	.61	.85	1.45	2.50
Div'ds Decl'd per sh (B)(■)	.10	.11	.12	.12	.12	.12	.13	.21	.18	.21	.26	.31	.39	.53	.60	.60	.60	.80
Cap'l Spending per sh	.23	.30	.38	.23	.29	.29	.32	.30	.50	.53	.57	.82	1.56	1.51	.91	.85	.85	.70
Book Value per sh (C)	2.19	2.28	2.27	2.25	2.52	2.52	3.27	3.97	4.51	5.12	5.81	6.51	8.16	9.34	9.27	9.40	10.15	14.30
Common Shs Outst'g (D)	12.37	12.85	13.88	13.94	13.91	13.91	13.89	14.20	13.54	13.52	13.55	13.60	13.65	13.77	13.77	13.80	13.80	14.00
Avg Ann'l P/E Ratio	15.1	14.1	17.3	13.3	8.3		4.4	4.5	6.1	6.7	8.0	11.1	12.2	14.1	25.1			11.0
Avg Ann'l Earn's Yield	6.6%	7.1%	5.8%	2.9%	7.5%	12.1%	22.7%	22.2%	16.4%	14.9%	12.5%	9.0%	8.2%	7.1%	4.0%			9.1%
Avg Ann'l Div'd Yield	2.0%	2.2%	3.5%	3.8%			3.3%	5.2%	3.9%	3.9%	3.9%	3.4%	1.6%	2.0%				2.9%

Bold figures are Value Line estimates.

Financial data

	1974	1975	1976	1977	1978	1979	1980	1981	1982	1983	1984	86-88E
Sales ($mill)	391.0	338.4	347.8	381.7	468.0	630.9	761.0	611.2	499.1	580	645	900
Operating Margin	6.5%	7.2%	8.6%	8.5%	8.5%	7.4%	10.8%	11.0%	8.4%	9.0%	10.0%	11.0%
Depreciation ($mill)	2.6	3.0	3.3	4.4	5.0	6.4	7.8	8.8	10.5	11.5	12.0	13.0
Net Profit ($mill)	12.2	12.7	10.6	11.2	12.9	13.8	27.8	23.4	8.4	12.0	20.0	35.0
Income Tax Rate	53.0%	50.5%	49.3%	47.2%	50.5%	38.8%	49.5%	44.8%	46.0%	46.0%	46.0%	46.0%
Net Profit Margin	3.1%	3.8%	3.0%	2.9%	2.8%	2.2%	3.7%	3.8%	1.7%	2.1%	3.1%	3.9%
Working Cap'l ($mill)	45.0	51.9	59.3	62.8	78.5	75.0	82.8	89.5	100.6	95.0	105	150
Long-Term Debt ($mill)	29.8	29.9	38.2	42.9	56.7	53.1	54.8	56.7	75.7	70.0	75.0	70.0
Net Worth ($mill)	45.4	56.4	61.0	69.3	78.7	88.5	111.4	128.6	127.6	130	140	200
% Earned Total Cap'l	18.0%	16.2%	11.9%	11.3%	11.1%	11.7%	18.4%	14.2%	6.3%	8.0%	11.0%	14.5%
% Earned Net Worth	27.0%	22.5%	17.3%	16.1%	16.4%	15.6%	24.9%	18.2%	6.5%	9.0%	14.5%	17.5%
% Retained to Comm Eq	23.0%	17.3%	13.2%	11.9%	11.9%	10.8%	20.0%	12.6%	1%	3.0%	8.5%	12.0%
% All Div'ds to Net Prof	15%	23%	24%	26%	28%	31%	19%	31%	99%	69%	41%	32%

CAPITAL STRUCTURE as of 3/31/83

Total Debt $180.2 mill. Due in 5 Yrs $163.1 mill.
LT Debt $74.8 mill. LT Interest $8.8 mill.
Incl. $16.2 mill. capitalized leases.
(LT interest earned: 2.6x: total interest coverage: 1.8x) (37% of Cap'l)
Leases, Uncapitalized Annual rentals $4.7 mill.
Pension Liability None vs. None in 1981
Pfd Stock None
Common Stock 13,774,000 shs. (63% of Cap'l)
as of 5/10/83

Source: Value Line Ratings & Reports. Reprinted by permission of the publisher. Copyright, Value Line Inc.

Sabine, Southland Royalty, and others were exceptions. (I suspect this group of exceptions was due to the continuing world oil crisis.) Were there no other exceptions? There are always exceptions—but you have to work to find them. You don't have to find every good potential investment. You merely need to insure that you make good ones. It is easy to find the ones that aren't exceptions. Throughout the 1960s and 1970s, PSRs would have proven a uniquely valuable tool for assessing potential opportunities and avoiding potential disasters.

PSRs and the Great American Smokestack Stock

What about basic industry stocks—the companies that plug along without much fanfare making the essential materials and parts we all need in our daily lives? What about companies in the steel, auto, chemical, paper, mining, or machinery industries? What about all the lesser-known, medium-size, and smaller companies? How does the concept of Price Sales Ratios fit?

Quite well. The Price Sales Ratio is often lower for these than for more exciting companies. Most of these companies don't earn exceptionally high margins and don't grow at significantly rapid rates—therefore justifying lower Price Sales Ratios.

Our rule, if you want to invest in these stocks is:

Buy them at PSRs under 0.4.

Sell them as their PSR approaches 0.8.

Often these stocks never achieve PSRs as high as 0.8 and may need to be sold sooner. If a company has particularly poor future prospects, it may be better to sell at PSRs closer to 0.6. As with any other stock, margin analysis is the key (see Chapters 10 and 11). A smokestack stock often will rise nicely from a very low level. It may then "stall out" at PSRs around 0.5 to 0.6. (Since I only recommend owning Super Companies, I tend to be gun-shy: I would sell out these lesser-quality companies quickly, at a profit, rather than hold on hoping the PSR may rise.)

Below is a copy of *Value Line* on Alcoa. Alcoa is an almost-perfect example of a smokestack stock. From the numbers in *Value Line,* you can calculate the PSRs:

Alcoa—High and Low PSRs for 1972–1981

	1972	1973	1974	1975	1976	1977	1978	1979	1980	1981
High	.71	.82	.64	.73	.72	.61	.46	.44	.54	.56
Low	.48	.48	.32	.40	.45	.41	.33	.34	.37	.34

Comparing the high and low PSRs with the high and low points of the stock, you sense how PSRs could be used on a smokestack stock. You would have done well if you had:

Sold Alcoa, or failed to own it at the times when its PSR began to approach 0.8.

Bought it when the PSR was below 0.4.

Following these steps would have allowed you to trade the stock almost perfectly to maximize short-term profits. (Trading is a risky business I don't recommend. If you do trade, PSRs are, nevertheless, a valuable tool.) (See Illustration 6–10.)

Consider Standard Oil of California (SOCAL). (See Illustration 6–11.) Following is a copy of the *Value Line* report on it. Using our concept of PSRs you could have:

Avoided the stock at its highs in 1972 and 1973, thus avoiding losses.

Bought it any time between 1974 and 1981, except for part of 1980 and 1981 when it hit its peak. This would have been nicely profitable.

International Minerals and Chemical is another example. (See Illustration 6–12.) It is the free world's largest producer of fertilizers. Below are *Value Line* statistics. Using our rule, it could have been bought any year between 1969 and 1974 except 1973. Any purchase would have been profitable. It could have been held until 1979 or 1980. Between 1974 and 1979, the PSR fell in the middle of our range—between 0.4 and 0.8. During 1979, it approached a PSR of 0.8. In 1980, it would briefly break through this level. Our rule would have forced sales at these levels. The stock subsequently fell and has not regained its prior highs.

The Williams Companies is one of International Mineral's leading competitors. (See Illustration 6–13.) Here, too, the rules work. This stock traded "out of synch" with the overall level of the stock market—peaking as the stock market was low. As the stock market rose, Williams fell. The PSR rules would have taken you out close to the top. It would have put you back in later at lower prices that would have been profitable.

By 1983—with the market up, many smokestack stocks were too high to be held.

Use PSRs as THE Stock Market Timing Device

PSRs are a great—maybe THE great—stock market timing device. Chapter 12 indicates that stock market timing devices tend not to work. PSRs are as effective as any existing timing device because

ILLUSTRATION 6–10

ALCOA NYSE-AA

RECENT PRICE	P/E RATIO	EARN'S YLD	DIV'D YLD	
43	14.4 (Trailing NMF Median: 9.5)	6.9%	2.9%	1212

TIMELINESS **3** (Relative Price Perform-ance Next 12 Mos.) Average

SAFETY **3** (Scale: 1 Highest to 5 Lowest) Average

BETA 1.05 (1.00 = Market)

1986-88 PROJECTIONS	Price	Gain	Ann'l Total Return
High	90	(+110%)	22%
Low	60	(+ 40%)	7%

Target Price Range 1986 1987 1988 1989

Value Line

6.5 × "Cash Flow" p sh

3-for-2 split

2-for-1 split

Relative Price Strength

Options Trade On CBO

Percent 9.0 shares 6.0 traded 3.0

Insider Decisions

1982: J A S O N D J F M A M J J A S 1983

to Buy 0 0 0 0 0 0 0 0 0 0 0 0 0 0 0

to Sell 0 0 0 0 0 0 0 0 0 0 0 0 0 0 0

Institutional Decisions

	2Q'82	3Q'82	4Q'82	1Q'83	2Q'83
to Buy	49	77	69	75	66
to Sell	88	68	63	84	84
Hdg's(000)	41787	42853	44610	48782	46599

	1968	1969	1970	1971	1972	1973	1974	1975	1976	1977	1978	1979	1980	1981	1982	1983	1984	1985	86-88E
Sales per sh	20.98	23.95	23.60	22.16	26.72	32.61	40.85	34.05	42.59	49.24	57.79	68.04	70.45	66.85	58.89	66.90	71.05		78.40
"Cash Flow" per sh	3.34	3.75	3.71	2.93	3.83	3.93	5.02	3.44	4.84	5.72	7.67	10.65	9.97	7.93	3.96	6.10	9.50		11.20
Earnings per sh	1.58	1.86	1.73	82	1.54	1.55	2.57	93	2.07	2.79	4.45	7.15	6.54	3.97	0.15	1.76	4.00		6.75
Div'ds Decl'd per sh	60	60	60	60	60	65	67	67	70	68	95	1.30	1.60	1.80	1.65	1.20	1.25		2.10
Cap'l Spending per sh	2.75	3.83	4.42	3.07	2.13	2.98	5.33	5.64	3.55	4.06	4.99	5.97	8.73	9.10	6.33	5.15	6.20		7.85
Book Value per sh	16.23	17.49	18.34	18.49	19.41	20.30	22.18	22.29	23.64	25.76	29.20	35.02	39.25	41.24	38.60	39.16	42.70		52.50
Common Shs Outst'g	64.50	64.51	64.52	65.03	65.61	66.15	66.15	67.72	68.66	69.38	70.11	70.34	73.07	74.46	78.92	80.70	80.72		81.00
Avg Ann'l P/E Ratio	14.9	13.2	11.1	22.9	13.6	8.2	12.7	21.8	9.1	5.0	3.7	4.9	7.4	NMF	11.0				
Avg Ann'l Earn's Yield	6.7%	7.6%	9.0%	4.4%	11.1%	7.4%	12.2%	4.6%	7.9%	11.0%	27.0%	20.4%	13.5%	NMF	9.1%				
Avg Ann'l Div'd Yield	2.5%	2.5%	3.1%	3.2%	3.5%	3.1%	3.2%	3.3%	2.6%	2.7%	4.3%	4.9%	5.0%	6.1%	6.4%	2.6%			
Sales ($mill)							2727.3	2305.9	2924.4	3416.5	4051.8	4785.6	5147.6	4977.5	4647.6	5200	5600		6800
Operating Margin							19.4%	14.2%	17.1%	17.1%	19.7%	21.5%	19.3%	14.9%	6.9%	11.5%	15.5%		20.0%
Depreciation ($mill)							164.7	170.8	191.3	203.9	227.5	247.0	261.3	297.1	323.8	350	380		450
Net Profit ($mill)							173.1	64.8	143.8	195.2	312.7	504.6	469.9	296.2	d9.1	144	390		560
Income Tax Rate							48.8%	35.3%	34.3%	33.3%	37.7%	34.9%	34.8%	23.3%	--	16.0%	35.0%		35.0%
Net Profit Margin							6.4%	2.8%	4.9%	5.7%	7.7%	10.5%	9.1%	6.0%	NMF	2.3%	6.7%		8.1%
Working Cap'l ($mill)							568.7	644.2	581.6	667.1	735.6	859.0	820.0	950.4	965.8	940	1185		1030
Long-Term Debt ($mill)							931.9	1254.0	1158.1	1166.0	1130.0	1020.6	1017.5	1381.9	1702.6	1660	1710		1825
Net Worth ($mill)							1547.0	1575.4	1689.1	1853.1	2113.0	2529.1	2933.8	3136.7	3112.5	3225	3510		4740
% Earned Total Cap'l							8.1%	3.7%	6.7%	7.8%	10.9%	15.4%	12.8%	7.7%	NMF	5.5%	9.0%		9.5%
% Earned Net Worth							11.2%	4.1%	8.5%	10.5%	14.8%	20.0%	16.0%	9.4%	NMF	4.5%	11.0%		11.5%
% Retained to Comm Eq							8.5%	1.1%	5.8%	8.2%	11.9%	16.7%	12.3%	5.2%	NMF	1.5%	8.0%		8.0%
% All Div'ds to Net Prof							27%	74%	35%	25%	22%	19%	25%	46%	NMF	68%	27%		31%

CAPITAL STRUCTURE as of 6/30/83

Total Debt $1729.2 mill. Due in 5 Yrs $267.3 mill.

LT Debt $1693.5 mill. LT Interest $168.6 mill.

Excl. debt discount of $267.0 mill.

(Interest not earned) (35% of Cap'l)

Leases, Uncapitalized Annual rentals $40.1 mill.

Pension Liability None in 1982 vs. None in 1981

Pfd Stock $66.0 mill. Pfd Div'd $2.5 mill.

659,909 shares $3.75 cum. pfd. ($100 par) callable $100. (1% of Cap'l)

Common Stock 80,667,090 shs (64% of Cap'l) (83.0 mill. fully diluted shares)

as of 9/30/83

Nov. 18, 1983

© Value Line, Inc.

Source: *Value Line Ratings & Reports.* Reprinted by permission of the publisher. Copyright, Value Line Inc.

ILLUSTRATION 6-11

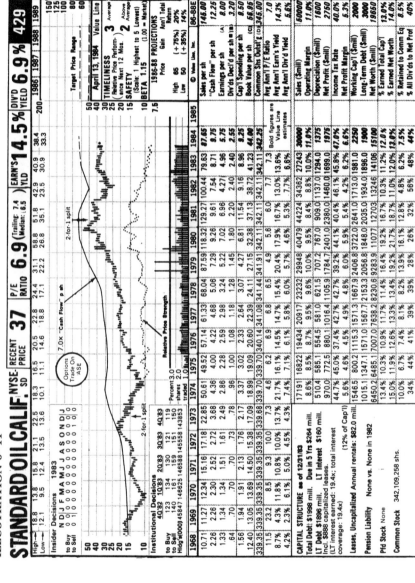

Source: *Value Line Ratings & Reports.* Reprinted by permission of the publisher. Copyright, Value Line Inc.

ILLUSTRATION 6–12

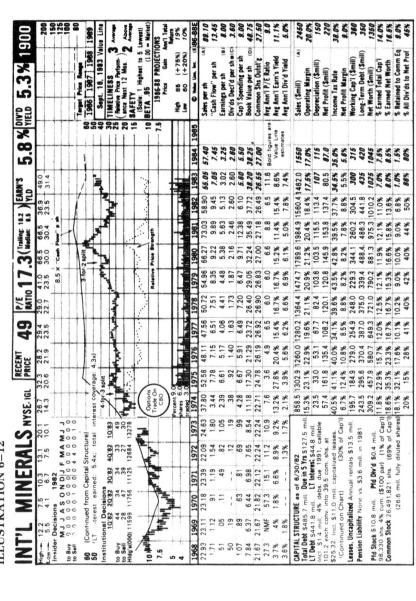

Source: Value Line Ratings & Reports. Reprinted by permission of the publisher. Copyright, Value Line Inc.

ILLUSTRATION 6–13

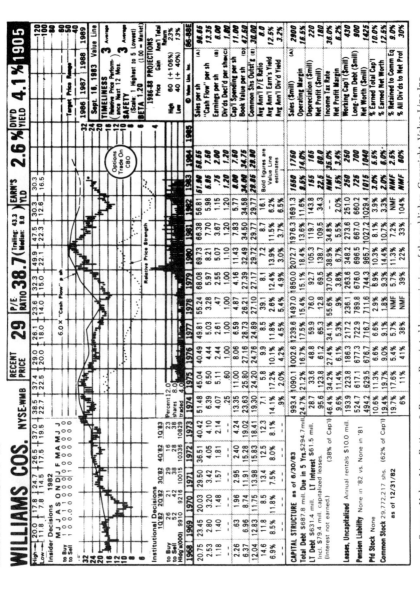

Source: *Value Line Ratings & Reports*. Reprinted by permission of the publisher. Copyright, Value Line Inc.

they are specific rather than systemic. Most timing devices try to describe what is happening to the overall level of the market. They are systemic by nature. They attempt to provide a valuation for the whole system. They don't work—history proves this. (See Chapter 12.)

PSRs are calculated for specific companies at specific points in time. They are specific rather than systemic. If you want to time the stock market, just look at specific stocks. Here is how to do it.

Fisher's Rules for Timing the Stock Market

1. When a company is selling at a (sufficiently) low PSR—BUY it.
2. If you can't find companies selling at (sufficiently) low PSRs, DON'T buy stocks.

You have just learned how to time the stock market. You now know virtually everything on the subject that I know. The concept is quite simple. When things can be found that are cheap enough to buy, the time is ripe to buy. When prices are so high that nothing can be found at appropriate PSRs, the market is too high—don't buy.

If you can't find many companies selling at reasonable PSRs, the market is probably high. At a time like 1974 or 1982, vast numbers of companies sold at outrageously low PSRs. It was perfectly obvious from the PSRs that the market was low then. In the late 1960s, with so few companies selling at low PSRs, it was obvious the market was high. Let your use of PSRs on specific companies tell you if the market is high or not. You buy only stocks—not the stock market.

PSRs in the "Garbage Dump" of the Stock Market

I screen for opportunities among companies reporting quarterly earnings losses (see Chapter 12). While often not of interest in my search for Super Companies, I see fascinating little companies selling at low PSRs such as 0.20, 0.10, 0.06 or even lower. What does this mean? It means that a company with $100 million of sales is selling at a market value of perhaps only $6 million. A $20 million company may be selling with a market value of only $1 to $2 million.

Consider a stock selling at a PSR of 0.05. If, years later, the market revalues that stock at some middle-of-the-road PSR like 0.50, the stock will have increased tenfold. If the company has doubled in size over the years, it means a twentyfold increase. If someone buys one of these and the market becomes really hot on it, the profit potential could be larger still. Among these low PSR stocks, there are some spectacular future opportunities. Profits will be awesome for the few who can detect a company with a "Sleepy Dog" future from one that can take off and soar.

"But these must be terrible companies," you say? Not at all. Some of them are, to be sure. Some have terrible records. Most have records that are just boring. They are losing money now or have for several years. Maybe they only made 2 percent margins in earlier and better years. They've averaged modest returns on assets and equity. Over the years, they grew, but not particularly any more than the economy. With the recession/depression of 1981–1982, the stock fell apart from already boringly low levels.

In Chapter 7, we explore some stocks from the garbage dump of the Great Depression that went on to make spectacular profits for their owners—profits of 2,000 to 5,000 percent in only three to five years—fortunes from failure.

Fortunes from Failures—
The Myth of the 1930s

Through the Time Warp

Long-term cyclical trends take years—even decades—to reverse. High stock markets are fueled by fat profit margins and rising earnings which mask the level of stock prices. Low stock markets are kept down by poor margins and profit stagnation. The long-term pendulum of profitability swings back and forth. These trends take so long to play out that we often don't notice changes—much the same way we don't see the minute hand revolving around the clock. Current conditions, whether good or not, are apt to be nothing but vague memories in a few years. The farther back in time we go, the more vague are the memories.

Studying the PSRs of the 1930s is like going back through a time warp. It's easy to recall the well-regarded companies of 5, 10, or 15 years ago. (Some are still well regarded, and others, not so. Some have even gone belly-up. AM International, Equity Funding, and Magnussen Computer are easy to remember.)

Lots of people recall Transitron and its kind in the 1950s and 1960s. Memories don't work as well going back 50 years. How many remember Auburn Automobile from the 1930s? We tend to remember only survivors. Everyone knows IBM must have been around then. The same can safely be assumed for most of the Fortune 500.

The 1933 *Moody's* in the San Francisco Business Library is so dilapidated, it's held together with rubber bands. (Sifting through it, the dust made me sneeze endlessly.) The results of looking back are both reassuring and shocking—and nothing to sneeze at.

Fisher Investments has tracked market values versus asset values, earnings, and sales in more than 150 major companies from 1926 to 1939. Twelve were studied in detail up through 1957:

Bethlehem Steel	Caterpillar Tractor
Dow Chemical	Eastman Kodak
FMC (Food Machinery)	General Electric
IBM	J. C. Penney
Mead Corporation	Remington Rand
SCM (Smith-Corona)	Sears

The myth of the 1930s says: "Stocks got so badly battered between 1929 and 1933 that great companies could be bought at bargain-basement prices." One conjures up visions of shrewd investors picking up great names like IBM or Dow Chemical at low price-earnings ratios and low market values compared to assets. One imagines stocks almost given away. Like most myths, there is some truth there—also some pure fantasy.

Many stocks were extraordinarily cheap for a few years. Other stocks *never* had the low valuations the myth would lead you to expect. Many stocks were simply not at bargain-basement levels at the very bottom of the 1933 market. Some stocks appeared cheap based on some single valuation technique. Perhaps they had a low price-earnings ratio. Or their price may have been very low in relation to book value.

Using other measures of value, they were not cheap. Outstanding stocks *all* started with low Price Sales Ratios (PSRs). Stocks at high PSRs did not perform well by comparison. This tended to be the case regardless of price-earnings ratios or whatever.

IBM Not a Growth Stock?

Consider IBM. This all-time growth company performed so spectacularly for so long it is an exception to the rule—but not much of an exception. It was an exception in the same sense that Intel was in the 1970s—not quite enough of one to qualify as a Super Stock. That may seem to be an outrageous statement. (I can hear the conscience of Wall Street screaming, "IBM not a Super Stock?") Consider the facts.

IBM stock hit its low at 52½ in 1932. It ranged from there to a high of 117. In 1933, its range was from 75¾ to 153¼. It then rose and fell on its way to setting a long-term high of 194 in 1936. It briefly broke through to 195¾ in 1939 but fell back. It would not hit 195 again until 1945 when it broke through to another plateau at 250.

It vacillated below this level into the early 1950s. In 1956, it reached its last peak in our 30-year time study. At that time, it was at $550 per share. What does all this mean?

Suppose you had perfect luck. Suppose you had bought IBM at the very bottom in 1932 and sold it at the very top in 1956. What's the bottom line? One dollar invested in IBM at 52½ in 1932 would have increased to $10.48. That's the good news. The bad news is that it would have taken 24 years for this to happen. Your annual compound rate of return would have been only 10 percent over the quarter century—hardly what one would have expected from the myth of the 1930s. You buy the all-time-great growth "Super" Stock at the very bottom of the greatest market crash of all time. You hold it for a quarter of a century. Your timing is impeccable, and you sell it at its peak. And you only end up with a 10 percent annual compound rate of return. Is that possible?

Worse yet, what would have happened if your timing wasn't perfect? Rarely would one be lucky enough to buy at the very bottom and sell at the very top. Suppose, instead, you only were lucky enough to buy at the midpoint of IBM's price range in 1932. Suppose you sold at the midpoint of its price range in 1956—at least this is possible. What would your rate of return have been? The midpoints would have been as follows:

	1932	1956
High	117	550
Low	52½	400
Midpoint	84¾	475

If you bought at 84¾ and sold at 475, a $1 investment would have become $5.61. Generating this increase would have meant a rate of return of only 7.5 percent over the 24 years. And this in "The all-time-great growth company." How can this be? Was IBM not everything people have always heard it was? Of course it was. It was all of that and more. It was spectacular. During the time period involved, it grew from being less than $20 million in sales to over $1 billion. The problem is that IBM was never extraordinarily "cheap"—even at the bottom of the Great Depression. It did almost triple in the year after its absolute bottom in 1932. By 1936, it hit a peak of almost 30 percent higher than its highest 1933 price.

These results are not exceptional, considering the uniqueness of the period involved. Many stocks increased 20 to 100 times in value

Yearly Range for IBM Common Stock, 1929–1939

	1929	1930	1931	1932	1933	1934	1935	1936	1937	1938	1939
High	255	197	179	117	153	164	190.5	194	189	185	195
Low	109	131	92	52.5	75	131	149	160	127.5	130	145

in the first few years after their lows. They were very cheap at their lowest prices. IBM was not.

There is only one measure by which IBM might have been considered cheap. Below are the high and low price-earnings ratios for IBM for 1926 through 1935:

High-Low Price-Earnings Ratios for IBM, 1926–1935

	1926	1927	1928	1929	1930	1931	1932	1933	1934	1935
High	8.9	15.9	19.1	23.1	17.1	16.2	13.0	19.0	17.7	19.3
Low	6.0	7.1	13.1	9.9	11.3	8.3	5.8	9.1	14.1	15.1

At times, it had a low price-earnings ratio. This was not because the prices were low. If IBM were extremely low in 1932, it would have increased much more than it did. Instead, the P/E was low because IBM earned so much. (The P/Es were low because the profits were too high.) Nobody—*nobody*—makes the kind of profits today that IBM made in the 1920s and 1930s.

During the 1930s, IBM consistently earned net after-tax profit margins greater than 23 percent. In 1935, the net after-tax profit margin was a whopping 32.4 percent. Can you imagine a company today earning 32 percent of its sales dollar as after-tax profit? It is very far from the reality we know. Return on stockholder's equity (ROE is net income divided by shareholder's equity) was consistently outstanding at more than 12 percent. This company seems to have never felt the effects of The Great Depression.

The stock, which started out very high in the 1920s, never became extremely cheap. If you thought IBM was cheap because its price-earnings ratio was low in 1932, you also would have thought it was cheap at much higher prices in 1929 and 1927. Clearly, price-earnings ratios don't give us the answers we need to assess the value of IBM in the 1930s.

What will? Lets look at Price Sales Ratios. At its very lowest point in 1932, IBM had a PSR of 2.3. At its highest point in 1932, it had a PSR of 5.1. Below are high and low PSRs for IBM from 1932 through 1939:

High-Low PSRs for IBM, 1932–1939

	1932	1933	1934	1935	1936	1937	1938	1939
High	5.1	6.0	5.5	6.2	5.5	4.6	4.3	4.2
Low	2.3	3.0	4.4	4.9	4.5	3.1	3.0	3.1

It does not take much imagination to see that IBM's original high PSR acted like a weight around its neck, making it hard for the stock to rise. The stock rose as the sales rose—and no faster. It just couldn't get up over the ceiling that existed at the level of 5 to 6. While it was making exceptional profit margins (therefore its price-earnings ratios were not exceptionally high), the market knew, as only it can, that those margins were not sustainable over the long term. The market listened more to the PSR than to the P/E.

The fact that IBM was making so much money in the short term tended to make the lowest PSR that it sold at rather high.

This is the paradox of value for exceptionally profitable companies. The already-high PSR keeps the stock from increasing significantly. The fat, short-term profits keep the PSR from contracting too far (admittedly, a little like the chicken and the egg). When and if profitability fades away, a stock like this is extremely vulnerable. If, as was the case with a few companies like IBM, growth continues unabated for years, the stock will improve—but not at spectacular rates. It will improve as the company "grows into its britches."

IBM gained much of its growth-stock reputation in the 1950s and 1960s, during which time it performed beautifully. A large part of its better performance was because, by the mid-to-late 1940s, the company had "grown into its britches." In 1946, IBM's PSR hit its 50-year low, at 0.51—a Super Stock level. In 8 of the 10 years between 1946 and 1955, IBM sold at PSRs below one. In four of them, it sold at PSRs of 0.75 or below. From this time frame, over the next 20 years, IBM stock soared, gaining the legendary reputation which has remained with it ever since. It grew and its valuation rose. As IBM again became fashionable and highly valued, its PSR rose. By the mid-to-late 1960s, IBM's PSR was again bouncing around the stratosphere between four and six, and again, the stock stopped performing. The key to making significantly above-average long-term profits in IBM, throughout the last 50 years, lay in buying the stock when it sold at low PSRs.

IBM was not alone in the 1930s. Other companies sold at high valuations. Some deserved it. Most did not. Coca-Cola was a case similar to IBM. It consistently generated outstanding returns. Its stock briefly sold at low price-earnings ratios, but mostly at high Price Sales Ratios. AND the stock was an unspectacular performer in the five years after its "bottom" in 1932.

Most stocks that sold at high prices based on their PSRs did not deserve their rich valuations—they subsequently performed poorly. Burroughs started off at high values. At the end of the 1930s, despite a tremendous Bull Market, it was still selling at the same levels it had in the early 1930s. The market was up. Its business was up, but Burroughs wasn't up.

Likewise, Gillette Safety Razor sold at lower prices in 1938 and 1939 than it did in 1932 and 1933. The principle cause was that it started out at excessive valuations. At its highest in 1932 and 1933, it had a PSR of 4.4. By 1939, its highest PSR was only 1.5. Gillette had grown, but people had become discouraged. After-tax margins and return on equity had both slipped from the mid-30s down into the mid-teens. Compared to its past, this was a disappointment. Today, anyone would be delighted with after-tax margins as high as Gillette's very lowest during the Great Depression. The market wanted more.

Most stocks did well from their lows of the 1930s. Some did exceptionally well. It was not rare to see tenfold increases (1,000 percent) in the five years beginning 1932–1933—a compound annual ratè of return of 59 percent. Others did even better. Some stocks increased 20 to 40 times in value and more. These were stocks that, at their lows, were being almost given away.

Spectacular Profits with Low-PSR Stocks

Revere Copper and Brass, for instance, sold at a total market value of only $200,000 at its low. For more than three years, it could be bought at a market value of less than $600,000. For a cool half-million dollars or less, you could have bought control of the company. It had more than $15 million in sales (about the same as IBM's at the time). That made its PSR ridiculously low at only 0.04. It had a balance sheet that was stronger than that of most companies of a comparable size today. From its low, the stock increased more than 45 times in value. If it had been bought at three times its low, it still would have increased in value more than 15 times thereafter. A 45-fold increase in value over five years is a compound rate of return of 115 percent per year.

Other low-PSR stocks turned in stellar performances. Deere & Co. increased more than 20 times in price in three years (171 percent-plus rate of return). So did Remington Rand and Cutler-Hammer. Borg-Warner increased more than 25 times in value in four years (123 percent-plus rate of return). Caterpillar Tractor increased 20 times in price in four years (111 percent-plus rate of return). Cooper-Bessemer, now Cooper Industries, increased more than 30 times in value in three years (a whopping 210 percent rate of return). L. C. Smith & Corona Typewriters increased 40 times in price in four years (150 percent-plus rate of return). Other stocks did this well, also. Unfortunately, many of them are names that are no longer familiar. Who ever heard of Campbell, Wyant and Cannon Foundry? Who remembers Houdaille-Hershey? American Seating? Flintkote? McGraw Electric? Bullard Co.? Fairbanks, Morse & Co.? General Cable? They, along with other low-PSR stocks, increased 20 times or more in value. Throughout our study, we have been unable to find a single stock starting at a PSR over 1.5 which increased nearly this much.

Consider L. C. Smith & Corona Typewriters—one of the all-time giveaways (now called SCM Corporation). As the name implies, they sold typewriters. They also made and sold related products such as adding machines, duplicating machines, and carbon paper. Their business was what we would today call office automation. (Office-automation stocks such as Wang and NBI have been some of the very hottest stocks of the early 1980s.)

Today, SCM is a $2 billion giant in numerous businesses ranging from typewriters to chemicals. In 1933, it was only a $5 million company. Of course, a dollar was worth more then than it is now. It had a strong balance sheet and maintained excellent liquidity. At its worst, net current assets exceeded one third of total shareholder's equity.

By 1937, this ratio had improved to over 75 percent. Today, few companies have this kind of liquidity. As it turns out, this $5 million company had a total market value in 1932 and 1933 of less than $200,000. It had a PSR of only 0.04. They gave it away. True, it lost money through these years. But during the total period, less than 10 percent of its 1931 net worth was lost. Who could ask for more—a 150 percent per year compound rate of return backed by a strong balance sheet. (See Illustration 7–1.)

Cooper-Bessemer is another phenomenal example. In 1932, it was only a $2 million company. Total liabilities were negligible. Net current assets made up more than half of net worth. At its low, it had a market value of less than $100,000. Its PSR was only 0.02 (*phenomenal*). By the end of 1936, the stock was up more than 30 times in value. If you had bought half the company for $50,000, you soon would have had more than $1.5 million worth of stock. Today, Cooper Industries is more than $3 billion in sales.

The extremely profitable stocks of the 1930s were all low-PSR stocks. There are many more examples between the extremities. Dozens and dozens of companies with low PSRs increased 10 to 15 times in market value from 1932 and 1933 to 1935 and 1936. They generated annual rates of return between 75 percent and 140 percent, depending upon how long it took for them to achieve their increases.

What about All Those Great Companies?

What about all the *great* companies? Surely among them must be some exceptions—some that grew enough to justify high initial

ILLUSTRATION 7–1 *Smith-Corona Incorporated*

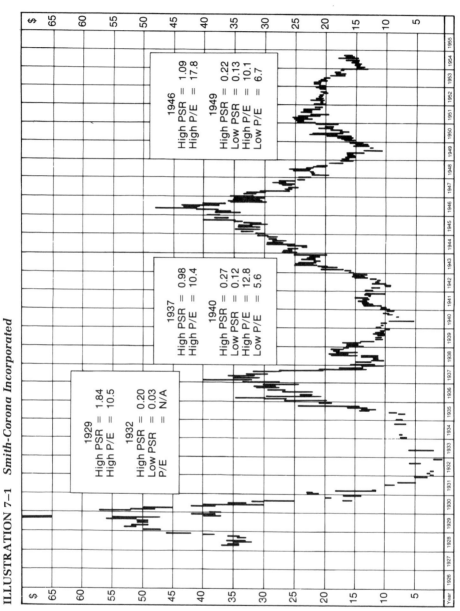

1929
High PSR = 1.84
High P/E = 10.5

1932
High PSR = 0.20
Low PSR = 0.03
P/E = N/A

1937
High PSR = 0.98
High P/E = 10.4

1940
High PSR = 0.27
Low PSR = 0.12
High P/E = 12.8
Low P/E = 5.6

1946
High PSR = 1.09
High P/E = 17.8

1949
High PSR = 0.22
Low PSR = 0.13
High P/E = 10.1
Low P/E = 6.7

Source: M. C. Horsey & Company, Inc., P.O. Box H, Salisbury, Md. 21801.

PSRs? IBM was the only exception we could find—not much of one at that. Instead, there were the "greats" with low PSRs. Most of them did well (we have already mentioned SCM, Caterpillar, and Remington). What about the others? Bethlehem Steel, FMC, Mead, and Sears were low-PSR stocks (less than 0.15, 0.33, 0.20, and 0.20) in which one could have made 1,000 to 2,000 percent in five years. Sears, for example, had its lowest price-earnings ratio in 1931 at 12. But at its absolute low in 1932, there wasn't a price-earnings ratio because there weren't any earnings. (See Illustration 7–2.)

J. C. Penney was a low-PSR stock (0.20 at the bottom), only increasing ninefold in value between 1932 and 1936 (still better than high-PSR stocks did). At its high, it had a PSR of only 1.1.

Three of the stocks had marginally high PSRs by our standards. Eastman Kodak was one. At its very low, it had a PSR of only 1.4, increasing 5.6 times during the 1930s. It did better than IBM—but not as well as the extremely low PSR stocks. Most of its increase came from growth: The PSR a little more than doubled to 3.3 at its peak. Dow Chemical, likewise, starting with a PSR of 1.1, increased 7.6 times in value by 1937—peaking out with a PSR of 6.6. General Electric increased 7.6 times in value from its absolute low in 1932 to its absolute high in 1937. Its low PSR was a moderate 0.93, while the high was 3.8.

From their highs in 1937, most stocks drifted generally lower. Those stocks with very high PSRs in 1937 (like IBM and Dow) did poorly. Consider Dow. Between 1937 and 1947, the company grew from $22 to $130 million in sales. Profits grew from $4.9 to $12.7 million. Logic and the "Growth Stock" school would lead you to believe the stock should have gone up. It didn't. In 1947, it sold at lower prices than in 1937. After 10 years of exceptional growth, in 1947, it finally had grown into its britches. It was then cheap by any standard and performed beautifully for the next few decades.

The stock prices of the late 1920s did not seem so high then. High prices were masked by fat profit margins which kept price-earnings ratios from getting too high. Many companies had very low price-earnings ratios in 1929. Investors couldn't get enough of these stocks. Several years later, many price-earnings ratios were infinite. Rigorous use of PSRs would have saved investors a lot of headaches and money in this time period. Had investors tempered their optimism in 1929 and pessimism in 1932–33 with PSR analysis, we might not talk today about the "Great Crash."

Both obscure and famous stocks showed the same recurrent patterns throughout the 1930s. High-PSR stocks tended to perform relatively poorly. The best performers had low PSRs. Most stocks were cheap during the 1930s. That is for sure. That is the part of the "Myth of the 1930s" that bears up under examination.

ILLUSTRATION 7–2 *Sears, Roebuck & Company*

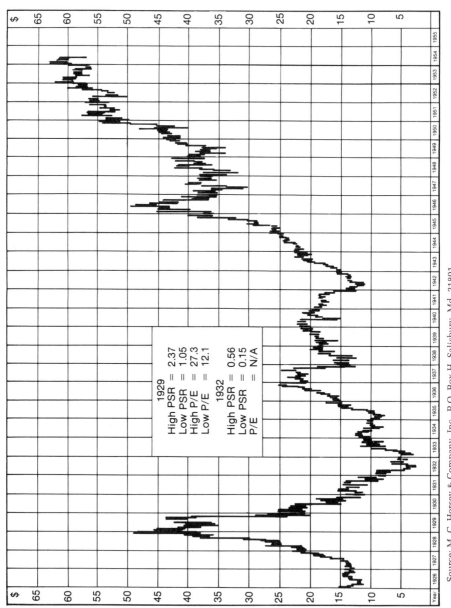

1929
High PSR = 2.37
Low PSR = 1.05
High P/E = 27.3
Low P/E = 12.1

1932
High PSR = 0.56
Low PSR = 0.15
P/E = N/A

Source: M. C. Horsey & Company, Inc., P.O. Box H, Salisbury, Md. 21801.

The part of the myth that doesn't bear up is the notion that the whole market was a giveaway. Some stocks weren't so cheap. They were the ones with high PSRs. The fortunes that were made coming out of the depression were made in stocks that had been thought of at the time as failures. "Fortunes from failures" is a recurrent theme in financial history. Fortunes from failures—stocks discarded as "garbage" while their basic values are overlooked (see Chapters 1 and 2—the glitch). Whether looking at the 1930s or any other time frame, the fortunes-from-failures concept applies. From among poorly regarded low-PSR stocks, some unique opportunities emerge.

Part Three

Fundamental Analysis

Super Companies: The Business Aspects— Stalking Excellence

Basic Business Traits

It is crucial to examine the business aspects that determine a Super Company. A key cornerstone to Super-Stock investment is buying stock in companies that are truly outstanding in their most-basic business fundamentals. True Super Stocks are Super Companies bought at the right price. You can buy stock in a poor company and have it later double or triple. Unless it is truly a Great Company, however, it is very, very unlikely that it will ever increase in value enough to qualify as a Super Stock.

A Super Company is a business which distinguishes itself because it can generate internally funded growth at well above average rates. As inflation rates vary, so too must the rate of growth a Super Company must attain through internally generated growth. A Super Company should be able to grow an average of at least 15 "real" (after inflation) percent per year. If inflation is 6 percent per year, a Super Company will be able to fund growth averaging at least 21 percent per year. If, instead, inflation rages at 15 percent per year, then a Super Company should be able to grow at least 30 percent per year. At any given time, only a few hundred Super Companies exist out of the tens of thousands of businesses in the world. Many are well recognized for their unique traits. Others are not well identified. It doesn't matter whether or not Wall Street thinks a company is fundamentally strong and likely to grow. What matters is that it be strong and able to grow. It is preferable if, at the time a stock is bought, the financial community thinks the company is terrible (see Chapter 2). It must have strong future-growth potential in a fundamental business sense. Its business aspects must distinguish it as a Super Company.

In their most abbreviated form, the business aspects of a Super Company must include:

1. *Growth orientation:* A burning desire in all senior personnel (which percolates down through the organization) for growth. This need manifest itself not only in growth markets but, more importantly, throughout the daily lives of the employees that make growth happen.
2. *Marketing excellence:* A broad understanding of changes in the nature of its market—at least as soon as the customer first perceives them—along with an organization capable of attaining and continuing to maintain customer satisfaction.
3. *An unfair advantage:* A competitive superiority over all current or potential competitors—usually being the lowest-cost producer—and/or having established a unique or semiproprietary position in at least a major portion of its product lines.
4. *Creative personnel relations:* A company "culture" that makes employees feel they are treated with dignity, that they have been and will be offered fair promotion opportunities, and that they exist in an atmosphere where constructive ideas from subordinates are encouraged and financially rewarded.
5. *The best in financial controls:* Financial controls which learn quickly if results are not as planned. This must be coupled with a constant desire to seek continual creative evolutionary improvements in financial controls relative to the competition. A Super Company must never be content with controls merely comparable to what others have.

There is a great deal more required of a Super Company—high margins, high market share, better management, leading product positioning, a quality image, and many other specific characteristics. These are qualities which anyone would look for in a Super Company. Yet, a Super Company is one because of the above five mentioned aspects. For example, the company must have the potential for high gross margins, high pre-tax profit margins, and high net-profit margins. But margins are a result. They come from the same causes and are the result of the basics being in place. The employees and management, and their actions, are the causes.

In other words, the company must have those aspects within its employee force which indicate the overwhelming likelihood of rapidly rising sales and potentially strong future profit margins. The rapidly rising sales potential is at least heavily dependent upon a growth orientation.

Growth Orientation

Growth does not just happen. It starts in the minds of management. It is a burning obsession. The mental traits that foster a growth orientation in an individual have been understood for decades. They are inherently positive personal qualities. They have been chronicled in works such as Napoleon Hill and W. Clement Stone, *Success through a Positive Mental Attitude* (Englewood Cliffs, N.J.: Prentice-Hall, 1960), and Norman Vincent Peale, *The Power of Positive Thinking* (Englewood Cliffs, N.J.: Prentice-Hall, 1952).

While any individual can develop these traits, it is difficult to build them in others. This is the role of a true leader. For good or bad, there is a leader within any long-lasting grouping of people. Within any group dynamic, at the very start, some natural pecking order unfolds. Leaders have power thrust upon them by the combined will of their followers. Many incorrectly assume that leaders seize power. That isn't usually true. Instead, power is given to leaders by the followers they cultivate. Followers want what the leader has: vision, confidence, respect of others, and respect for the followers.

Followers absorb these qualities through association with their leaders and peers. It is beautiful to watch. In a Super Company, the key employees have a sparkle in their eyes as they talk about their fellows. When describing superiors, they often resort to fable-like stories. It is not this way at normal companies when employees talk about co-workers.

A friend went to work for Verbatim recently. A former marketing manager for a huge electronics firm, he exhibited an advanced state of "job burnout." He had respect for his former firm but displayed a bitterness toward his boss and peers. The first day at Verbatim, he was approached by the chairman who already knew a certain amount about him. My friend's eyes glowed as he told the story. With his former employer, he never met anyone higher than a regional vice president. Now he was talking to the chairman of the board. It just amazed him that the chairman knew more about him than he did about the chairman. The chairman impressed him as few ever had before. This burned-out reject from Corporate America applied himself with a vigor that showed no display of job burnout. In the early weeks, he worked 15-hour days and was tickled pink at the opportunity. He had found a job with people he could follow with respect. Just so—in any Super Company—the orientation of top management is absorbed by the followers.

A Super Company looks at problems as potential opportunities. Discovering hidden costs in manufacturing could be viewed as a problem. It could be an opportunity for future cost reduction—allowing lower product prices—and increased sales potential.

The introduction of a new product by a competitor can be viewed as a problem. It is also an opportunity to better learn a customer's inclinations as it reacts to the new market entry. For example, some participants in the PC (personal computer) market were intimidated by IBM's entry into that field. Others saw it as a validation of the future of the market. Others saw it as an immediate opportunity to sell complementary products. The management of a Super Company looks for a silver lining in every cloud.

The charisma of a Super Company's leader will be evident at the most casual meeting. Because the orientation must begin with him, it must be evident in him. His confidence must be unquestionable. His desire to be more than he is—and to be the leader of a growing, greater company—must be highlighted by a certain humility. He need speak of his subordinates with a high degree of pride. He will always seek subordinates whom he feels are more capable than himself—in whom he believes. Once he finds them, he will "talk them up" whenever possible. They will understand and appreciate that he is promoting them in the most basic sense. They, in turn, will promote his ideas to their subordinates.

The final outcome of this process of percolation is a group of people seeking opportunities to grow. Marketing, technology, and support concepts will be accumulated at each level of the company and communicated horizontally and vertically within the organization. The company will not lack ideas for future growth—it draws from within. It will have to pick from among its best ideas. Lower levels of management will accept these ideas out of a true and natural respect for superiors. Respect in the decision-making process is an attribute which separates a Super Company from the garden-variety American corporation. In no place is it any more clear than in marketing.

Marketing Excellence

Marketing is an absolute key—perhaps the single most important aspect to success. More companies fail, or exist at a lackluster level, for lack of marketing excellence than for any other single reason.

Superb marketing is so important because it satisfies one of business's only reasons for existence: its customers.

Exceptional marketing is rare. It is rare because marketing is more of an art than any other portion of business. Corny, but true: Marketing in its simplest and best form is helping people. And it is hard to do a good job if you don't understand them. This ability to understand the customer is what makes good marketing so unique.

Everyone knows someone who mistakenly believes that marketing is nothing more than some form of eloquence in the gift of gab. These people, at best, confuse marketing with salesmanship. Salesmanship is an art form in itself. Beyond salesmanship, marketing includes:

1. Advertising.
2. Market research.
3. Merchandising.
4. Public relations.
5. Sales management.
6. Service.
7. Strategic and product planning.

The last point may be the most important. It is at the strategic level that companies so frequently get off on the wrong foot. In most small companies, in spite of the formal existence of a marketing vice president, the chief executive usually acts as the head of marketing. He must. It is at the chief-executive level that key strategic decisions are made regarding the market.

The key to strategic planning is an intuitive ability to determine how currently nonexistent market forces will develop. Strategic planning exceeds rationality. Rationality is restricted by logic. Logic is necessary but not sufficient. Many of the most-important decisions in life cannot be made by logic alone. It is here that the role of the chief executive comes in.

Regardless of the strength of the marketing organization, unless the chief executive is intuitively strong at marketing, the company is likely to stumble repeatedly over itself. A company run by a man with a strong intuitive understanding of his markets is stronger than one led by a logical man whose main strengths are in technology, production, or finance. The other skills can usually be purchased. True marketing grace is an art.

Still, no matter how strong the man at the top may be, he must develop under him subordinates who are skilled marketers—people with whom top management can work comfortably at all levels and in all circumstances. For example:

Quanta-Ray: "Underpromise; Overperform"—
Customers Are the Best Salesmen

Bob Mortensen had a Harvard MBA. He had been the world's first laser salesman—a corporate marketing manager and vice president with the world's leading laser firm, Spectra-Physics. He also had high-level experience in production and finance management. Now he was the president of his own laser company—Quanta-Ray— which meant he had to swim upstream against larger and more-entrenched competition.

One might expect him to lean on his unusually competent marketing background to make all the decisions. Far from it. After setting the basic product strategy, as only a chief executive can, he left the marketing decisions up to his exceptionally able marketing vice president, Gene Watson. Watson was effective, in part, because Mortensen—as a superb marketing man himself—knew just what he needed in a marketing manager. He linked himself to Watson and then got out of Watson's way.

Watson called all the shots, ranging from what color the product should be to how they should advertise. He determined what firms they would use for advertising and public relations. He decided what kind of salesmen they would hire. In this case, most of the salesmen Watson hired had absolutely no prior experience selling. He took the time to train them himself. Watson was particularly artistic in his handling of the advertising and public relations functions. His advertisements evidenced a degree of "class," causing customers to want to associate themselves with Quanta-Ray. He had a strong ability to interact with leading scientists to motivate them to write technical papers citing successful results using Quanta-Ray lasers. This is the best sort of PR possible.

From Watson and Mortensen I learned my single most useful lesson in advertising and public relations—it is usually best to cultivate a reputation for underpromising and overperforming. When customers perceive that they consistently will get more than they are promised, they become the supplier's allies in generating more customers. They generate referrals and buy more themselves. They get a psychic "high" from dealing with people they know aren't making excessive sales claims. (Most people have been shortchanged too many times in different areas of their lives—they get gun-shy.) People value relationships where they can trust those with whom they deal.

Customers went to great lengths to help land sales for Quanta-Ray. Watson cultivated this reputation for "underpromising and overperforming by always keeping his published product specifications substantially below the actual capability of the equipment.

This way customers quickly know they can rely on any claim made by the supplier. (The Japanese have mastered this technique and often use it to gain a premium price in the electronics industry.) At the same time, the customers feel they are purchasing inexpensively because the "cost of concern" has been lifted from their heads.

To be sure, as president, Mortensen did not divorce himself from the market. Almost every president of a small company absolutely must make key sales calls. In fact, for several years, Watson and Mortensen shared an office—with their desks butted up next to each other in one of the best forms of forced communication possible. It was impossible for Mortensen to divorce himself from the market. It was impossible for Watson not to infuse the marketing slant into everything that came into that office—production, research, and finance. In the process, Quanta-Ray developed markets in solid-state tunable lasers that other competent laser companies overlooked.[1]

Is Management in Control of Marketing?

In a less-successful company, the marketing vice president was stubborn and convinced that no one but he knew how the market should be handled. He was jealous and resentful of any contact made by the chief executive or anyone outside of marketing with any customer. If someone from R&D or finance contacted customers for any reason, the marketing vice president threw copious temper tantrums. This might have been all right had the marketing vice president really had a strong "handle" on his markets. Unfortunately, this wasn't the case. (If he had such a strong handle he wouldn't have been so paranoid.) In time, both the marketing vice president and the chief executive had to be replaced—but not before the company had successfully lost a large percentage of its former value.

Consider another company's salesmanship for extremely sophisticated electronic process control equipment.

A huge multinational, multidivision customer had recently committed to buying several systems, costing a few hundred thousand dollars each, for different locations. Purchase decisions had been made separately at the division management level. Since other firms supplied similar equipment, there should have been competitive bids for each of these installations. There weren't. Divisional buyers bought exclusively from this relatively small vendor without seriously considering other alternatives.

---

[1] In time, Quanta-Ray was bought by Spectra-Physics, the industry leader, and became the heart of Spectra's solid-state laser activities. This was five years after my investment in 1976. It realized a profit of more than 30 times my cost—concrete testimonial to the contribution a vivid spirit, or in this case, two vivid spirits, in marketing can make to a Super Company.

"How could this be?" I asked the customer's corporate management. "Don't you require divisional decision makers to seek out competitive bids?" The man in charge of equipment procurement at headquarters explained that even he didn't understand. The salespeople apparently convinced divisional decision makers to sign letters of intent so quickly that there was no talk of the purchase at the corporate level. Since the letters of intent included money-back guarantees (if not satisfied after six months), the buyers felt they weren't risking much. The buyers were persuaded by the guarantor to take the risk without checking either other competition or corporate headquarters.

The installations were completely successful. None of the systems was ever returned. The whole thing still sounds like something right out of a Dale Carnegie book. Afterward, I asked the management of this small electronics company what single functional area it would most like to improve. To my amazement, the three top officers of the company, without consultation or hesitation, picked marketing—where they were already so strong—as the key area for improvement.

How Are Sales and Service Handled?

In an area as artistically volatile as marketing, it is impossible to establish absolute rules. Some guidelines are helpful. If a business manufactures sophisticated or expensive products, a strong direct field sales force is usually best. By contrast, be concerned by an organization that markets through a distributor network.

Firms marketing through distributors can have difficulty in directing marketing efforts. It may be harder to train, motivate, discipline, and reorient sales people who aren't fully dedicated to a single employer's product line. On the other hand, some distributor "reps" may oversell the company's product with excessive promises. When these promises fail to materialize, a product or firm can have its reputation damaged (underpromise; overperform).

Many small firms get started with distributors because they can't afford their own dedicated sales force. As they grow, they tend to switch to their own force. This is less true for businesses selling low-priced items than for firms producing sophisticated products.

Service is an area often overlooked by the casual business observer. It can be an effective sales tool—or an Achilles' heel. Talking with a few customers ascertains the quality of a firm's service. Be skeptical of firms hiring third-party sources to act as their servicing agents. As with distributors' representatives, a third-party servicing agent is hard to train, motivate, and control. I am amazed by the number of firms that hire their own competitors to act as third-party servicing agents.

Recently I visited a highly regarded, small, high-technology company. Its stock is high by any method of determination. Its principle competitor is DEC. To my surprise, it is completely dependent upon DEC to service its products in the continental United States. DEC is a fine firm, but it doesn't take much imagination to envision its doing less than it might to service a competitor's products. (Would your heart be as dedicated to servicing someone else's customers as it would be to helping your own?)

The key to marketing management lies in the interplay of salespeople, marketing managers, marketing vice president, and the chief executive. Each is vital. Each is an artisan. Yet each may be fairly difficult to deal with from a management point of view. On the surface, these exceptional individuals will be intelligent, suave, and charming. Inside, many often feel insecure.

The salepeople are apt to be hard to manage because they are used to being out there on their own, thinking for themselves. In many respects, they view their lives from a sense of independence. Business-school case histories abound with tales of field sales organizations gone out of control. Marketing managers are hard to manage because so many of them are just "Peter-Principled" salespeople. If excellence is to exist in marketing, it must be fostered between the CEO and the marketing vice president and grow down through the organization. If you can't see it at the top, you won't see it at all. The potential investor must scrutinize the top two marketing people most carefully. A correct judgment of them is prerequisite to making a correct judgment of the company.

Find the Unfair Advantage

A Super Company must have a competitive superiority over all current or potential competitors. This usually involves being the lowest-cost producer and/or having established a unique or semi-proprietary position in at least a major portion of its product lines.

Above my desk hangs a small sign that reads, "All I really want in life is an unfair advantage." Something proprietary or unique gives a company an advantage over others that allows for potentially large gross margins.[2] These margins allow for the internal generation of enough profits to fund rapid future growth. It is essential in a Super Company.

The unique advantage may come in different forms. The advantage may be more obvious in some businesses than in others. In mining, for instance, the advantage may be merely better reserves in

---

[2] Gross margin means gross profit divided by sales. Gross profit is sales minus cost of goods sold. Cost of goods sold are those direct production-oriented costs associated with making the product.

the ground. In consumer items, a trade name or patent may be sufficient. Lower-cost production through better production techniques is a common and, at times, absolutely necessary form. Marketing and research teams that work well together in product development may provide the advantage by helping to keep one step ahead of the competition.

The ultimate test of research is whether the product can offer the desired feature with a cost low enough to allow a reasonable gross margin. When marketing gives a product idea to top management, the proposal includes those specific features the product needs to satisfy customers. Marketing also will supply estimates of necessary product pricing.

With these product features and prices assumed, marketing will provide specific volume forecasts over time. Accordingly, engineering needs to work within these constraints. The product must be designed to be *producible* with the *specified features* in the *right volumes* with a sufficiently *low cost per unit*.

The largest single area where research efficiency plays a creative role is in this area of design-to-cost considerations. There is no other function that plays so important a role for the future profitability of the product and yet is so completely determined by the engineering effort. Can we cut on costs here? Can we skimp over there? Should we be extra careful not to cut costs on this feature? The design-to-cost function is one where businesses frequently get off on the wrong foot with products. It is the major impact that research efficiency has on gross margins and subsequent net margins.

Once a product is designed with inherently high costs, it is difficult to alter that deficiency. It is likely never remedied. Products that start off with poor gross margins tend to stay that way forever.

IBM is not my idea of a Super Stock, yet many believe it to be a Super Company. It is certainly a Super Competitor—with a lot of advantages. One from which they never cease to benefit is the IBM name. Everyone in the computer business knows that an IBM salesperson can get in doors that remain closed to others. Customers react with favor to the name IBM. Customers react with favor to most forms of supplier advantage.

The financial community easily accepts the notion of a proprietary advantage among technology companies. Since investors accept the notion that technology companies offer something unique, they are often prone to bid up the stock to high levels.

It is easy to devise a list of companies with unique advantages in technology. Still, low-technology or no-technology examples abound. Warren Buffett, the legendary Omaha investor, is fond of newspapers having a "local business franchise"—another way to describe a business advantage. McDonald's ("Does it all for you") and Toys-R-Us created advantages through exploiting catchy marketing logos.

Sometimes companies create an advantage in economies of scale generated by acquisitions in related fields. (See Chapter 10 to discover why profit margins often are tied to market share.) To have a Super Stock, you must have at least a Super Company. A Super Company will have an unusual competitive advantage that allows it to make outstanding profitability, expressed in gross and net margins.

Nucor Corporation developed its competitive advantage in the extremely mundane steel industry. They developed processes with costs low enough to compete with foreign steel, while still making outstanding returns. Continuous casting has been well understood in the steel business for years. In the late 1960s, Nucor pioneered coupling continuous casting—fed by cheap scrap steel—with a local minimill concept.

By the mid-1970s, Nucor's mills were so efficient that steel never stopped moving from the time it was first hot until it was a finished piece of inventory. The process improvements Nucor developed reduced energy requirements, capital costs, and labor per ton of steel produced. Nucor created a cost structure that allowed good profits and continued plant expansion in depressed times (1977 and 1982) when the rest of the U.S. and foreign steel industries were losing money.

A Super Company receives numerous benefits from the advantages it maintains over competitors. These ought to generate the basis for superior market share. It doesn't have to have the market share at the time of the investment. When I first invested in Nucor, for example, it had low market share in most product lines. A Super Company ought to be able, if it has a true advantage over competition, to gain market share or at least to keep market share to the extent it desires. The analyst's standard question, aimed at finding intermediate to long-term goals should be: "What are you doing now to make margins better in the future?" This is often the same as asking: "What are you doing to increase your future market share?"

There are a lot of wrong answers to these questions. Management may explain it is cutting various forms of selling and administrative expense. It may even be cutting research. All of that may be fine, but the real solution has to lie at the gross-margin level.[3] Better to ask: "What are you doing to improve gross margins?" What a company does to improve gross margins tends to be the same things that allow it to improve market share.

---

[3] Gross margin means gross profit divided by sales. Gross profit is sales minus cost of goods sold. Cost of goods sold are those direct production-oriented costs associated with making the product.

Profitability and market share are so closely wed that it often becomes futile to invest long-term money in anything other than an industry's market-share leader. The only good long-term investment in a company with low market share is when you expect it to eventually upset the leader and take the leading market-share position away (see Chapters 10 and 11).

Does the Customer Get the "Best Bang for the Buck"?

An advantage is often achieved through product differentiation in the eyes of customers. By designing a product that addresses a slightly different market niche or by offering price performance advantages with unique features, a company can often command a premium price. Marketing excellence enables a company to identify which product characteristics are most important to customers. In stressing these features while trimming costs in other areas, it is possible to give the customer the most "bang for the buck." (The introduction of portability to personal computers is a perfect example.) This almost always pays off for all concerned. Market share may be defined in this case in terms of the so-called market niche. Size differentiation falls into this category and is one of the most useful analytical tools for staying out of trouble. (It is so important that a substantial portion of Chapter 9 is devoted to size differentiation.)

Labor Relations Are Critical

Labor relations are a key element of a Super Company. Business and trade journals regularly report labor difficulties suffered by business—an unfortunate and usually unnecessary misery.

Super Companies seldom face labor unions, much less any form of visible labor dispute, because they have more than suitable labor relations. An enlightened management views labor as being just as much a contributor as management to the success of a company.

In recent years, participatory management (where employees participate in creative changes and product ideas) has become popular as more and more U.S. companies attempt to duplicate or modify Japanese ways to achieve Japaneselike results. The key is not any one labor or employee relations method. The key is a willingness and continual desire to seek out improvements in the employee environment, encouraging him or her to generate greater efficiency.

Nucor, again, is a perfect example. Nucor annual reports are dotted with tiny printed names—the names of each and every employee of the company. Nucor does more than put their employees on the cover. Each employee is compensated according to the success of a small team (of which he or she is a member). There is no theoretical limit to how much an employee can make. Nucor wants each individual to earn as much as possible—the result of producing a lot of steel efficiently. The efficiency of the small team is directly proportional to the contributions of each member. Consequently, each team member works to insure that every other team member stays in gear and contributes. Laggards aren't fired. They are socially ostracized by team co-members and, in time, quit. Typical Nucor steelworkers make in excess of $30,000 per year—not too shabby for a minority blue-collar worker with a limited education. They would earn far less with the Steelworkers Union.[4]

But Nucor doesn't stop there. To encourage employees toward a better future, Nucor additionally pays $1,400 per year toward the college education of any child of any employee of the company—no strings attached. If an employee has four college-age children, that means $5,600 a year. The policy is enlightened self-interest because the employee good will generated by the grants is worth much more than the actual cost.

Finally, to show employees and stockholders as well that they are willing to put their money where their mouth is, over half the total compensation of all Nucor officers is directly tied to net earnings of the company. If the company does well, so do the officers. In a bad recession year, such as 1982, officers received relatively little.

Other companies utilize numerous methods to improve employee relations—ranging from company parties to employee fitness centers. They may implement day-care centers for employees' children or a weekly 5 P.M. company cocktail party. Some produce company movies made by and for the employees. The list goes on, limited only by the imagination and will of the participants.

A Super Company is blessed with a management that is both willing and possesses a never-ceasing imagination. The key is for management to keep searching for new ideas to improve the employee environment which fosters productivity and the flow of ideas to management.

Financial Controls—Question the Answers

Financial controls may seem boring. They are an absolute requirement for success. The process of rapid growth requires keeping track

---

[4] In 1980, a typical member of the Steelworkers Union made an average wage of $26,450 compared to $31,000 at Nucor. Source: *Business Week*, September 21, 1981, pp. 42Z–n16.

of all elements involved—a good set of current numbers reflecting developments at a detailed level.

The finance department of a Super Company routinely generates reports (within three weeks or less of the end of a month) that include, at least, the following:

1. Consistent financial statements for the most recent month and quarter and for the year to date.
2. Financial statements at the operating level for the most recent month by product line and profit center.
3. Order, backlog, shipment, and inventory analysis for the most recent month.
4. Monthly and year-to-date expenses by category, compared against budget for all categories of expenses falling below the gross margin line of an income statement.
5. Head count by type of employee and area of assignment to keep track of manpower by function. Good management knows where and when it needs to add or subtract personnel.

There is no limit to the inventiveness that may be used to analyze how a business is doing. The Super Company is always seeking new and better ways to accumulate and analyze data. The Super Company is not resistant to change in its management information systems but encourages change and suggestions of change at all levels.

Financial controls are the responsibility of the financial vice president of the firm. Sometimes this function has other names (such as chief financial officer or vice president—finance). In a smaller company, the function may rest with an executive vice president responsible for administrative areas outside of marketing, research, and production. He will have a treasurer and a controller reporting to him.

Financial people are often conservative and conventional by nature. It is the responsibility of the chief financial officer to hire or transform the treasurer and controller so that they become leaders in an evolutionary process of controls refinement.

Look for a clue to the mental outlook of key financial executives by asking questions that "force them out of the bushes" on these issues. Questions should be reasonable yet detailed—the kind they will naturally have answers to on the tips of their tongues.

Questions should not be so sensitive that executives might have any hesitation answering freely. A typical question might be: "On a percentage basis, how much does marketing expense vary month to month and what has been the variance from budget in the last few months?"

Answers to such questions shouldn't be terribly sensitive to management. At the same time, the way they are given, will—when asked by a skilled and experienced interviewer—indicate important aspects of the company's financial controls. They can reveal what the company has available at its finger tips. They also may reveal how the company reacts to issues they may not have considered or kept track of in the past. An attitude toward change is as important as available information.

Top financial officers of a Super Company will have the answer to almost any question in one of two forms—in the forefront of their minds or through ready access to a paper report or computer terminal within a short physical distance of their normal working environment. Remember that these men live with numbers. They are prone to remember large amounts of numbers that most men would forget. Likewise, because numbers are their "staff of life," it is essential to them to have instant access to almost anything and everything conceivable.

Take, for example, Bob Frick, vice president-finance for Measurex Corporation in the mid-1970s. (He is now the chief financial officer at the Bank of America.) Bob could remember tremendous amounts of data. It's immediately clear on meeting him that he has a tremendous intellect. When asked for facts he didn't have in his head, he would turn to a battery of binders behind his desk. They contained up-to-date minutiae on every detail of the business. His binders were sufficiently well organized that it never took him more than a few moments to find what was needed. Today, of course, computer power allows instant retrieval Bob didn't have.

From time to time, new ideas pop up for handling things better or differently. Ask top financial officers what they think about these ideas. Answers may reveal their emotional reactions to the all-important aspect of seeking change and improvements in financial controls. Some may not have considered the ideas and may immediately resist something new. Others may have considered the ideas and be able to explain why they are not good ideas for their particular company.

Financial managements of Super Companies will embrace new ideas and will be apt to know virtually any idea you propose. They may not have chosen to implement an idea because it spawned an even better solution to the same goal. The key is in the desire to seek progress.

Marketing, financial controls, and employee relations must be outstanding in Super Companies. They must be coupled with a major advantage—a basic purpose for being in business—against which others can't easily compete. These qualities must exist within an environment where employees are preoccupied with a pervasive growth orientation. Smart businesspeople don't waste energy in areas liable to yield poor rewards. Beating the competition is fine. *Avoiding competition is still better.* It is usually wise to avoid direct competition whenever possible. Let's take a look at avoiding competition—both from other companies and other investors.

Chapter 9

Avoid Risk—
Avoid Competition

David and The Anteaters

Life is too short, and there are lots of big bad guys out there who just love to eat somebody else's lunch. Stay away from them. In business, the point is fully valid. At times, a David will slay a Goliath. More likely, a Goliath may just trip over himself and crush two or three Davids without even meaning to do so.

My sons watch "anteater" cartoons on Saturday television. Anteaters eat ants. Anteaters may step on ants. They may even sit on ants. Any way you figure it, it's the ant that gets it. Anteaters are not very noble, and they may not command a lot of respect. If I were running the Ark, anteaters would be just about the last creatures I'd let on board. Nevertheless, they can make life awfully miserable for the poor ants.

Avoid the Places Anteaters Hang Out

Big companies do well in big markets. Small companies do well in small markets. It is rare for a big company to do well in a small market or for a small company to do well in a big market.

Big markets, particularly big markets with good growth potential, attract big companies. A multibillion dollar company will not hesitate for a moment to go after a huge market. But it will hesitate to go after a small market, even if it is growing fairly rapidly.

Consider the personal computer (PC) market. In just a few years, it has become a $6 billion market, and it is still growing quite rapidly. Before the very first byte had been taken out of an Apple, companies like DEC, Hewlett-Packard (HP), IBM, and Texas Instruments (TI) had all identified the market potential for personal computers.

Yet none entered the market then. Apple, Kaypro, Osborne, Radio Shack, and other smaller companies carved out places for themselves in the small, fast-growing market while the big guys were still figuring out if it was for real.

In 1982, as a bigger market, the bigger players were on the field. IBM, for example, had captured a huge share of this now vast PC market in a short period of time. They accomplished this with a product many observers feel is inferior to numerous other alternatives. Superior alternative hardware is readily available from established-but-smaller vendors—but doesn't sell as well. These firms don't have IBM's clout in large markets. Independent software firms write programs for the IBM PC because they know IBM will do well whether the hardware is the best or not. Because so much software is being written for the IBM PC, it becomes attractive even with mundane hardware.

In 1983 and 1984, the anteaters are apt to have their way. More than a few ants are apt to suffer along the way. Look at the way Texas Instruments priced its personal computer. It doesn't matter whether or not they make money at those prices. They can afford to lose money for a long time, if they choose to win a market they desire. Look at what TI did in calculators and watches. Bowmar was the early leader in calculators. Remember the Bowmar Brain? Texas Instruments calculator pricing drove Bowmar right into Chapter 11 bankruptcy.

Avoid markets which are apt to face direct competition from giants. Giants can cause you losses while not making money themselves. (I am just as afraid of having an anteater sit on me as eat me.) A company should address markets appropriate to its size. Ant companies (small) should address markets too small to hold much interest to anteater companies. In a small market, a big company is apt to be lost.

Any company has only a limited number of people who think like generals. Most people think like colonels, majors, captains, sergeants, and privates. Most companies will address their best brains toward their most important markets. A big company is apt to address its best brains toward big markets. Consider DEC, HP, or TI, each with $4 billion in annual sales.[1] Each tries to grow at 20 percent

---

[1] Based on 1983 sales.

per year. That required $800 million of additional sales in 1983 and requires an additional billion dollars in sales in 1984. If you were running those companies, would you fool around with a market that was only a few hundred million in sales? Wouldn't you be even more deterred if those markets already had a host of well-entrenched smaller and more entrepreneurial competitors?

The Japanese Zap Large Markets—Sometimes

The Japanese are a major fear among American businesspeople. They get a lot of press. Fear abounds that they may enter other markets. "Perhaps they will do to us what they did to the auto, steel, and TV industries."

The Japanese style does its best in large markets. They do well in fields requiring mass consumer marketing or price marketing. They do relatively poorly in markets intensive in direct selling to sophisticated customers or markets that require significant strategic market planning.

Consider the laser market. After 20 years, it is only a several hundred million dollar market at the component-parts level. That, too, is made up of a number of niches based on different technologies for getting the devices to "lase." There are families of products: argon lasers, CO_2, diodes, dyes, eximers, HeNes, rubies, semiconductor lasers, and YAG lasers, among others. These markets are dominated by Spectra-Physics of San Jose and Coherent in Palo Alto. They were both among the early founders of the industry in its fledgling years. In 1983, Spectra was a $135 million company. The third largest player, Control Laser, in Florida, had less than $15 million in annual sales. The dozens of other vendors are even smaller.

Big companies have been unable to capture a significant share of this market in spite of efforts by a number of them. The United States is a significant exporter of lasers to Japan. The big Japanese firms make lasers in Japan, but the Japanese market is small. They have difficulty selling their products well in the United States because the sale would require intensive marketing. Each laser sale requires a high level of technical sales and service support. It is hard for any firm that isn't local to provide this. Because the Japanese can't get a toehold in the U.S. market, they have low volume; their costs are high—they can't achieve economies of scale like they do in the auto industry. U.S. laser companies, with higher volume and lower costs, do a significant amount of business in Japan. The same is true of industry after industry. In small markets, the Japanese do relatively poorly.

Consider floppy disks. Disks are an almost perfect "play" on the personal computer phenomenon. They are the "razor blades" of the personal computer industry. Any serious personal computer user buys hundreds of dollars of disks within a year of buying a computer. They go hand in hand.

When I bought my stock in Verbatim Corporation, the total market for "floppies" was less than $250 million. It was primarily 8-inch disks and, to a lesser degree, 5¼-inch disks. The latter market was smaller but growing at a faster rate. IBM made 8-inch but not 5¼-inch disks. 3M was in the market. Hitachi was there. All three made good products. None of them marketed well.

The market was dominated by smaller firms. With 35 percent of the 5¼-inch disk market, Verbatim was postured perfectly. Other small vendors like Dysan and Xidex have carved off their shares. To the large companies like 3M, this was a rather small market. It is true that the Japanese, via Hitachi—and others—had a limited presence in floppy disks. Still, they haven't done well.

The Japanese and the big U.S. firms have never captured a significant market share in this rapidly growing area, try as they might. As the market grows, some will. Meanwhile, by growing with a small market, Verbatim has been able to maintain its 35 percent market share.

Small (and Different) Is Beautiful

It is as appropriate to avoid mainstream technologies as it is to avoid big markets. This is true for many of the same reasons. Whenever possible, try to avoid the areas of technology that the major research labs around the country are stressing. The major thrusts of the IBMs, the TIs, and the Bell Labs are apt to result in time in major commercial efforts for themselves or other companies.

Look, instead, at areas where the big guys aren't throwing major research dollars—just like throwing playing cards into a hat. The big companies tend to spend the bulk of their research money where they foresee large future market opportunities. A small company can spend years developing a better mousetrap only to be thwarted by the $50 million research breakthrough of a huge institution. Avoiding the mainstream technologies is often the same as avoiding large markets.

A small company does best to address itself to markets that are rapidly growing but too small to attract anteaters. Some small company executives who don't understand this pursue big markets. Often they get hurt. A company with $50 million a year of sales is usually much better off in a $150 million market which is rapidly growing than it is in a much bigger and faster growing market. (The reason for this won't become fully apparent until Chapter 10.) Part of the reason is that the company won't be tempted to try to grow too fast (see Chapter 2). The main reason is that this is a way to avoid anteaters.

Remember Your Teddy Roosevelt—Walk Softly but Carry a Strong Balance Sheet

An ant can carry away from a picnic a piece of bread every bit as big as itself—even bigger. We aren't like that. We store up our resources in little chunks, more like squirrels preparing for winter.

A strong balance sheet is worth a great deal of Excedrin. Risk is reduced substantially by investing in companies with them. Don't be concerned about investing in a company that is losing money if it has a bright future. But be very concerned about investing in a company that is losing money if the losses are significant in relation to its war chest—it may not have a future at all. Balance-sheet analysis is fairly mundane. The basics are easily learned in an introductory accounting course for nonaccounting majors at most colleges.

As a general principle, it is safest to consider how much money a company might lose in the period ahead (see Chapter 10 on margin analysis) and then make sure the balance sheet is strong enough to support these losses and more. A Super Company should have free working capital sufficient to support at least five years of the worst losses imaginable for the company. This is what I call future-loss coverage. The more future-loss coverage, the better.

It helps if a company has less than 40 percent of its total assets financed by debt. The less debt a company has, the lower the risks. This is just common sense. In the consideration of total debt, it is important to take into account potential contingent liabilities.[2]

Cash flow is crucial. Many unsophisticated investors are unaware businesses can lose money and still generate substantial amounts of cash. Net cash generated by the accounting entry of "depreciation" on the income statement can go a long way toward keeping a company solvent in rough times. It provides the cash to pay bills and keep the wolves from the door.

Temporarily losing money in an accounting sense is acceptable, but beware of a negative cash flow. Net free working capital should be sufficient to cover at least three years of negative cash flow. (If you run out of cash, you are apt to run out of business.) When a Super Company has a positive cash flow through depreciation or amortization, it drastically reduces the risks of buying the stock of a loss-ridden corporation.

---

[2] This could include unfunded pension liabilities, risks from litigation, or future environmental or regulatory deficiency corrections.

Who Stands behind the Financials?

Expect the company to be audited by one of the "Big Eight" accounting firms: Arthur Andersen & Co.; Arthur Young & Co.; Coopers & Lybrand; Peat, Marwick, Mitchell & Co.; Touche Ross & Co.; Deloitte Haskins & Sells; Price Waterhouse & Co.; or Ernst & Whinney. Ninety-five percent of all Super Companies are audited by one of these firms. Probably more than 80 percent of all publicly owned companies are audited by them. As they grow, many smaller companies will switch to the Big Eight.

A Big Eight audit is not a guarantee of the accuracy of the balance sheet. Everybody makes mistakes. But a Big Eight audit tends to indicate normal procedures were closely followed. The signature of Arthur Andersen & Co. or Peat, Marwick, Mitchell & Co. on an annual report gives some reason for believing the balance sheet is approximately what it appears to be.

Smaller regional firms may do a fine job, but many do not routinely provide audits. They may not be equipped to deal with unusual incidents or procedures. When a regional firm provides the audit, it is good to ask how many other public companies it audits and who they are. Often they have little activity and experience in this area.

Who Has Controlling Interest?

Super Companies generally have a substantial ownership by top management. Management is likely to have company founders among its members. If management came in later, they were probably given options as an incentive to increase the value of the stock by improving the company.

If management owns substantial amounts of stock, they are the stockholder's partners. They have every incentive to make the shares become more valuable. They will be particularly protective of the company's balance sheet. The company's balance sheet is one you share in common with management if you buy the stock. There are not any firm rules as to how much stock management should own, but there are some ideas which help. Management should get a reasonable salary—but small in relation to the value of the stock it owns. Be skeptical when management owns an amount of stock not much larger than their salary. They may be more interested in their salary than in the value of their stockholder's company. It is best if management's stock ownership is at least 10 times its combined annual salary.

Be skeptical when one or two individuals own controlling interest in a company—the results may be anything from fantastic to terrible. It all depends on the people.

If no one has controlling interest and management fails to perform, the board of directors is likely to throw out management and bring in a new one. If one or two people have control, the future of the company is more completely in their hands. Those with control can make a big success of their company—or a complete failure. There isn't anything a board of directors can or will do in a situation like this to protect minority shareholders.

A suitable controlling management views shareholders as entitled business owners with a right to future prosperity. A poor controlling management sees minority shareholders as a pain in the neck. A poor chief executive, with control, may view the company as his—and minority shareholders as second-class citizens.

The poor chief executive with control can continue his inept management for reasons of pride or ego. He may replace himself with a poor choice, perhaps a friend. He may feel rich enough and have lost the burning desire to build his company (and his wealth). Plenty of chief executives with controlling interest have gone on to make big successes for themselves and all their shareholders. Plenty were failures. There are usually more failures than successes in any area.

When a few closely aligned people control a company, it is more essential than ever to have a strong sense of what these controlling people are like as individuals. If you can't assess this, it may be better to play it safe and invest elsewhere.

Chapter 10

Margin Analysis—
All I Really Want in Life Is an Unfair Advantage

The Problem

The analysis of future profit margins is at the heart of the investment problem. It ties together market valuations, sales, and earnings. It also ties Price Sales Ratios and price-earnings ratios together. It ties fundamental analysis together with valuation analysis. It can't be overemphasized. Margin analysis is not a new concept. It is a very old idea.

What is margin analysis all about? It is being able to project approximately how much money a business should earn in the future. It is being able to do so even if there may be little or no profitability at present. Many people focus on how much a business should earn next quarter or next year. I don't. (This chapter and the next will focus on how to approximate margins over the coming years—ideally, five years.)

Margin analysis is critical to Super-Stock analysis as it gives a rational basis to valuing businesses suffering an earnings glitch. Most investors don't have a rational basis for valuing companies when a glitch occurs. You can—a real edge over other investors. You can value a company while it is hurting and the stock is down. The benefit of long-term margin analysis is that you can predict with some accuracy how profitable a business may or may not be in a few years.

You've decided that American Widgetronics may well be a Super Company. Perhaps you aren't sure yet. You've done some checking. Everything so far smells right. Now you want to carry through to a conclusion. Margin analysis will be the last step in deciding if it is a Super Company. It will be the first step in deciding if it is a Super Stock.

Margin analysis is a bridge between business analysis and security valuation. Margin analysis ties together fragmentary information collected about a business during the period of investigation. It is a multifaceted method to see the broad future overview.

Some Definitions

Margins	= After-tax earnings divided by total sales.
Pre-tax margin	= Total sales, minus all expenses except taxes, divided by total sales.
Gross margin	= Total sales, minus cost of goods sold, divided by total sales.
Total sales	= All revenue generated from products sold or services rendered.

Look for Clues from the Past: Who Kicked the Sleeping Dog?

Look at the history of the company's margins. Then decide whether future margins should be the same as, above, or below historical margins. Companies have varying histories. Some consistently earn margins of 5 to 7 percent. Others earn 10 percent for several years and then earn no money at all for several years, averaging halfway between. Some have a long history of low margins. Some earn little in good years and lose large amounts in bad years. An elite few have long histories of consistently high margins—in the 10 percent range.

Almost by definition, a Super Company will average better margins than its competitors and others in its industry. A manufacturing Super Company must earn margins which average about 5 percent over the long term. Few, no matter how super, earn margins much above 10 percent in the long term. This is particularly true if the company is growing rapidly. New competitive forces are apt to be sucked into these high-margin high-growth areas, as if into a vacuum. New entrants may not be successful but will likely bring margins down for the rest of the industry, even for the industry leader—our Super Company. For nonmanufacturing Super Companies, margins may be much lower.

Always remember that a high Price Sales Ratio (PSR) for one company or industry may be a low PSR for another company or industry. The PSR you should be willing to pay is heavily affected by future margins. (See Table 4–1.) Low future margins mean a given current PSR will translate into a relatively high future price-earnings ratio. High future margins mean a given current PSR will translate into a relatively low future price-earnings ratio.

The financial history of a company reveals the financial culture that has developed there. Consider the case of a manufacturing company that has made less than 2 percent margins in each of the last five years. You wonder whether or not it may be a Super Company.

The low margins tell you something. They say the management then in power found it acceptable (or at least livable) to generate poor results. (They certainly became accustomed to not earning good margins.) The board of directors didn't get too upset. Management didn't get too upset. Perhaps some disgruntled shareholders sold shares to others who, with lower expectations, were willing to take on the lackluster results—at a lower price. Still, no one made a big fuss.

Without something to shake them up, this company would not likely be a Super Company. It is more like a sleeping dog. Without a good swift "kick," it is apt to remain asleep. If it's to be a Super Company, you need to identify what kick woke the dog. Who did the kicking? What direction is the dog going as it awakens? In my experience, I have rarely seen a "Sleeping Dog" awake without a "kick" that included new management.

A kick requires more than new management. It also requires a violent upheaval to shake up the corporate culture. The old guys have to be thrown out and branded as Sleeping Dogs. A new group has to be brought in with great fanfare to perform the corporate rebirth. Without this shake-up, middle- to lower-level employees won't view the potential for a better future with much credibility. It will be hard to motivate them to a different way of corporate life. They will react in a "ho-hum" manner to any talk of improved profitability and growth. It will sound like talk, nothing more. Without a cultural rebirth, it is unlikely a Sleeping Dog will become a Super Company. So look for new management.

Now consider a company with an impressive record of growth and good margins. It is likely the board of directors will forgive management mistakes as long as management is trying. After all, they've performed before. Don't they deserve another chance? This management has a previous record for understanding the importance of earning high margins. High margins don't just happen.

There are more ways to waste margins than to earn them. High margins happen because people make them happen. This management may be having problems but will strive for excellence.

When In Doubt, Ask!

It never hurts to be sure. It is very easy to ask management its long-term margin goals. I have never found a company that didn't have a goal for what its margins should be. While some haven't thought it out well, they all have some number to offer. Ask! Then listen! This can be the beginning of a dialogue that provides clues to how the company thinks—one of the key ingredients for margin analysis.

The corporate goal will usually be higher than current margins. Frequently, and particularly in the case of a Sleeping Dog with a new management, the stated margin goal will be quite high in relation to historical margins. To achieve this new level, the company will have to do some things quite differently than in the past. Do they understand how much they must function differently? Many don't. They drastically underestimate what needs to be done and, as a result, never achieve their goals. Super Companies do and will. Avoid leading questions which may allow management to tell you what they think you want them to say. Ask management to lay out their strategy for improving margins. Look for radical departures in the case of a Sleeping Dog.

From Rags to Riches

Responses will fall into one of two classes:

A company may plan improvements that would result in a higher gross margin. This would allow more profit to slip past the same amount of research expenses, administrative and general expenses, and sales expenses (rags).

They may plan raising profits by cutting selling or research expense or reducing administrative costs (again, rags).

The most enduring way to raise profitability is to raise gross margins. This usually requires doing something fundamentally different than in the past. Products may be designed with lower production costs. Products may be designed with unique features that support a higher sales price in relation to production costs. Pinching pennies in overhead, selling expense, and R&D is not likely to have enduring effects because competition too easily can do the same things. More leverage is achieved by managing and getting results from rags than by cutting. It is hard to develop the products, processes, and markets to raise gross margins without spending significantly on marketing and research.

Most good companies need to spend at least 20 percent of their sales dollar on rags. If a company is to earn a minimum of 5 percent margins, given a 50 percent tax rate, it needs gross margins better than 30 percent. Let's examine why.

On the table below are two companies. Company A makes 30 percent gross margins. Company B makes 40 percent gross margins. They each spend 20 percent of their sales dollar on rags. Look at the difference in after-tax profit margins. Company A, with a 30 percent gross margin, just barely meets our 5 percent hurdle. Company B, on the other hand, with a 40 percent gross margin, is able to earn twice that net margin at 10 percent.

	Company A	Company B
Gross margin	30%	40%
Sales/Revenue	100	100
Cost of goods sold	70	60
Gross profit margin	30	40
Expenses:		
Research	5	5
Marketing	10	10
General and administrative	5	5
Total rags	20	20
Pre-tax margin	10	20
Income taxes	5	10
Net profit margin	5%	10%

The percentage of money spent on rags could increase because:

Sales start to decline against fixed rags spending.

The company elects to spend more on rags to develop potential for future growth.

Suppose a company needs to spend more on rags. Maybe they want to develop new products or promote existing lines. Maybe they want to build their financial accounting and controls functions. It really doesn't matter why; rags spending as a percent of sales increases. Consider what happens when it does. Below, Companies A and B earn the same gross margins as they did in our last example, but now they spend 25 percent of sales on rags.

	Company A	Company B
Gross margin	30%	40%
Sales/Revenue	100	100
Cost of goods sold	70	60
Gross profit margin	30	40
Expenses:		
Research	7	7
Marketing	11	11
General and administrative	7	7
Total rags	25	25
Pre-tax margin	5	15
Income taxes	2.5	7.5
Net profit margin	2.5%	7.5%

In this scenario, Company A earns inadequate margins to meet our 5 percent hurdle. Company B, with the greater gross margin, easily meets the hurdle. These two examples show the value of high gross margins. It would be a nice goal to make 50-plus percent gross margins. This would leave more room still for profit and more rags oriented toward future growth. A very nice income statement might look as follows:

Gross margin	50%
Sales/Revenue	100
Cost of goods sold	50
Gross profit margin	50
Expenses:	
Research	8
Marketing	11
General and administrative	7
Total rags	26
Pre-tax margin	24
Income taxes	12
Net profit margin	12%

This income statement affords room for spending for the future while providing current profits to finance the future. While this is a nice goal, the numbers need not be cast in concrete.

Unfortunately, accounting is not perfect. What may be included as cost of goods sold at one firm may be included as a marketing expense or general and administrative expense at another firm. It is hard for management to decide how to account for certain expenses. In many firms, the service arm can be a very effective sales tool. Should certain parts of service be considered cost of goods sold, associated with service revenues, or should they be considered marketing expenses, associated with trying to persuade a customer to buy additional quantities?

Likewise, product sales requiring technical installation often involve interaction between salespeople, technical people, and production people. An estimate of how much of each person's time goes to each function will determine the financial statement's makeup. Much of what shows as either cost of goods sold, gross margin, sales expense, research, or general and administrative costs will be allocated based on management assumptions.

Something Rather Unique Must Be Done

Since managements make different assumptions, it is usually a mistake to attempt to be too precise with respect to appropriate levels for any one component of a company's income statement. It can be more of an art than a science. Don't niggle and naggle over whether it spends 8 percent or 9 percent on marketing. It is not important whether the overall goal for gross margins is 39 percent or 41 percent. It is important the overall plan for margin improvement make sense—a must if the goals are to be reached. All parts combined must make sense. If a high gross margin is to be achieved, something rather unique must be done.

High gross margins come because of:

Product planning (marketing) which correctly ascertains the nature of future customer demand and competition. This allows for meaningful future product pricing and volume estimates.

Design-to-cost product engineering with low material and production process costs in relation to future pricing. The product must be designed to be mass produced at very low costs and yet still fill the customer's needs.

Efficient manufacturing costs with continuous attention to detail at each step of production.

Look for what it is in the company's plan that allows them to provide service to the customer in a fashion that will be hard for others to duplicate. This may not necessarily be unique technology. It is more likely a unique understanding of customers. If management does not have the "unfair advantage" well articulated in its own mind, it isn't a Super Company.

Asking management how they propose to achieve their margin

goals generates interesting answers. Classify these as management actions which are truly innovative or as actions management should have been taking all along. Running with leaner inventories, increasing production efficiency, shortening length of time of the average receivable, cutting advertising expenses, and other "screw-tightening" operations are all well and good, but they are hardly an unfair advantage. They are the things your competitors are apt to be doing. They are all necessary—just not sufficient.

When a company aims to meet margin goals through screw-tightening operations, it admits it previously hasn't been well run. If it still has the same management, it is unlikely to be superbly run in the future. Why should they change? Sleeping-Dog managements claiming to tighten the screws never seem to get them very tight. A Sleeping Dog with new management may be able to tighten the screws somewhat.

In the case of new management personnel, it is not difficult to check out patterns in their former employment. Where had they been previously, and what had they done at their prior positions? Had they been able to tighten the screws in their former assignments?

Be skeptical of getting superior returns from doing the same old things better. Simple textbook management alone will generate better-than-average—but not outstanding—results. Be skeptical of claims that good margins can be generated quickly from poor ones. It is rarely true, except when emerging from a general recession. A dramatic sustained long-term improvement in margins will necessarily be the result of sweeping changes in the nature of the business. Super Companies will have an unfair advantage over competition that will allow them to make fat margins.

All I Really Want in Life Is an Unfair Advantage

"Unfair advantages" come in many forms. They tend to fall into three major categories—marketing advantages, production advantages, and research. In years past, when research was more than a commodity item, proprietary technology was often an unfair advantage. This is less-often true today. Sometimes, unique technology still can provide an unfair advantage.

Unfair advantages in marketing come in many forms. One is simply a better knowledge of how to motivate customers. This is quite common. Joe Blow spends his early years in the savings and loan industry. Later he leaves the S&Ls to start selling products or services to them. Nothing could really be simpler. When he wants to learn about something new, he approaches the contacts in his "buddy-buddy" network. He quickly discovers what is going on in the market, while other salespeople may get stopped at the purchasing-agent level. The others aren't often in situations where the key, high-level decision makers let their hair down. Joe Blow crosses this threshold easily. It is not only that he knows them but also, to a large extent, he thinks as they do.

Consider Dataquest, the famous information services company, now a subsidiary of A. C. Nielsen. Its semiconductor industry service in its early years was a success, in large part because it was run and marketed by Jim Reilly. Reilly had come out of Signetics, Intersil and Fairchild with a long and successful career in marketing in the semiconductor industry. When he called to sell Dataquest services to bigwigs in the semiconductor industry, he could get in doors and attract the attention of people that others couldn't. Within a very short period, the semiconductor service became far and away the biggest part of Dataquest's operations.

Let's focus further on the so-called unfair advantage. Some types of advantages include:

> Distribution advantages and the ability to fan out a product base, cost base, or technology base into different markets.
>
> Economies of scale by advertising closely aligned products.
>
> Trade secrets.
>
> A lengthy time lead.
>
> Lower-cost production techniques.
>
> A quality image for which customers will pay a premium.

The list goes on and on. The point is to look for an unfair advantage as a key determinant to whether or not your investment would earn above-average future margins. Determine if there are sound reasons to believe the company can maintain its advantage over competitors.

High Market Share Can Be an Unfair Advantage

High market share is a long-recognized form of unfair advantage. The Boston Consulting Group brought this concept into the realm of modern margin analysis, popularizing it as a key to determining potential profitability.

The concept was intuitively understood by many decades earlier. In its extreme, this concept gave birth to the aged Sherman and Clayton antitrust acts. The government thought extremely high market share to be so unfair they made it illegal. Market share is forever apt to hold its place, in the rationality of business schools, as a key tool for understanding future profitability. Just why market share is so important to future margins should be obvious.

The issue is a little like the chicken and the egg. The Super

Company builds market share over time and comes to dominate an industry. Then, through its market share, it is able to: (1) maintain high margins and, thereby, (2) finance the developmental expenses to perpetuate its dominance.

Relative Market Share Is More Powerful Still

Consider why. Generally, a 30 percent market share is considered a high share. Is it really the market share that counts? Market share is important, but the relative market share is most important. Below are three companies, all in different industries. Each has a 30 percent share of its market:

	Company A	Company B	Company C
Market share	30%	30%	30%
Market share of its largest competitor	50%	30%	12%
Market share of its next largest competitor	20%	15%	7%
Total number of competitors	3	9	18

In spite of the fact that each of these three companies has a 30 percent market share, their relative shares are all different. Therefore, differences are implied for their potential profitability. Company C is likely to be in the best position by far. It has a dominant position in its industry. It is likely to have the lowest per-unit production costs since it spreads costs over a larger volume of units produced. It will be able to afford development costs and market studies due to its volume: items its smaller competitors must forgo. In a weak economy, it probably can cut prices further than industry stragglers.

The only time high market share is liable to move against Company C is if a rapid change takes place in production technology. Huge fixed investments in plants with old processes, for instance, may work against the market-share leader. High market share never protected U. S. Steel from competitive inroads by foreign steel and domestic minimills in the 1960s and 1970s. Japanese and other foreign steel producers built new technology plants to compete against aging U. S. Steel plants, many of which were still using old, open-hearth technology.

More damaging, but less well known, is the effect of the U.S. minimills. In only 10 years, domestic minimills—employing continuous casting and other innovations—swept the market away from the big steel companies in rods, flats, re-bars, angles, and other long, thin shapes. A bed frame or oil rig tower, formerly made of USS steel, is now made of steel by Chapparel, Florida Steel, Georgetown, Nucor, and others. These were real-life Davids slaying Goliaths.

On the other hand, if consumer preferences change and Company C is not responsive, it can lose market share. General Motors and Ford lost market share as they disregarded America's shift in preference in the 1960s and 1970s toward smaller cars. Theoretically, the market-share leader ought to be able to spend much more than competitors studying markets and understanding shifts in consumer preferences. Companies may not always take advantage of the potential that exists in their unfair advantage of high market share. Management may fail to be responsive to market changes or simply fail to produce efficiently. Still, the potential power of high market share is great.

Company B is in worse shape. Still quite strong relative to the industry, it has all the inherent muscle that Company C enjoys in its industry. Unfortunately for Company B, its chief competitor has just as much muscle. They both have the natural potential to inflict great damage on one another. This is a little like Muhammud Ali against Joe Frazier—both clearly champions in their own right, but after 15 rounds against each other, both are a bit done in. There is no obvious reason why one should do particularly better than the other. The outcome is largely the result of personal factors.

Now consider Company A with a high absolute market share but a low relative market share. Its share is low compared to the industry leader. It is obviously not in a strong position—vulnerable to the whim of its larger and more powerful competitor. In an industry like this, with few competitors and each having a respectable market share, all are likely to have good margins in times of prosperity as profitability becomes foremost in their minds. This is likely to promote informal meetings of the minds to avoid strenuous price competition in what, in the early 1970s, Dow Chemical called "statesman-like pricing." Statesmanship is likely to fade when prosperity does. In a poor economic environment, these companies are likely to slug it out to the fullest in price wars. Company A is then liable to feel the full wrath of its larger competitor who has many of the same advantages over it that Company C has over its competitors.

Another factor further complicates things—growth. Each firm will find itself in quite a different situation if its industry is in a strong demand—growth environment—than if the industry suffers from shrinking demand. This should be intuitively obvious to the most casual observer. If Company C is in an industry widely perceived to have rapid growth prospects, it may find new and increased competition from smaller competitors who have been able to raise additional equity and debt financing.

If, instead, the industry were shrinking, it would be unlikely these smaller firms would find anyone to provide the financing. Look at the differences. First, you have numerous high-technology firms being formed and financed with venture capital and public equity offerings at high Price Sales Ratios. Then you have their counterparts in the auto and related industries, which have been shrinking in relative importance for years. Growth doesn't eliminate the validity of the market-share argument by any means. It just alters it somewhat.

Chapter 11

Margin Analysis Continued—
Formulas and Rules

A Forecasting Formula for Margin Analysis

Some years ago, I put together a simple profit margin forecasting formula. It ties margin analysis together in a quantitative fashion. The formula is intended to be more thought provoking than practical. No one formula could possibly explain all the different variables affecting margins. Mine certainly can't. It won't allow you to forecast margins precisely. Rather, it is useful because it raises questions about the future margin potential of a company.

The formula in its most reduced form is:

$$\text{Average long-term potential margin} = \frac{.13(\text{Market share})^2(1 + \text{Industry growth rate})}{\text{Market share of largest competitor}}$$

This formula's utility may not be obvious. It is powerful and easy to use. It takes into account market share, relative market share, and growth rates. While it may look confusing at first, it is easy to compute.

Knowing market shares and growth rate, you can compute this formula on a calculator in seconds. The formula ignores the total number of industry participants because, if there are many industry participants, most will be marginal. If there are only a few industry participants, the economics will be covered by the formula. The formula assumes a constant tax rate of 50 percent.

Note the formula doesn't allow for a 100 percent market share by any party. One hundred percent market share means no competitors. In the real world, monopolies don't exist unless the government creates or regulates them. If they do, as in the case of regulated utilities and the like, they don't usually allow fat profit margins.

What would happen if your competitor has 100 percent market share? You must have no business and therefore can't possibly make any margin. If your company has 100 percent market share, its monopoly position should allow an infinite profit margin. Logic would say this is possible. An economist would argue it isn't likely.[1]

The formula allows for varying market shares and extremely rapid or negative growth rates. The coefficient of 0.13 is arbitrary and was determined by experimentation over time. A prime variable is the exact market and industry within which a company competes. This can be very difficult. What market does Federal Express exist in? What is its market share? In a multi-industry firm or a conglomerate, it may be quite confusing also. Within a single industry, there are frequently a number of different markets. Markets may be defined, for example, geographically by freight-cost limitations (the cement industry, for instance), or socially (most prestige consumer items). A Kaypro Computer, the Volkswagen of its industry, really does not compete with the Mercedes-like Grid Systems Computer at six times the price. They just aren't the same markets.

Some Examples

To test the theoretical validity of the formula, consider some examples. Suppose a company has a 30 percent market share in an industry you believe will grow at a 40 percent rate for the next five years. Its largest competitor has a 12 percent market share. The formula says the company has the *potential* for a 13.7 percent profit margin.

$$\frac{\text{Potential}}{\text{margin}} = \frac{.13(.30)(.30)(1 + 0.40)}{.12} = .137$$

This company is in just about the most ideal position imaginable. It has a high and dominant market share in a rapidly growing market where its largest competitor is less than half its size. Common sense points to good future prospects. (Fortunately, so does my formula.) If this company earns poor margins, it has tripped over

---

Even most monopoly producers shouldn't be able to get extraordinarily high profit margins. Unless they are one of the few having an "extremely inelastic demand," it would be impossible.

itself in some regard. It likely failed to develop good strategies or to execute them well. The formula does not say the company will earn a 13.7 percent profit margin—rather that it has the *potential* to earn good profit margins if it tends its business properly (Company C in the previous chapter, with the assumption its industry grows quite rapidly).

Consider Company B from that same example. It has a 30 percent market share, as does its largest competitor. If you envision a 5 percent growth rate, the formula shows it having the potential for margins of only 4.1 percent. The formula places a heavy bias against the firm in a low- or slow-growth industry, even with a fairly high market share.

$$\frac{\text{Potential}}{\text{margin}} = \frac{.13(.30)(.30)(1.0 + 0.05)}{.30} = .041$$

If a company is in a low-growth or declining industry and wants to achieve above-average profits, things are more difficult. It had better have some very unfair advantages. The average profitability of companies in the steel industry over recent years—even those with high market share—has been very poor. Nucor Corporation produces commodity steel: angle irons, re-bars, flat strips, channels, I-beams, and other structural shapes. These are commoditylike products with little or no growth prospects. Nucor started in the early 1970s with a very low market share. In spite of these disadvantages, it exploited several unfair advantages to achieve above-average profitability and growth.

This is the point of the formula: It allows an investor to focus on how much of an exceptional unfair advantage is necessary for a company to achieve its margin goals. In Nucor's case, the formula would say that low margins were all that was possible. While investigating Nucor, this placed all the emphasis on the magnitude and quality of the unfair advantages. Everything else became secondary.

Note the formula generates no negative numbers. Every business has the potential for profitability—regardless of market share, growth rates, or competition. Potential is different than actualization. Companies lose money long term by failing to match their potential—not because they never had any.

Regardless of potential, companies must seek out advantages at every opportunity. Certainly the competition will. It also is important to consider competitors with respect to margins. What are their margins and what does that say about the company you are considering? Does the competition have some unfair advantage over "your" company? Virtually no firm will admit that competition has serious advantages. This is where talking to customers, suppliers, and competition pays off in spades. The "Scuttlebutt" method, described in

Common Stocks and Uncommon Profits (New York: Harper & Row, 1958), is a necessary step in learning the relative competitive situation:

> What kind of margins do competitors achieve and why? If the competition gets very high margins, should the company you are considering also get good margins? Why? Perhaps competition has the "unfair advantage."

This is an important point in the evaluation process. Once past this point, some simple rules help to approximate future margins.

Rules for Margin Analysis

The following are useful rules for analyzing profit margins:

RULE 1: If your potential Super Company has a high potential margin indicated by the forecasting formula (and no competitor appears to have an unfair advantage over it) the actual margin will short-fall from the potential by the lack of general management operating ability.

It is important to have a strong sense of management's operating ability based on the histories of the key individuals—particularly the chief operating officer (COO) as opposed to the chief executive officer (CEO). If the COO has a strong history of success in operations, there is no reason that the company should not approach its potential margins. If the COO has a history of relatively poor operating results, then this is not a Super Company and should be avoided. Use an assessment of the COO's abilities to scale margin assessments back from the potential for the company.

RULE 2: If a company has high potential margins indicated by the forecasting formula and there appears some likelihood competition has an unfair advantage, the unfair advantage should be equivalent to a reduction of the estimated growth rate for the industry as stated in the formula.

Precision is impossible. If a competitor has an important unfair advantage, the company being considered is not a Super Company—the competitor will have first crack at whatever growth lies ahead. By that logic, the industry growth rate for companies, other than the one with the advantage, is not as great as it may have seemed on the surface. Estimating the effect of the competition allows an estimate of the potential margin. After adjusting for this, Rule 1 applies as well.

RULE 3: If a company has low potential margins indicated by the formula, additional focus must be put on unfair advantages. If the company does not have clear unfair advantages over competition, it is unlikely to earn margins higher than its low potential and is unlikely to be a Super Company.

This is the case for most industrial companies. They have low potential margins and no unfair advantages over competition. Try as they might, they are unlikely to achieve attractive margins. Only extreme luck will reward this type of company. (Maybe an earthquake will wipe out the competition.) Since they aren't Super Companies, they are less in control of their own destinies. They can be hurt as badly or worse by bad luck as they can be helped by good luck.

RULE 4: If the company has low potential margins indicated by the formula, additional focus must be put on unfair advantages. If the company does have clear unfair advantages over competition, this is the equivalent to an increase in the estimated industry growth rate.

This is the hardest case to estimate. It's often extremely difficult to get a good handle on the magnitude of the economic significance of an advantage. Probe management's thinking to see if their rationale for margin improvement is completely based on doing things differently than in the past. Does their logic make rational business sense? Assess management's basic operating capability and history. If they rank high, it is reasonable to accept management's margin goals after providing a "haircut."

The "haircut" is necessary because managements tend to be a bit optimistic about what they can achieve. They almost have to be. It is their life. Some companies pull this off with elegance. Ken Iverson of Nucor had not achieved adequate financial results when I first visited the company. Yet it was apparent he was a man who could maximize his advantages for long-term profit potential. Recognizing this capability in management is almost an art form. It is like looking at a young boxer and knowing if he has the right stuff to go on to become a contender.

RULE 5: If a company had the same management for years, earned good margins, and is currently less profitable, check if long-term industry conditions have changed. Are the changes for the better or the worse? If industry conditions are no worse than before, it is likely, in time, margins almost as good as before will return. Allow three years for this metamorphosis to take place.

Rapidly growing young companies frequently make mistakes. The best learn from them. (See Chapters 1 and 2.) If long-term industry conditions are no worse than during its period of good margins, this management (which has shown the determination and ability to achieve before) will earn good margins again. It is safer to be conservative on margin analysis. Here again, a haircut from prior historical margins is prudent. Good managements fight back at their difficulties and, in time, win out. The young management of California Microwave made marketing mistakes in 1979—which made a significant dent in their financial results (see Chapter 15). Gradually, the nature of its business was altered. In time, margins—while not up to previous levels—became clearly suitable for Super-Company status.

No One Is Perfect—You Don't Have to Be

These five rules, while not all inclusive, form a basis for estimating future margins. No one can, nor need, estimate perfectly. It is an art rather than science. It can be done well enough to allow people to make consistent profits when combined with appropriate valuation techniques. It isn't that you can predict that the future margin of XYZ in 1987 will be 5.7 percent. That kind of precision just isn't possible. What can be known with fair certainty is whether a given company is likely to earn above- or below-average profit margins over the long term. Those earning above-average long-term returns may be Super Companies. Bought properly, they can be Super Stocks.

Knowing whether a company's future margins will be closer to 5 percent or 10 percent is important. Perhaps its margins will be closer to 1 percent. This knowledge makes or breaks fortunes. Focusing on long-term margins allows you to ignore the short term. It allows you to think as—and become—a long-term investor.

No astute business owner would decide to sell out based on what happened to earnings in a single day, week, month, quarter, or even year. The successful investor looks beyond the year to what the business can earn over a long period of time. Even if you know for an absolute fact earnings will be terrible next year, you will do better to focus on business prospects over the long haul. It is here fortunes are made and lost. (Rome was not built in a day.)

You can't overemphasize the importance of margin analysis. (A whole book could easily be devoted to the subject.) Margin analysis is slightly different for every industry and slightly different for each company. Yet the basic thrust is similar.

Understand the basic business and probe for unfair advantages. Margin analysis is not precise enough to allow accurate detailed security-analyst type, quarter-by-quarter earnings per share numbers. Margin analysis is precise enough to form the final step in deciding if a potential business may or may not be a Super Company.

Margin analysis also is the first step in the valuation process to determine if a Super Company is a Super Stock. Suppose you have decided a particular business is a Super Company. You have studied its potential, and you are satisfied. It meets our margin requirements. What price should you be willing to pay?

It does little good knowing a certain business is a Super Company and will earn good long-term average profit margins without also knowing what price to pay for that business. By the same token, it does little good knowing a certain business you have owned, perhaps for years, is a Super Company without knowing what circumstances justify its sale.

The next chapter establishes the methodology of investing—putting together the dynamics of margin analysis and investigation of Price Sales Ratios and Price Research Ratios.

Part Four

Dynamics

Chapter 12

Into Action—
There's Method to
the Madness

Where Is the Magic Key?

Now we will look at the process for analyzing and valuing Super Stocks. Many readers have neither the time nor the inclination to do all the basic steps necessary to insure investment success. But each portion is an important subcomponent to the overall desired result.

There has been little discussion so far regarding the overall stock market (one paragraph in Chapter 6 only). It is here that our discussion of the market resides. Will the stock market rise or will it fall? It usually isn't very important. What is important is to find Super Companies and to buy them inexpensively—finding Super Stocks. A Super Stock can rise right through a severe bear market (see Verbatim case history in Chapter 14).

Too much investment time is spent on the direction of the stock market. Varying factors blend together, leading investors to conclude which direction they think the market will move. People use this background basis for formulating their investment tactics. If they think the market is strong and rising, they buy, focusing on which stocks should perform well in "this" market. If they think the market looks weak, they sell or even sell short. This is all a little silly. People don't outguess the stock market with any consistency. Most investors are wrong most of the time. Why play a losing game? Have you ever met someone who could forecast market trends consistently? I have never even heard about anyone who could. Still, imagine what it would be like if you could.

Assume, for a moment, you could predict the market perfectly with respect to major moves of more than 100 points in the Dow Jones Industrial Averages. Assume, further, that you sold short successfully on every single down move and bought stocks in every single 100-point bull move. To make it better still, let us assume no brokerage or tax costs.

How much could you make? You could make a good return to be sure, but no better than with a Super Stock. Table 12–1 is a list

---

TABLE 12–1
Results of Being Able to Call Every 100-Point Move of the DJIA for Five Years Ended December 31, 1982

Period of Change	DJIA Top and Bottom	DJIA Points Gained/Lost	Percent Change	Value of $1 Compounded
1/78	n/a*	0	0	1.000
3/78–9/78	737/917	180	24.4	1.244
9/78–11/78	917/780	−137	−14.9	1.430
11/78–10/79	780/903	123	15.8	1.656
10/79–11/79	903/795	−108	−12.0	1.854
11/79–2/80	795/918	123	15.5	2.140
2/80–3/80	918/730	−188	−20.5	2.579
3/80–11/80	730/1,009	279	38.2	3.564
11/80–12/80	1,009/895	−114	−11.3	3.967
12/80–4/81	895/1,031	136	15.2	4.570
4/81–8/82	1,031/772	−259	−25.1	5.718
8/82–12/82	772/1,078	306	39.6	7.984

* Not apply.

---

showing each such move for the five years ended December 31, 1982, along with the percentage gain you would have realized from the move.

Not bad! Almost eight times your money in five years—a compound rate of return of 51.5-percent. While a worthy goal, no one comes even close to this attempting to outguess the market—most lose money at this game. In reality, you would suffer regular income tax rates (as opposed to tax-advantaged long-term capital gains rates) and brokerage commissions on 11 turns of the portfolio at about 1 to 10 percent per turn (depending on when the turn occurred and discounting it back to the present).

Many have made reputations as stock market seers. Those who stick their necks out the farthest usually end up with egg on their faces. There is no end to the lengths people go to try to find the magic key to the stock market. People have tried:

Computers.

Astrology.

Demographic studies.

Sunspots.

Economics.

Technical analysis.

Tea leaves.

The skin of a dried lizard at sunset cast to the wind.

Political analysis.

Just about anything else you could think to name.

None of it works well. (The dried lizard is my favorite—"flakey," but at least once it had life in it.)

At best, one could hope to be right about the stock market perhaps half the time. At worst, one is apt to be wrong most of the time. Stock-market seers run hot for a couple of years. Then most embarrass themselves.

Probably the most dramatic recent example is Joe Granville. As Granville gained an ever-bigger following for his deadly accurate calls of the 1979 through 1981 market turning points, his predictions became more extreme. He must have had faith in the accuracy of his predictions to have proclaimed them so strongly. It must have been painful for him as the market went its own way against his will. (The market may be one of God's best mechanisms for teaching people humility.) Don't play games that can't be won. There are better things to do with your time. And if you found a magic key to unlock all the market's secrets, you would still make no more than is possible with Super Stocks.

People buy stocks—not the whole stock market. It is much better to focus on the stocks and the businesses—not on the market. Focus on what is possible. It is possible to find and buy Super Stocks. With a Super Stock, it is possible to get the same kind of returns as if you had found the long-desired magic key to the market—and at tax-advantaged capital gains rates.

Focus on what you can do—not on what you can't do. It is much better to use the market for its original purpose—a place to buy a fractional ownership in a business. Focus on the businesses. Buy great ones when they can be purchased inexpensively. Forget about the rest of the market.

Opportunities Are Seldom Labeled

A client gave me a small plaque. I keep it by my chalk board so I'll see it regularly. It says:

Opportunities Are Seldom Labeled

This is true for stocks as well as for many areas of life. If something is already well touted, it isn't apt to be worthwhile. If someone wants you to buy something, someone wants to sell it to you. The "sure thing" that everyone knows is a sure-fire money-maker is usually a sure-fire money-loser. As Bernard Baruch said in his autobiography, "When beggars and shoeshine boys, barbers and beauticians can tell you how to get rich, it is time to remind yourself that there is no more dangerous illusion than the belief that one can get something for nothing."[1]

All of the retailer's advertisements crying out for you to "save here" really mean "spend here." People are amazed at an individual's good fortune in picking up some little "gem" when no one else wanted it. It only could have been an "unwanted" gem because it was not already known as a gem. Opportunities are seldom labeled.

One of the beauties of Wall Street is that some labeling exists. The problem is to avoid confusion while reading the labels. The labels aren't perfect. But many aren't bad. I tend to focus my search for potential investments among three kinds of labels:

- Low PSRs and PRRs among the industries in which I am knowledgeable.
- Money-losing companies with which I am not already familiar.
- Qualitative assessments by others of outstanding businesses with strong future prospects.

Scan for Low PSRs

This is relatively easy to do. First, get a personal computer. Almost any kind will do. An Apple or IBM or whatever. Millions already have computers because they can help with so many things. It would help to have two disk drives. Then get a modem and communications software. (The total cost of this entire system would be about $2,000 to $4,000 at 1983 prices, depending on what you buy.)

Through a normal push-button telephone line and modem, computers can access broad data-base services such as "The Source," by *Reader's Digest*. Make sure the one you use offers Media General Financial Services or an equivalent. (I use "The Source," which I find convenient. You can get the same service from other "sources.") Media General has a service providing statistical scans of financial data for specific industry groups.

For example, you might be interested in advertising agencies or the cement industry or business data processing computers or whatever. By entering into the computer, when prompted, an industry's

---

[1] Bernard M. Baruch, *My Own Story* (New York: Henry Holt & Company, 1957), p. 258.

code number, which they provide, you can scan the entire industry. Of if you wish, you can scan specific stocks only. They offer 12 "screens." Use Screen 6. This includes PSRs, which they call "% MKT TO REV." Screen 6 also has a lot of other information such as the current stock price and the price divided by stockholder's equity per share, as well as information many investors use but which I purposefully ignore—such as betas.

You can use any of the other screens to gather still more useful information if you wish. Screen 10, for instance, shows each company's most recent annual sales, profit margin, return on equity, debt-to-equity ratio, and the most recent quarter's debt-to-equity ratio.

Presto—you have a universe of low PSR stocks to consider as potential Super Companies. All of this information can be saved on diskette for future use. Further, the stored files can be accessed and edited using one of the standard and easy-to-use word processing programs such as Wordstar. (This book was written on Wordstar.) If desired, these files can be printed out on "hard-paper" copy using any printer.

Looking through these stocks, you can pick out those that have PSRs warranting further consideration. For example, in the summer of 1983, I looked through the list of publishers and found that all but three had PSRs too high to have the potential warranting further consideration. This saves lots of time.

The use of personal computers is one place where the small investor actually has an advantage over most professionals. These data-base services charge by the minute for usage. They offer steep discounts for nonprime-time usage to encourage your use when their lines are least busy. As an amateur, at home at night, you can avail yourself of these services at a third the cost, or less, of the normal daytime business user. To get these low rates, business users must either work night shifts or, as we do at Fisher Investments, use portable computers that commute to work and use the phone lines at home at night. (Current least-load "Source" rates are 10 cents per minute versus 34 cents per minute during weekdays.)

Put together a list of low-PSR stocks to consider as potential Super Companies. Clearly, most of them won't qualify. The few you find that ARE Super Companies are Super Stocks. The key is to find out if they are Super Companies or not. Quality assessment is the hard part. (The stocks that I compile from this computer scan go into my "To the Library Pile File"—to be studied further.)

Scan for Money-Losing Companies

Why would anyone scan for money-losing companies? Money-losing companies are not apt to be inundated with financial-community support. A very few darlings of Wall Street, like the biotechnology stocks, are allowed regularly to lose money without losing financial-community favor. They are exceptions.

Most companies losing money, even for a short time, are in the financial doghouse. Every day I go through the "Digest of Earnings Reports" in *The Wall Street Journal* looking for money-losing companies. I am particularly interested in ones with names unfamiliar to me. There are so many companies, it is virtually impossible to know most of them. Everyone knows the big-capitalization stocks. Many people know the glamour stocks. No one knows all the stocks. The total number of publicly traded businesses is so vast it is quite hard to fathom. For years, I've been searching the earnings digest. I never seem to run out of companies I've never heard of before.

Unfamiliar companies that are losing money I circle in blue pen. I then give the earnings digest to a co-worker, who looks up each company in *Standard & Poor's*. On a single sheet of paper, she writes out a brief summary of what they do, along with some brief financial data that includes the PSR. If the PSR is greater than 0.75, she throws out the paper. If the PSR is less than 0.75, she returns the paper to me. I either discard it or I put it in the "To the Library Pile File." Some I discard because I'm not interested or I don't think I know much about the industry. I'm sure I pass up a lot of opportunities. (Life is too short to spend a lot of time in areas you're uncomfortable with or ignorant about. Stick to things understandable.)

Scan for Qualitative Assessments of Superior Companies

This area may be more useful than either of the previous two. It probably won't lead to ideas that can be quickly implemented. (It has been the source of most of my investments.) The information found here tends to pop out, perhaps years later, when something you learned becomes of later use. Over time, by reading trade journals, going to financial and technical conferences, and talking to people in industry and Wall Street, I get a sense of who is doing "what well, where, and why." Let me repeat that: *Who is doing What Well, Where, and Why?*

Here's an example: For years, I had heard and read great things about microwave technology in general and California Microwave in particular (see Chapter 15). I heard these things at conferences and from people in the financial world. I was fairly certain this company deserved close inspection as a potential Super Company. I had not yet made a detailed study of the company. When they had a glitch in 1980, the stock fell—this was time to look closer. The process of information accumulation had given me a qualitative scan on California Microwave several years before I was ready to use it.

You can expect to hear rosy things about a company with whom Wall Street is in love. As we learned in Chapters 1 and 2, many of these are likely true. As we also saw, it is quite common for most of the financial community to turn its back on a company suffering a glitch. So through this qualitative screening process, it is possible to learn who is doing what well, where, and why—and then (perhaps) years later, at a low price, have an opportunity to invest in that company. Reading trade journals helps one keep abreast of what is happening. Advertisements frequently are as interesting as articles because they depict (as they are supposed to) in an easily understood format who is doing what. Articles may range from short news quips to in-depth analyses of specific product lines. File the most interesting parts.

Beyond subscriptions, I make a once-a-month library sojourn for trade journals alone. San Francisco has an outstanding business library. Across town, in the Main Branch, the city houses more technical journals than I could hope to consume. These magazines help keep an investor familiar with the established players in the field. Who produces top-quality products? Who are other people talking about as the "top dog" in the field? Who is receiving technical or commercial awards?

Attending financial and technical conferences not only helps learn who does what where but also can help answer some of the all-important wells and whys. Brokerage firms and industry groups sponsor financial conferences where companies make investment- and business-oriented presentations. It is possible to learn quite a lot from these presentations and other people in attendance. Take a lot of the "Contrarian" with you when you go—agreement within the crowd can be so thick you could cut it with a knife.[2] Consider events such as the spring and fall conferences of The American Electronics Association. They are legendary due to the size and prestige of their attendance.

Attendees come both from industry and the investment world. Talk with both. Follow through with them between conferences. A given security analyst may or may not be a good investor but is likely to know a tremendous amount about the industry he or she follows. If you want specific information, or just want to know what people think about an industry, who could be better? These people are invaluable in assessing what is going on. Remember, many of these people won't have correct investment conclusions on a company

---

[2] "Contrarians" seem to be spiritual descendents of Missouri settlers—with a "show-me" attitude. Contrarians believe that if most people say a stock should rise, it will fall and vice versa. They believe whatever the crowd thinks is wrong. While that tends to be true, it is often hard to identify what the crowd thinks.

you are considering, but that doesn't negate the fact that they know a lot.

Security analysts are interesting because they know so much. I gain some of the "who does what well, where, and why" from them. I do not seek their investment conclusions. I ask their impressions of the merits of Product X versus Product Y. I ask who makes the best double-density widgets. I ask if it is true that Company A is developing a new solid-state widget. Many of the best analysts prefer it this way.

Unfortunately, many investors don't have access to analysts—whose employers expect them to be compensated through a significant amount of brokerage business. But even if you don't have enough brokerage, you should be able to get their attention if you can catch them at the right conferences, trade shows, and so forth. Most people are friendly and like to talk if you just approach them correctly. The important thing is to approach them in a time and way so that you aren't infringing on their busy schedules.

Other professional investors also may be quite knowledgeable. In fact, some may know more about certain areas of industry than the security analysts. Seeking them out helps build a data base against which one can apply contrarian thinking. Remember from earlier discussions that it is necessary (but not sufficient) to go against the crowd. To go against the crowd, you need to know which way the crowd is going.

People in industry are interesting because they are out on the firing line day in and day out. They live, eat, sleep, and breathe their industry. Again, they have a very strong sense of who may be doing things well. They tend to be less biased about Wall Street attitudes toward a company than many investors and analysts because their focus is more at the operating level. At a conference, these people are usually friendly and willing to swap ideas, "war stories," and fears. Learn what you can from all these people. At some time in the future it will pay off.

The Best Research Facilities Cost Nothing to Use

Gradually, leads are gathered—some from scanning for low PSRs. Some come from scanning the "Digest of Earnings Reports" of *The Wall Street Journal* for money-losing companies that are not familiar names. Others come from qualitative screening of ideas of other people. Which ideas are worthy of heavy research? Which ideas would it be better to waste little time on?

Now, it's time to do a minimal amount of work to determine if more work is warranted. This is the time to go to the library—a wonderful place because so much information is in one place costing the users only their time. This also is time to apply discipline, keeping both eyes on the ball. Avoid stumbling into this or that interesting, but useless, time drain. I've learned some fascinating tidbits in libraries which did me relatively little financial good. Save your time—you'll need it for the Super Companies.

Start with *Standard & Poor's* or *Moody's*. I use *Standard & Poor's* out of habit. This material is quickly digested for each company. Frequently, you can decide right there that additional time in investigation would bear little fruit. Perhaps a company violates one or more of the principles regarding Super Companies in Chapters 8 or 9. The sooner I can decide a company is not of interest, the sooner I can divert my time to those companies that might be of investment interest.

Take an Important Side Step in Time

At this point, I would like to introduce a concept which may seem tangential. It has helped me a lot. *Time is scarce.* There is never enough to do everything I'd like. I need all the help possible determining where to best spend my time.

How long is a day in blocks of time I can use? There are 1,440 minutes per day. If you sleep eight hours a day, you are awake about 1,000 minutes. If you spend an hour on something, you've devoted 6 percent of your day to it:

$$\text{One hour} = 60 \text{ minutes}$$
$$\frac{60}{1,000} = .06 = 6\%$$

Thirty minutes is 3 percent of your day. Twenty minutes is 2 percent, and two hours—120 minutes—is 12 percent of your day. When people ask me to lunch, I wonder if seeing them is worth 12 percent of my day. It may be or may not be. Perhaps we can chat on the phone for 20 minutes instead (2 percent of my day). If so, I have saved 10 percent of my day for more productive efforts.

If businesses struggle for small savings, why shouldn't I? I don't have blocks of time I can afford to waste. Do I have two hours to waste in the library on interesting companies and ideas I won't pursue further? Not if it costs me 12 percent of my day. Do I have two hours to spend in the library learning about a business I will want to invest in? Of course! I will do whatever I can to save myself time in the screening process. What I want to know is what I *need* to decide if a stock warrants more time.

The Key to Esoteric and Little-Known Publications

If a company is still of interest at this point, I do two things. First, I get its address and write for its most recent annual report, subsequent quarterly reports, SEC Forms 10-K and 10-Q, and proxy statement. Reviewing this material will either generate disinterest or form the basis for the next step in the investigation. If I detect that it violates the fundamental principles set down in Chapters 8, 9, 10, or 11, the company isn't worth additional time or effort. It may be possible to eliminate it from further consideration.

If not, I grab the *F&S Index*—one of the most useful publications with which I am familiar. Unfortunately, it is not well known outside the research world. It's like a *Reader's Guide to Periodical Literature*, specializing in industrial and commercial information. It is possible to look up any company for any recent year or quarter or even the most-recent few weeks and find everything in print about it in any normal publication. The *F&S Index* catalogs information from extremely esoteric and little-known publications as well as from common sources such as *Business Week, Electronic News, Laser Focus, Paper Trade Journal, The Wall Street Journal,* and virtually every other trade or finance journal. It covers domestic as well as many foreign publications. It is easy to use. A larger problem can be getting your hands on some of the more-obscure periodicals.

I accumulate all publicly available published information about the company. There is still the realm of brokerage-firm reports and coverage. Regularly, I browse through the *Wall Street Transcript* because it gives an outstanding collection of comments showing what different people in the financial community are thinking. It shows their conclusions and, frequently, the body of brokerage-firm research reports. These reports may provide additional information about a company. They provide useful insights into Wall Street's attitudes toward a stock. I want to find few (or even, no) brokerage-firm reports on a company because it means the stock is not already broadly promoted within Wall Street.

Avoid Competition from Wall Street

A Super Company usually gets little attention from Wall Street before its stock starts to rise (see Chapters 1 and 2). Reduce risk by avoiding competition from Wall Street.

How many brokerage firms write research comments or reports on the stock? If the company has an investor relations contact, you can phone and ask how many analysts visit the company and write reports on it and who they are. Investor relations contacts readily give out this information because it makes their job easier. If the company doesn't have an investors relations contact, you can speak with the president's secretary (a good opportunity to make friends—you're likely to need that person's help later).

If more than a few analysts write reports on the stock, it has a moderate amount of financial-community interest. If more than about six analysts write on the firm, it has substantial financial-community interest. If more than 15 investment professionals visit the company and maintain phone contact on a regular basis, it has considerable financial-community support.

Consider Table 12–2. It provides a general (not hard-and-fast) guideline to the approximate maximum number of analysts who

TABLE 12–2
Approximate Maximum Number of Professionals Following a Super Company on a Regular Basis before the Company Is Overrun by Financial-Community Interest

Approximate Size of Company in $ Millions of Revenue	Approximate Number of Written Brokerage Reports	Approximate Total Number of Visiting Investment Professionals
$ 0–20	2	5
21–50	3	10
51–100	4	15
100–200	5	20
200–500	8	30
500–1,000	20	60

follow Super Companies of varying sizes before the stock becomes overrun with financial-community interest.[3]

Table 12–2 is based on the experience of Fisher Investments. The term *approximate* is simply a guide in the table. It gives an idea of financial-community interest in companies of different sizes. The percentage of brokerage reports written compared with the number of visiting professionals is higher for both the smallest and the largest companies. There are two reasons. Small companies get a high percentage because those few willing to go out of their way to visit small, out-of-favor stocks are often more zealous in their approach. If they like a small, obscure-but-exciting company, they will visit it regularly. They may believe in it enough to stick their necks out in support.

As companies get bigger, around the $50 to $200 million range, they tend to attract less-strident followers. Among more casual fol-

---

[3] Determining how many is too artful to be quantified into hard-and-fast rules.

lowers, the percentage of reports written tends to fall. As a Super Company gets much bigger, in the $200 million to $1 billion range, the success that helped achieve its size tends to attract financial community support. It falls into more and more institutional portfolios.

You want to see little or no Wall Street interest in the company you are considering. Note the concept of a maximum number. Many companies have no professional investor (or just one or two) regularly following its activities—the less the better from a buyer's viewpoint.

By contrast, a company in the financial-community limelight will have a large body of followers. When a company you are considering has lots of followers, don't waste further time on it. Life is too short. (It is even a bad sign if they have the above-mentioned investor relations contact. They shouldn't have enough investor relations to warrant such a function.)

Visit the Company

Having digested everything in print, you know a considerable amount about the company. Gaps in knowledge and understanding also are likely. Make a list of questions. Some may be factual, such as the number of managers and salespeople in its marketing organization. Others may be oriented toward how management thinks. Making the list is essential. It forces you to think about what you might not know. "What do I know and what don't I know?" I jot questions down as they occur to me. Later, I organize them the way I plan to use them.

Appendix 1 lists the most commonly asked questions—the ones asked over and over again. A number of specific questions are tailored for each unique company. Since time is so valuable, it is disrespectful to request management time for information easily learned elsewhere. (I am embarrassed if management answers saying, "That's on page such and such in the 10-K." I should already know what is and isn't in the 10-K before taking management time.) With a good list of questions prepared, I am ready to contact the company.

Sometimes it is hard to convince management to see you. Whenever possible, get a personal introduction to top-management personnel from someone who knows them closely. Do I have connections at the board-of-directors level or among the company's auditors, legal counsel, bankers, or investment bankers? Usually, I don't.

For years, I tried phoning to explain my intent in the hope management would see me. Often, I couldn't get past a secretary. Some secretaries see their job as protecting the boss from the outside world. (Maybe some bosses think that way, too.) She would ask what I wanted. I would explain. She would tell me that she would check with Mr. So and So (her boss).

Weeks would pass and I wouldn't hear back. I'd phone again. Finally, I'd reach the same secretary, who would seem to have difficulty remembering me—finally responding that she was sorry, but her boss and the other key officers were too busy to see me in the coming months. In time, through perseverance, I'd "build a ladder" to management and convince them to see me. I'd do this by "building" some mutual acquaintances. I'd look for people to meet who might be a "step" on the "ladder." Whom do I know that should know someone that knows these people? Their customers perhaps? An existing acquaintance that does business in their town? Trade and financial conferences are great places to meet "steps" on the "ladder." This process often got quite involved and took close to forever. Sometimes I still have to do this—but not often.

Getting Your Foot in the Door

Since then, I have found it is easier to write a letter. When I want to meet a management, I write to the chief executive. I tell him in the first few lines why I want to see him. I explain my potential financial interest and that I have already put effort into studying his company. I detail how much stock I am potentially interested in buying. Then I explain a little about myself and my firm. I usually mention some of the companies in which I have investments (in case he wants to verify that I am who I say I am by talking to them.) I offer further references. I volunteer that I would meet with someone else there if he thinks it more appropriate or if he is going to be "out of town." (This way it is hard for him to refuse me totally.)

Finally, I offer about five alternative dates when my schedule allows me to come to his corporate headquarters. I suggest he pick the date and time most convenient to him. If all of these dates are bad, I offer that he pick an alternate date which I would try to make. This way, I let him know the degree to which this is serious and important to me. I then suggest he have his secretary call to set up the date and time. I thank him in advance for his time.

These letters get about a 95 percent successful response—phenomenally high for a "cold-call" letter. His secretary, when responding, knows when the meeting is and always is as prompt, courteous, and helpful as possible. I strongly suggest letters of self-introduction.

On the date of the appointment, I review my questions and all the information in my files. With this information fresh in mind, and with questions and notes in hand, I meet with whomever I am scheduled. This first meeting rarely lasts more than two hours. Most of my questions are answered in full, but a few more still are not clear. In the next 24 hours, new questions will come to mind, triggered by what I've learned.

Contact Customers, Competitors, Suppliers, and Investment Professionals

One goal is to learn more about the business. Another is to learn the financial-community view of the company. The ultimate goal is to hear from customers, competitors, and suppliers that the company is wonderful, while hearing from Wall Street that the company is one in which they have little interest.

The process of investigation to date should have uncovered names of individuals in firms that do business with, or in competition with, the firm. Compiling a list of at least several customers, competitors, and suppliers should be easy. Ask them about the company. The image that these people have, in composite, will be vivid and penetrating. Usually, these people can be reached by phone. Again, if I have difficulty, I write a letter explaining why I want to talk to them and ask for some time on the phone. Most people are surprisingly cooperative. Most people love to have someone ask them their opinion.

Questions logically come to mind. Ask a customer if he buys only from the company or also from the company's competitors. Ask why he buys from whom he does. Ask the customer's on-going impression of the company. Have they serviced the product well? Would he buy from that company again? How do they stack up to competition? What does he think are their strongest and weakest points as a supplier? Have they been getting better or worse over time? If he were running the company's business, what would he do differently? How does he perceive the market for the product changing? Customers usually love to talk about these kinds of questions because you are asking them to talk about their own lives. Take notes for later reference.

Suppliers also are good sources of information, although sometimes biased. A supplier may fear losing future business if word gets back that something unfavorable was mentioned. A supplier may be biased because most people tend to think positively about their customers. ("Of course, XYZ is going to grow. I've budgeted twice as much for them to buy from me next year as this.") Still, useful information can be gained.

Suppliers may be willing to compare their different customers. They may indicate how much they sell to different customers. If they have had trouble getting orders from the company recently (say an order has been cut back), they may ask if you know what is going on—a significant reason for them to talk to you. After all, you have been studying their customer. They only see their customer from one vantage point. They are likely interested in any broader view you offer them. Helping them understand their customer is helping them make sales.

It may be hard to get competitors to talk freely. Why should they talk to you? After all, you are contemplating investing money in their competitor! Who wants to help someone invest in a competitor? Conferences are, again, a very good solution to this problem. The competitor is probably at the conference and expects business questions from strangers. It wants to present itself in the best possible light. Ask about the competitor's business. During the discussion, steer the conversation toward the company you are studying. Throw in leading questions to get to information about "your" company.

Competitors are likely to talk freely about their "superiority" over the other company. Listen very carefully. They may be right about their superiority. Take notes. Compare what you hear from each of the competitors to sense how they all stack up—back to back. To what extent do the different competitors agree? Ask each whom they consider their most serious competitors? Who are the two or three competitors with the best technology? Who has the best marketing organization? Why?

Suppose the customers, competitors, and suppliers all reinforce your image of the company as a Super Company. It would be nice to have the financial community tell you that it is a real dog. Corporate managements will freely indicate which investment professionals regularly stay abreast of the company. They also will disclose who used to be interested but doesn't seem to be now. Seek out the latter group. Compare how their sense of the company conflicts with those who are currently visiting the company and with you.

Compare what the financial community tells you with what the customers, competitors, and suppliers tell you. Be particularly sensitive to "old" information in the hands of investment people. Is it no longer true? Sense if the investment people really know what they are talking about. Or are they instead reacting to rumors or bitter emotions from the past?

It's Time to Reach a Conclusion

The information gathered should be reviewed once more as a refresher to provide a rapid overview. A final judgment should be made using margin analysis. Is this or is this not a company that can grow rapidly with a fair degree of certainty? Can it do so without requiring dilutive outside financing? What kind of margins should it make long term? What problems will it have to overcome to grow at these rates? What are the three largest risks that might upset all of this?

The PSR and the PRR must have been low, or we never would have allowed the investigation to consume this much time. But, if convinced the business has strong prospects for the future and qualifies as a Super Company, I still need a process applying discipline to the analysis of price. I make a "Pre-Buy Valuation—Projection." It has all the information I need to come to a final conclusion on a single page. At the top, it shows the stock market price and the fully diluted number of shares, along with where I have to go to buy the stock (traded on the New York Stock Exchange, the AMEX, or over the counter—with OTC market makers listed). Next are PSR and PRR calculations. Below this, I have a section for conclusions. The conclusions cover:

1. What factors might make the stock decline?
2. At what rate do I predict sales growth over the next five years?
3. What is a reasonable future margin goal for the company to attain?
4. What is a reasonable and conservative valuation for the market to place on the company sometime in the next several years—when it is attaining these margins?
5. What does this translate into in terms of an approximate price-earnings ratio in three to five years?
6. To buy the total amount of the stock I want, how much money is involved and what percentage of the business does this buy?

In the middle of the page, I make a graph which shows my sales forecast and a sense of what could happen to the market value. The market-value forecast assumes that someplace along the line the price sales multiple rises, then falls back down, and then, later still, rises again. This gives a sense of what can be gained through potential multiple expansion versus what might be gained in simple growth. I try to keep it simple. I don't take into account future dilution through equity offerings or new stock options or anything else too fancy.

Illustration 12–1 is a sample "Pre-Buy Valuation—Projection." As I draw the chart in the middle, I compare the cost of the stock to the two high points when the stock supposedly has met my projections both for future sales and PSR. Assuming the stock reaches the points on the graph in the time horizon drawn (which is only guess work), I have reference points I can use to calculate projected rates of return. Using the "future value" keys on my calculator, I compute the "projected" rates of return for the stock (assuming it meets my guesstimates as to timing).

ILLUSTRATION 12–1

Current date

XYZ CORP. PRE-BUY
VALUATION—PROJECTION

Buy thru:
h&q, lfr, mrl,
dnw, mtg

1. Company has 4.9 million fully diluted shares at a market price of $12 offered OTC. Market value = $59 million.
2. Last 12 months' revenue = $84 million
   PSR = 0.70 o.k.
   Last 12 months' R&D = $5 million
   PRR = 11.8 o.k.

CONCLUSIONS

1. Stock is likely to drop some unless the company starts earning some profit in the next 12 months. Market assumes some turn-around.
2. Revenue can easily grow at 25 percent average rate over the next five years.
3. The company ought to be averaging 7 percent net margins after 36 months.

PROJECTION

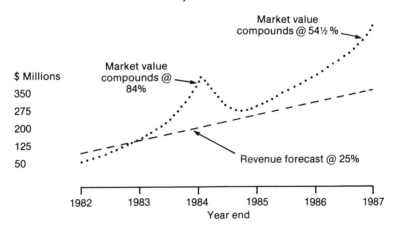

4. At some point in time, this stock ought to be able to sell at two times sales. Maybe it happens in 1983–84, or maybe in 1987.
5. If they earn 7 percent margins and sell at a PSR of 2, they will have a price-earnings ratio of 29.
6. If I am to buy $1 million of stock and, in the process, the stock rises to 15, I will have bought at about an average of $13.5/share. This means I will have bought 74,000 shares, or 1.5% of the total business.

A Super Stock needs (by definition) to yield a long-term rate of return in excess of 25 percent—hopefully, it will offer even more. I always need lots of room for "slippage." So I always require the lowest projected rate of return to be more than 40 percent. If, after all this work, I have that, it is time to buy the stock. The next logical concern is when to sell the stock, which is what Chapter 13 is about.

Bringing It All Back Home—When to sell

When Is the Bloom off the Rose?

When is the "right" time to sell a Super Stock? Almost never. The time to sell is when one of two things happens:

Its PSRs get outrageously high.

The company ceases to have those traits which qualified it as a Super Company.

It is useless to own a stock unless it increases in value at a respectable—if irregular—rate. Unless the stock rises over time, it would be better to own municipal bonds or some other safe asset. Very few would doubt that it is wise to sell a stock if the inherent quality of the business has deteriorated over time.

If the basic business aspects of the company no longer point toward internally financed growth, it may be doubly rough on the company's future. Managements used to a growth environment may have difficulty with the psychology of an environment devoid of growth. The portfolios of the world are cluttered with former growth stocks that have long lost their head of steam. When a good company goes bad, its stock follows quickly.

To stay on top of what is going on, look at the business regularly as if it were your first opportunity to learn about it. Look at the company with open eyes—play the contrarian. Has anything changed in the basic business aspects? Has management changed?

167

Have they become a bit complacent or rigid from too much success? Have the markets changed? Perhaps new products made by different competitors or even industries are replacing the old guard? Has the technology changed? Has the competition changed? Perhaps there are major new entrants in the business.

It is hard to look at a holding in a truly objective light—close to impossible. If a stock has done poorly for an investor, it may be perceived through bitter eyes. If a company performed well for years and an investor made profits of 500, 1,000, 2,000 percent, or more, it is certain management deserves tremendous credit.

An investor, over time, builds a superhumanlike mental image of the management which generated such rewarding results. That image, slowly built with proven success, is likely to be correct for years and years. As the image gets stronger and more entrenched, it is harder and harder to look at management as if for the first time. When mistakes are made, it is easy to forgive them. (No one is perfect.)

Maintain objectivity. I wish I could say I do an excellent job in this area. I don't. It is among the hardest things in the entire investment process. If prior experiences tell me a management is exceptionally capable, I want to believe in them. I don't think I'm unique in this. Knowing when the bloom is off the rose is very difficult.

Beware of Heights

Another perfect time to sell is when the PSR of a Super Stock gets outrageously high. Compare the PSR of your company with that of other companies of similar size. Studying PSRs helps get a sense of how high is "up." A stock selling at five times sales is equivalent to a company that earns 10 percent margins selling at 50 times earnings (see Table 4–1). A stock selling at 10 times sales is equivalent to a company that earns 10 percent margins selling at 100 times earnings. In Appendix 2 is "Relationships between Price Sales Ratios and Size of the Companies Covered in the H&Q Statistical Summary" of February 1983 and May 1983. (These use the same format as Table 4–1.)

It is startling to see so many companies selling at 5, 10, 15, 20, and even up to 30 (29.67) times sales. Thirty times sales is equivalent to 300 times earnings for a company making 10 percent after-tax profit margins. Remember that in 1978, the highest PSR was only 2.5. The change in this Bull Market has been spectacular. In November of 1982, there were only eight companies on the list with PSRs over 6. By May 1983, there were 16.

To me, anything over three times sales is a real concern. Anything over five times sales is just plain scary. I cannot conceive of a long-term holding in the stocks selling at 5 to 30 times sales. They are a phenomenon of the Bull Market.

There Is Nothing Like a Good Long Ride

If a Super Stock is bought correctly and continues to display the fundamentals necessary to insure above-average internally financed growth—and the PSR stays reasonably low, I would hold it forever. As the company grows, the increased size will build a pressure under the price of the stock, and it will rise in value at about the rate of growth. A Super Stock with a PSR of 0.6 and growth in revenues of 25 percent per year (or more) will yield a very nice return. If it never ever has a PSR over 0.6, it is likely to grow in value—perhaps irregularly—by an average of 25 percent per year—the minimum hurdle to meet Super-Stock status. At the end of five years, it is likely to be worth three times its original value. This is the power of compound interest at work. At the end of 10 years, it could be worth nine times its original value. After 20 years, it could be worth more than 85 times its original cost.

On the other hand, as financial-community awareness of this Super Stock increases, its price sales multiple may rise. Should its PSR rise to 3 by the end of five years, it would have increased in value about 15 times. Were its multiple to rise to 3 in 20 years—which isn't likely because the company would be huge by then and big companies have low PSRs—it would be worth over 400 times its original cost.

So, why would anyone ever sell a Super Stock? Isn't it better to just buy and hold on forever and make a lot of money? Yes, if the PSR doesn't get too high. Remember, as companies grow bigger, there is a downward pressure on PSRs (see Chapter 4). We saw that few huge companies—only a handful—have a billion dollars in sales and PSRs greater than 1.

Big companies have less speculative appeal for most investors than do small ones with exciting stories. Everyone expects good things from IBM, but few expect revolutionary results in a company so large.

In a little company, people can exercise their fantasies freely. If a company has $200 million in revenues and a PSR of 6, it has a market value of $1.2 billion. When it gets to be $1 billion in revenue, it is apt to have a market value no higher—certainly not much higher. When the company achieves $2 billion in revenue, it still may not have a higher market value. High PSRs may have fully discounted most, if not all, future growth for decades to come. That is why it is appropriate to sell a stock if its PSR becomes excessively high. At a billion dollars in sales, our Super Stock is more likely to have PSR of 0.75—about what we paid for it.

A PSR is high only in relation to the size of a company and its future prospects. Three is a very high PSR for a company with a billion dollars in sales. Three may be a low PSR for a company with $3 million in sales and an explosive future immediately ahead. In most Super-Stock situations, PSRs begin to get excessively high at some level between 2 and 5. There are few companies, except perhaps in the start-up phase, where greater PSRs can be justified on a long-term basis. Many of those who choose to hold on to extremely high PSR stocks will, in time, be hurt rather badly.

After You've Sold, You've Reached the End of the Line

So you have it—the anatomy of a Super Stock. The emphasis is on fundamental business analysis—finding what makes the business unique—and buying it inexpensively.

The rest is all refinement. A Super Stock should be held for the long term until its PSR becomes excessively high or until it loses the fundamental business aspects that make it a Super Company. Pay less attention to the level and direction of the stock market. Pay more attention to the details of businesses. Consider the examples in the next two chapters.

Chapter 14

Verbatim Corporation— Disco Baby

Early History

Verbatim began as Information Terminals Corporation in 1969 in Sunnyvale, California. In November 1978, its name changed to Verbatim Corporation. It was founded by J. Reid Anderson to make and market removable memory media for computer-related industries. Anderson was an experienced veteran of high-tech entrepreneurialism—having been a founder of Anderson-Jacobsen, a successful electronic terminal manufacturer.[1]

Today, Verbatim is the world's leading manufacturer of flexible (floppy) diskettes—used as permanent yet removable memory storage media in personal computers, small computers, and word processing systems. (This book, for example, was composed and edited on a small computer using Verbatim 5¼-inch disks for storage of the information.) An older and slower-growing market exists for 8-inch disks. A new market is rapidly developing for 3½-inch "micro" diskettes.

At the time of Verbatim's founding, floppy-disk technology had not yet been developed. Verbatim's early revenues were derived mainly from sales of removable tape data cassettes. Removable data cassettes are computer-grade magnetic tape on two small reels in a plastic case (similar to consumer audio-cassette systems). Data cas-

---

[1] See *Forbes*, January 31, 1983, Appendix 3.

171

settes are used for slow but low-cost storage of data in relatively small quantities. They are used in terminals, point-of-sales terminals, small computers, and telecommunications equipment. In 1974, cassettes were 95 percent of Verbatim's sales.[2]

Floppy-disk technology, developed at IBM, was introduced in 1974. In the year ended June 30, 1978, floppy disks were just over half Verbatim's $22 million of sales. They were growing at a much faster rate than data cassettes—comprising two thirds of sales for the last six months of the year.[3]

Verbatim Corporation

Sales and Profits For the Five Years Ended June 30, 1978
($000, Except Per-Share Data)

	1974	1975	1976	1977	1978
Sales	$4,327	$6,761	$12,261	$15,462	$22,485
Net profits	390	520	787	887	1,464
Net per share	.18	.33	.48	.52	.83

Source: Prospectus to Verbatim's initial stock offering, February 15, 1978, p. 13.

At the time, Verbatim had approximately half the worldwide market for data cassettes and one third the market for floppy disks. With such a record, it was not difficult for Verbatim to go public, even in a lackluster stock market. Verbatim's initial public offering of stock on February 15, 1979, was at $17¾, and the stock ranged that year from $17¾ to $29. After the offering, Reid Anderson still owned more than 30 percent of the total company. His involvement was decreasing steadily. He was 62. President and chief operating officer, Dr. Peter A. McCuen, was responsible for day-to-day decisions.

Notes to the 1979 annual report hinted at potential problems. Fourth-quarter profits were said to have been impacted by production inefficiencies in its standard 8-inch disk product. Still, financial-community assessments remained optimistic. Hambrecht & Quist, for example, co-underwriter of Verbatim's stock offering, issued a 14-page report on September 5, 1979, recommending the stock for purchase. In the long term, its recommendation would be profitable—in the short term, it wouldn't.

After seven good years without a "down" quarter, Verbatim

---

[2] Source: Prospectus to Verbatim's initial public stock offering, February 15, 1978, p. 13.

[3] Ibid.

stubbed its toe in their second quarter as a publicly held company. They lost control of the process involved with making diskettes. The liner material for the inner jackets of the diskettes was changed without sufficient testing. The new liners absorbed too much lubricant, causing diskette failure. A change in the chemical coating on the disks also resulted in shorter product life.

Quality problems first surfaced in June 1979 as some small number of diskettes were returned for poor quality. Through December 1979, the quantity of bad product produced increased, but the company wasn't catching it yet. In the spring of 1980, the problem reached its zenith, and by December 1980, the problems were caught and corrected.[4]

Problems were mainly in the 8-inch disk lines, where market share dropped from 45 percent to 15 percent. Recalls of bad products were required, and sales dropped. The 5¼-inch markets were still emerging and so less affected. Also, in early fiscal 1980, Verbatim wrote off a major development effort in rigid (nonflexible, Winchester-type) disk media.[5] In the fourth quarter of fiscal 1980 (ended June 30, 1980), their first loss as a publicly held company was reported.

The President Is Gone

Peter McCuen was dismissed as president.[6] The situation was beyond control and worse than portrayed in the 1980 annual report. Management had not seen the magnitude of its problems because discussion of the problems had been toned down. The stock fell steadily from its high of $29 in 1979 to below $10 in mid-1980.

Losses continued. As yields fell, costs of goods sold rose both in absolute terms and as a percentage of sales. In the quarter ended December 31, 1980, a loss of $1,203,000 on sales of $11,316,000 was reported. The losses included inventory write-downs of more than $1.5 million. Employment had been cut from 1,538 employees to 1,242.[7] Illustration 14–1 shows the inside cover from Verbatim's 1981 annual report giving the quarterly results. The losses, write-downs, and falling stock price piqued my curiosity.

A Competitor by Comparison

Meanwhile, Dysan Corporation had entered the floppy-disk market with perfect timing—just as Verbatim's problems started. Dysan pos-

---

[4] Conversations with Wiley Carter, vice president-finance of Verbatim, January 27, 1981.

[5] *Forbes,* January 31, 1983, p. 47.

[6] *The Wall Street Journal,* January 13, 1981, p. 18.

[7] From Verbatim 2d quarter 1980 shareholder's report.

ILLUSTRATION 14–1

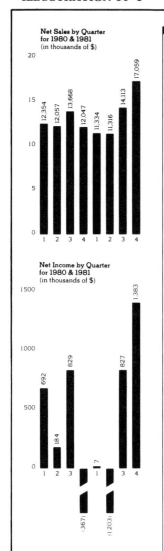

Financial Highlights

	1981	1980
Sales	$53,822,000	$50,126,000
Net Income	$ 1,014,000	$ 1,338,000
Net Income Per Share	$.45	$.61
Shareholders' Equity	$16,072,000	$14,227,000
Working Capital	$11,085,000	$13,208,000
Total Assets	$39,148,000	$36,124,000
Shares Outstanding at Year-End	2,211,368	2,133,664

Corporate Profile

Verbatim Corporation makes and sells removable magnetic data storage media. Its products, used by a myriad of computers and word processing systems to record and store digital information, are sold through a worldwide network of distributors and directly to original equipment manufacturers. Flexible disks, data cartridges and cassettes are manufactured by Verbatim at its facilities in Sunnyvale, California and in Limerick, Ireland, Tokyo, Japan and Melbourne, Australia. These facilities, together with sales offices in the United States, Switzerland, Germany, Japan and Australia, make Verbatim's premium magnetic media available to a worldwide customer base.

tured itself at the high end of the quality market and benefited from those scared off by quality problems at Verbatim. It was a masterful job of public relations, conveying themselves as the technology leader. Strongly tied to Wall Street through major leading venture-capital holdings, the cry went out (quickly and eagerly) that Dysan was THE technology leader and would soon overtake Verbatim.

Financial-community support disappeared. Verbatim's underwriter, Hambrecht & Quist, had supported the stock only months before. Now, weeks after the stock's low, they wrote: "We believe the stock will continue under pressure until there is some resolution of the problems discussed."

Hambrecht revised down its estimates for sales and earnings for 1980 and 1981.[8] I could find no other investment firm writing *any-thing* about the company. The company informed me at the time that they knew of only one other firm, Gruntal & Co., which wrote about the stock.[9]

When asked about a turn-around at Verbatim, Wall Streeters responded, "So what—even if it turns around, Dysan is going to eat their lunch in the long term." What about Dysan? The claim on Wall Street was that Dysan had better technology, better management, and better products. The big question was: "What effect would Dysan have on Verbatim in the long term? At that point, I asked an independent consultant to run life-cycle tests on random boxes of Dysan and Verbatim disks. The results showed no significant quality differences.

Dysan was selling at $17 per share with 13.6 million shares of stock outstanding. That gave them a market value of $231 million. Sales were only $71 million. That meant their PSR was 3.26—some seven and a half times higher than Verbatim's—clearly a darling of Wall Street.

With Dysan so much in financial-community favor, I was skeptical of claims about superiority. A lot of investors had built-in vested reasons to believe in Dysan's superiority—whether it was true or not.

I had previously met Norm Dion, Dysan's founder/president, at a financial-community conference. I had seen him several other times. In my brief interactions, I was skeptical about how well he listened—he seemed too much of a showman for my tastes. A manager must be a great listener to benefit from the input of subordinates. I doubted Dysan would do as well as the financial people thought it would. The herd aspect was just too strong.

Through early 1981, there were no favorable recommendations of Verbatim stock. Hambrecht & Quist later called it "appropriate for risk-oriented investors willing to discount this period of uncertainty." Results were "below our expectations."[10]

Informally, there were those who would say worse about Verba-

---

[8] Hambrecht & Quist interoffice memorandum, July 21, 1980.

[9] Wiley Carter notes, January 27, 1981.

[10] Hambrecht & Quist report, October 23, 1980. Its next report, using almost exactly the same wording, appeared on February 2, 1981.

tim. As I spoke casually to investment people, I was told by various sources that:

- Management was bad at Verbatim.
- There were questions of integrity involved.
- Dysan would take significant further market share away from Verbatim.
- Verbatim might be driven right out of business as more-capable firms (Dysan, 3M, IBM, Xidex, Japanese) took the markets.

The integrity issue was interesting. Several sources indicated they felt Wiley Carter, vice president-finance, had misled them as the problems unfolded. One analyst clearly confused his disappointment for the stock with his assessment of Carter's character—attacking Carter on personal grounds (including physical appearance and demeanor) that, through my own later interactions with Carter, I found completely groundless (see Chapter 2 for the psychology behind this).[11] People were skeptical about the timing of the original problems in relation to the 1979 stock offering. Several intimated that management probably knew about the problems before the offering and, in that sense, defrauded the public.

I spoke casually with more than 20 investment pros about Verbatim. In each case, I acted (and largely was) completely ignorant about facts.

I had kept a file of standard financial and news releases on Verbatim since 1979. I had not visited them. I felt no particular reason to hurry. January 1981 articles in *Electronics News* and *The Wall Street Journal* (see Illustrations 14–2 and 14–3) quickly changed all that. Verbatim brought in a new president and chief executive officer— Malcom Northrup—from Rockwell's Electronics Devices Division. I had no idea what his merits might be—but at least here was a sign that Verbatim might not be a Sleeping Dog (see Chapter 10). Things might change fast if this guy could make a strong impression on the financial community. I immediately went to work.

After quickly interviewing makers and buyers of disks, I arranged an initial visit with Verbatim on January 19, 1981. I met and spoke briefly with the functional heads of marketing and R&D. Most of my time was spent with Wiley Carter, Verbatim's vice president-finance.

I conducted interviews with people who had worked for, sold product to, and bought product from the new president prior to his

---

[11] Private conversations with a security analyst. In my several years interacting with Wiley Carter, I found him to be exceptionally honest and open about problems.

ILLUSTRATION 14–2

Verbatim Corp. Picks Northrup of Rockwell As New Chief Executive

By a WALL STREET JOURNAL *Staff Reporter*

SUNNYVALE, Calif. – Verbatim Corp. named Malcolm B. Northrup, executive vice president of Rockwell International Corp.'s electronic devices division, as president and chief executive officer, effective Jan. 21.

Mr. Northrup, 41 years old, will succeed J. Reid Anderson, the magnetic data storage products company's founder, who remains chairman. Mr. Anderson assumed the presidency last July when Peter McCuen was dismissed after the company ran into operating problems. In its fiscal first quarter, ended Sept. 30, Verbatim had net income of $7,000, compared with $692,000, or 31 cents a share, a year earlier.

* * *

Source: *The Wall Street Journal*, January 13, 1981.
Reprinted by permission of *The Wall Street Journal*, © Dow Jones & Company, Inc., 1981. All rights reserved.

---

employment at Verbatim. I even spoke to people he fired. Several impressions stood out in my mind:

1. The new president (not even there yet) had a good record. Not everyone liked him, but he was well respected even by those who didn't like him.
2. Disillusioned investors couldn't care less that there was a new president. They were still busy reliving their prior disappointments.
3. Verbatim's financial condition could withstand considerable further losses without disruption of activities.
4. Verbatim had a 35 percent market share (high) in the 5¼-inch floppy-disk market, widely projected to be the fastest growing major portion of the electronics industry. The remainder of their business would have no growth or moderate growth. (Eight-inch disks—moderate growth; data cassettes and cartridges—no growth.)

5. Verbatim was focusing early on how the marketing mechanism would change in the years ahead. They were planning for the day when the distribution channel would be less controlled by industrial sources (original equipment manufacturers, or OEMs) and more controlled by the large retail chains and distribution outlets.

Verbatim was particularly miffed at the good luck Dysan had had entering the market just as their own quality problems had begun. Carter told me with great pride that Verbatim had just won back the Apple Computer account from Dysan.

Growth of the floppy-disk market accelerated in 1981 due to the impact of the smaller, 5¼-inch disks.[12] Personal and small computer systems were just beginning to make a real impact in the marketplace. This had to be good for Verbatim. On the other hand, look at the chart of Verbatim's stock price up to early 1981 and the pages from Verbatim's second quarter 1981 shareholder's report (December 31, 1980). (See Illustration 14–4 and 14–5.)

The financial condition of the company is important. Verbatim had a sufficient current ratio of 2.1.[13] The quarter's loss had been $1.2 million. There were $13 million of stockholder's equity: Losses could continue to hemorrhage at that rate for at least 10 quarters. The company had time to get their act together. The cash flow was a plus. Large depreciation expenses gave Verbatim a strong cash flow for an electronics company. In fiscal 1980, while earning only $1.3 million, additional cash from depreciation amounted to $2 million, improving the liquidity of the balance sheet.[14]

Market share was important. In 5¼-inch disks, no one else had even half their market share. In 8-inch disks, with their market share way down due to their production problems, Verbatim was still tied for Number 1 position with IBM at 15 percent.[15] With high absolute and relative market share, it was obvious this company could be sold easily—lock, stock, and barrel—if the problems weren't remedied. But with such high share, they ought to be able to solve their problems on their own (see Chapter 10 on market share).

Because of the significant problems, Verbatim had swung to the

---

[12] *Chemical Week*, February 9, 1983, p. 38.

[13] The current ratio is simply derived from the balance sheet by dividing current assets by current liabilities. The standard rule most investors use is that the current ratio should exceed 2.0. As with everything else financial, there are always exceptions.

[14] Verbatim's 2d quarter 1981 shareholder's report and 1980 annual report.

[15] As told by Verbatim—Wiley Carter notes, January 27, 1981.

ILLUSTRATION 14–3

Northrup Exits Rockwell for Verbatim

By DENNY MOSIER

ANAHEIM, Calif. — Malcolm B. Northrup, executive vice-president of Rockwell's Electronic Devices division, has resigned after 18 years with the company to become president of a northern California disk media manufacturer.

Effective this week, Mr. Northrup assumes the post of president and chief executive at Verbatim Corp., Sunnyvale, Calif.

At Rockwell, Mr. Northrup leaves a position he has held for 14 months. Sharing the office of the president with Howard D. Walrath, EDD president, Mr. Northrup helped run an operation with annual sales of more than $200 million and about 4,100 employes.

The Rockwell division, which makes microprocessors and related circuits, bubble memories, microcomputer systems and interconnect systems, has been profitable since 1978, Mr. Northrup claimed.

Responsibilities for Mr. Northrup included running day-to-day operations for EDD on the West Coast, site of most of its MPU and related parts efforts. The division headquarters and Mr. Walrath are in Dallas.

"Positions like becoming chief executive officer of Verbatim don't come along very often," said Mr. Northrup. "That's literally it. It wasn't something I was anticipating. I thought about it a long time. It (Verbatim) is a good company . . . that's something every professional manager wants to be, a chief executive."

Mr. Northrup said he wasn't dissatisfied with Rockwell and scoffed at reports that his path to higher positions at Rockwell was blocked.

"I've never had (that) problem at Rockwell. I have a chance to run a public company. It's as big as what I'm running now. The challenges are different," he said, adding "Rockwell was pleasant."

Mr. Northrup said at least for the time being he doesn't expect Rockwell to replace him. Mr. Walrath is expected to assume Mr. Northrup's duties.

The Rockwell division Mr. Northrup helped run has agreed to second-source Motorola in making the 68000 16-bit microprocessor. Rockwell originally planned to start sampling the 68000 last summer, but missed that date (Antenna, June 30). Latest reports indicate EDD expects to sample the 68000 sometime this quarter.

Asked if the delay on the 68000 was part of his reason for leaving, Mr. Northrup said "Not a bit. Shortly, we'll be able to handle the 68000. I think it's in that range (first-quarter samples.)"

Mr. Northrup is the latest of several EDD managers to have left in recent months. Earlier, several EDD sales managers departed (EN, Aug. 11, Sept. 22). Asked if his departure is connected with those, Mr. Northrup said "Not a bit."

Also in recent months, Charles V. Kovac, a one-time general manager of EDD's Microelectronic Devices unit, was named marketing vice-president for EDD (EN, Aug. 18). Asked if Mr. Kovac's reassumption of a key management post within EDD was connected with his decision to leave EDD, Mr. Northrup said "There has never been a clash with Charles Kovac. He's an outstanding marketing executive. I was the instigator in centralizing marketing to provide for expanding."

One source familiar with Mr. Northrup's situation pointed out "It is interesting that he is going from bubble memories to a floppy disk manufacturer. That should tell you something."

In going to Verbatim, Mr. Northrup takes over duties from J. Reid Anderson, founder, who remains chairman. Noting his peripherals and semiconductor background, Mr. Northrup said he's been involved with semiconductors for the past 5 years but previously was in communications and computers, including designing tape and disk drives.

Source: *Electronics News*, January 19, 1981.

ILLUSTRATION 14–4
Verbatim Corporation

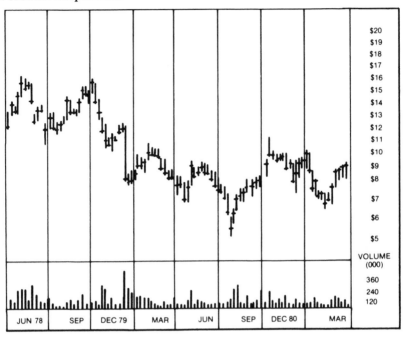

Source: Long Term Values, Robert M. Drislane 11915 La Grange Avenue, Los Angeles, CA 90025. A division of William O'Neil & Co. Incorporated.

extreme of caution in quality control. One hundred percent certification (*testing* in disk lingo) of every disk was required before shipment. This increased costs and losses, but the improved quality also overcame the bad quality image Verbatim had developed. With improved quality came increased orders.

The production problems had been solved before I ever visited the company—or, for that matter, before Malcolm Northrup began as president. Reid Anderson had done the dirty work. With the production process cleaned up and yields on the rise, operating results from the company had to improve.

My conclusion was that Verbatim was clearly a Super Company—a Super Company that had gone through a classic growth glitch. It had strong top management with all those sensitive characteristics necessary to foster and control growth (see Chapter 8), high

ILLUSTRATION 14–5

Verbatim Corporation
removable magnetic media

Second Quarter Report

For the six months ended December 31, 1980

More About Verbatim and Its People . . .

Our new President and Chief Executive Officer, **Malcolm Northrup**, brings to Verbatim an extensive knowledge of our industry. Mal has been with Rockwell International Corp. for the past 18 years, most recently as Executive Vice President of its Electronic Devices Division, a major multinational business area of Rockwell. Earlier, he held engineering management positions in its computer peripherals and communications divisions and general management positions in its semiconductor and magnetic component businesses. Mal has a B.S. degree in Physics from Southern Methodist University and began his career as a designer of disc and tape drives at Ampex Corporation.

Dr. George W. ("Bill") Brock has joined Verbatim Corporation as manager of its advanced technology department. Bill, who has a Ph.D. in Applied Mechanics from the University of Illinois, will be directing the work of our engineers and technicians who provide the technological foundations for Verbatim's product improvements and new product developments. Prior to joining Verbatim he was with IBM Corporation for 20 years where he worked on the development of disc and tape drives and was issued 17 U.S. patents. Bill's technical expertise and capabilities will help keep us at the forefront of technology in our industry.

Verbatim Corporation
Corporate Headquarters
323 Soquel Way
Sunnyvale, CA 94086
(408) 245-4400

Verbatim received a major contract from Hewlett Packard during the quarter for mini cassettes for a new H-P product, as well as significant orders for minidiskettes from Apple Computer, Lanier Business Products and Tandy Corporation. Additionally, I am pleased to report that our Datalife product introduction mentioned in last quarter's report has been very enthusiastically received in the marketplace, a recent development being the selection by Xerox of these products for sale in its retail stores.

Last July we embarked upon an extensive search for a new President and Chief Executive Officer. We were most fortunate in having our top choice, Malcolm Northrup, accept our offer and agree to join us on January 21st. Mal is an experienced professional who will be an important contributor to the Company's future and its growth in quality of people and products, in profits, and in sales and service to our customers. During the past quarter we also greatly strengthened our technical staff with the addition of Dr. Bill Brock who has had over 20 years experience in the magnetic recording field.

We have committed to the future growth of Verbatim with our purchase on January 8th of 38 acres of land in the University Research park near Charlotte, North Carolina. We expect to commence construction at this site within three years, making it our first U.S. tape coating and manufacturing plant outside of California.

Sincerely,

J. Reid Anderson

Chairman of the Board

January 26, 1981

ILLUSTRATION 14–5 (concluded)

To Our Shareholders:

Verbatim's net sales of $11,316,000 for the second quarter were 6% below the same quarter of the previous year. While our anticipated sales growth has been slowed by recessionary conditions in the United States and Europe, sales of our minidiskette and mini cassette products increased during the quarter compared to last year as did incoming new orders for all of our products.

The lower sales level, higher operating costs, and a decision to provide for a substantial write-down of inventory resulted in a loss of $1,203,000 for the quarter. After conducting a thorough evaluation of our inventories, we concluded that certain material did not measure up to the higher quality required in the products we have been shipping during the last several months. We provided for write-downs of more than $1,500,000 to ensure that these costs would not impact future profits. Steps also were taken during the quarter to reduce fixed and variable costs which will benefit us in the second half of our fiscal year. Verbatim's worldwide employment at the end of December was 1,242 versus 1,538 at the end of 1979, continuing a trend started last quarter of higher sales per employee.

In November, Verbatim Australia Pty. Ltd. began production at its facility near Melbourne, Australia. The opening coincided with the 8th World Computer Conference held in Melbourne where Verbatim had a major exhibit introducing its Datalife diskette products. Both the Datalife introduction and the announcement of the Verbatim Australia facility were enthusiastically received by our Australian distributors, dealers and customers. Production out of our Melbourne plant is right on schedule thanks to the excellent work of the Verbatim people involved in setting up the operations.

Verbatim Corporation and Subsidiaries
Consolidated Statements of Income (Unaudited)

	For the three months ended		For the six months ended	
	December 31 1980	December 31 1979*	December 31 1980	December 31 1979*
Sales	$11,316,000	$12,057,000	$22,650,000	$24,411,000
Costs and Expenses				
Cost of Products Sold	10,308,000	8,724,000	18,639,000	16,713,000
Research & Development	519,000	592,000	968,000	1,146,000
Selling, General & Administrative	2,270,000	2,053,000	4,464,000	4,366,000
Discontinued Product Development Program	—	203,000	—	260,000
Interest	445,000	216,000	794,000	289,000
Total Costs and Expenses	13,542,000	11,788,000	24,865,000	22,774,000
Income (Loss) Before Taxes	(2,226,000)	269,000	(2,215,000)	1,637,000
Provision for Income Taxes	(1,023,000)	85,000	(1,019,000)	761,000
Net Income (Loss)	$(1,203,000)	$ 184,000	$(1,196,000)	$ 876,000
Net Income (Loss) Per Share	$(.56)	$.08	$(.56)	$.40

Consolidated Balance Sheet Highlights (Unaudited)

	December 31 1980	December 31 1979*
Total Current Assets	$18,994,000	$18,429,000
Total Current Liabilities	$ 9,171,000	$11,079,000
Working Capital	$ 9,823,000	$ 7,350,000
Total Assets	$36,136,000	$30,244,000
Long Term Debt, Less Current Portion	$11,744,000	$ 4,458,000
Shareholders' Equity	$13,256,000	$13,567,000
Shares Outstanding	2,160,000	2,112,000

*Restated to give effect to capitalization of interest costs in accordance with I AS No. 34 which increased net income and net income per share, respectively, by $47,000 and $.02 for the three month period and $73,000 and $.04 for the six month period from amounts shown in the second quarter report for the period ended December 31, 1979.

absolute and relative market share in rapidly growing markets, and outstanding marketing skills. But what about the stock?

The Stock and the PSR

Consider Price Sales Ratios. At its initial public offering price of $17¾, Verbatim had a PSR of 1.70. At its 1981 peak of $29, the stock had a PSR of 2.71. At its low in midsummer 1980, with sales up and the stock price down, Verbatim's PSR was 0.43 (2.1 million shares times $10 per share divided by fiscal 1980 sales of $50.1 million). In January 1981, its PSR was only fractionally higher. At $10, Verbatim's Price Research Ratio was 10.4 (market value divided by annualized research expense).

Taking the Plunge

If Dysan didn't do awfully well, its stock would fall from its lofty PSR of 3.25. If Verbatim merely stayed alive, a major "player"-type corporation could be found to take it over at 10 times research and half of sales. With the quality-control problems behind it, there just wasn't much risk. Illustration 14–6 is my pre-buy valuation plan for Verbatim in February 1981. It has all the pertinent conclusions on it I needed to draw from to reach the final conclusion—to buy.

In the next few months, I bought slightly more than 22,000 shares—just more than 1 percent of Verbatim's total outstanding stock (later on I would buy another 12,000 shares at slightly higher prices.) The stock rose with my buying—usually a good sign (no supply around), costing from $12 to $17 per share.

The rest is sheer ecstasy. Verbatim's stock increased 10 to 15 times in value in only two years. It rose between 175 and 290 percent in the first year alone—a year in which the stock market took an awful beating. Table 14–1 shows the results for 1981 of 100 electronics stocks covered by *The Rosen Electronics letter*. Seventy-two declined. Of the 28 that rose in value, Verbatim topped the list for performance.

The first leg of the rise came as people began to see visible results of the turn-around. Verbatim's earnings rebounded in the third and fourth fiscal quarters of 1981. Orders rose steadily.[16] In the fourth quarter of fiscal 1981, it earned 61 cents per share, or an annual rate of $2.44. At $15 per share, the stock had only been six times earnings based on 1981 year-end's annual rate ($15/$2.44 = 6.2).

---

[16] 1981 Verbatim annual report to shareholders, p. 1.

ILLUSTRATION 14–6

February 15, 1981

VERBATIM CORPORATION PRE-BUY
VALUATION—PROJECTION*

Buy thru:
OCT: H&Q, GLD,
Paine, BEHR, DW
Kidder, Merrill

1. Verbatim has 2.16 million shares at a price of $13.5. Market value = $29 million.
2. Last 12 months' revenue = $48 million
   PSR = 0.60 o.k.
   Last 12 months' R&D = $2.132 million
   PRR = 13.6—barely o.k.

CONCLUSIONS

1. Stock is likely to drop if there are further write-offs. May drop if losses increase next quarter from current levels.
2. Revenue can easily grow at 25 percent average rate over the next five years.
3. Verbatim ought to be averaging 7.5 percent net margins after 36 months.

PROJECTION

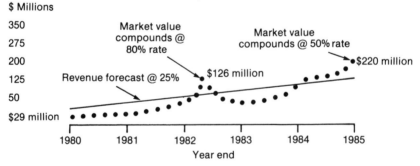

4. Some day this stock ought to sell at 1.5 times sales. Maybe it happens in 1983–84, or maybe in 1985.
5. If they earn 7.5 percent margins and sell at a PSR of 1.5, they will have a price-earnings ratio of 20—reasonable.
6. If I buy $0.5 million of stock and in the process the stock rises to 18, I will have bought at about an average of $15.75/share. This means I will have bought 31,700 shares, or 1.47 percent of the total business.

---

* Fisher Investments, standard procedure.

TABLE 14–1
Rosen 100 Stock Performance, Full-Year 1981, by Rank

Rank	Company	December 31, 1980	December 31, 1981	Year 1981 Percent Gain
1	Verbatim	$ 17.00	$46.75	175.00%
2	MCI Communications	13.25	34.00	156.60
3	Tandon	16.00	28.50	78.12
4	Northern Telecom	28.75	48.50	68.69
5	Unitrode	19.50	30.50	56.41
6	Computer & Comm Technology	16.00	25.00	56.25
7	Scientific-Atlanta	18.62	27.00	44.96
8	General Instrument	31.00	44.25	42.74
9	Intelligent Systems	16.00	22.50	40.62
10	Johnson, E F	17.50	24.00	37.14
11	Tandy	24.68	33.75	36.70
12	Dysan	13.50	18.37	36.11
13	Communications Industries	25.00	33.00	32.00
14	Comsat	48.12	63.50	31.94
15	CTS	22.00	28.75	30.68
16	Beckman Instruments	36.87	46.00	24.74
17	Ducommun	20.41	24.12	18.16
18	General Tel & Electronics	27.25	32.00	17.43
19	California Microwave	10.50	12.12	15.47
20	Sony	15.50	17.50	12.90
21	Intertec Data Systems	22.50	24.62	9.44
22	Kyoto Ceramic	31.25	34.12	9.20
23	Tracor	24.83	26.87	8.22
24	Varian	28.12	30.25	7.55
25	Siliconix	20.00	21.25	6.25
26	Alpha Industries	26.62	28.00	5.16
27	Avantek	16.25	17.00	4.61
28	E-systems	50.00	50.12	.24
29	AVNET	46.36	46.12	−.51
30	ITT	30.00	29.75	−.83
31	AMP	51.87	50.87	−1.92
32	Hazeltine	27.75	26.50	−4.50
33	Augat	27.16	25.25	−7.05
34	Superscope	3.50	3.25	−7.14
35	Dynascan	7.28	6.75	−7.29
36	Commodore International	49.75	46.00	−7.53
37	Drexler Technology	12.50	11.50	−8.00
38	Tektronix	61.12	55.00	−10.02
39	American Microsystems	29.25	26.00	−11.11
40	Hewlett-Packard	44.75	39.62	−11.45
41	Corning Glass	59.62	51.87	−12.99
42	Kollmorgen	24.83	21.37	−13.92
43	Fluke, John	23.57	19.25	−18.32
44	Computervision	40.25	32.50	−19.25
45	Analogic	32.00	25.75	−19.53
46	Motorola	73.00	57.75	−20.89
47	Harris	52.12	41.12	−21.10
48	M/A-COM	32.12	25.25	−21.40
49	Varo	10.25	8.00	−21.95
50	Perkin-Elmer	34.75	27.00	−22.30

continued

TABLE 14–1 (concluded)

Rank	Company	December 31, 1980	December 31, 1981	Year 1981 Percent Gain
51	Arrow Electronics	20.62	16.00	−22.42
52	Loral	43.25	33.50	−22.54
53	Vishay Intertechnology	12.85	9.87	−23.19
54	Plantronics	21.75	16.25	−25.28
55	Pioneer Standard	16.50	12.25	−25.75
56	Sanders Associates	62.50	45.87	−26.60
57	Regency Electronics	14.50	10.62	−26.72
58	Watkins-Johnson	40.00	29.00	−27.50
59	Teradyne	48.37	35.00	−27.64
60	Wyle Laboratories	11.25	8.12	−27.77
61	Energy Conversion Devices	16.75	11.75	−29.85
62	Anthem Electronics	19.50	13.50	−30.76
63	Rolm	46.75	32.00	−31.55
64	Raytheon	55.00	37.37	−32.04
65	Western Digital	9.87	6.62	−32.91
66	Cherry Electrical Products	16.50	11.00	−33.33
67	Texas Instruments	120.75	80.50	−33.33
68	International Rectifier	18.75	12.37	−34.00
69	Apple Computer	34.12	22.12	−35.16
70	Silicon systems	11.00	6.87	−37.50
71	RCA	29.37	18.25	−37.87
72	Analog Devices	28.20	17.50	−37.94
73	SEE Technologies	23.18	14.25	−38.52
74	Cado Systems	25.00	14.75	−41.00
75	KLA Instruments	32.00	18.50	−42.18
76	Genrad	24.00	13.87	−42.18
77	Standard Microsystems	10.87	6.25	−42.52
78	Zenith Radio	19.50	11.12	−42.94
79	Intel	40.25	22.50	−44.09
80	GCA	51.16	27.37	−46.49
81	Wavetek	19.50	10.25	−47.43
82	Veeco Instruments	27.41	14.25	−48.02
83	Coherent	29.50	15.25	−48.30
84	Advanced Micro Devices	34.50	17.62	−48.91
85	Applied Materials	27.66	14.00	−49.38
86	Nicolet Instrument	21.62	10.75	−50.28
87	Finnigan	15.62	7.50	−52.00
88	National Semiconductor	40.25	19.12	−52.48
89	Materials Research	33.93	15.75	−53.59
90	Marshall Industries	23.57	10.87	−53.86
91	Eeco	16.62	7.62	−54.13
92	AVX	30.50	13.87	−54.50
93	Kratos	20.25	9.00	−55.55
94	Micro Mask	17.00	7.50	−55.88
95	E-H International	5.25	2.12	−59.52
96	Spectra-Physics	53.75	21.25	−60.46
97	Harvey Group	7.75	3.00	−61.29
98	Kulicke & Soffa	32.00	12.25	−61.71
99	Solid State Scientific	19.25	6.50	−66.23
100	Threshold Technology	18.75	3.75	−80.00

Source: Reprinted with permission from RELease 1.0, formerly The Rosen Electronics Letter, January 15, 1982.

The Competitive Nappers Wake Up

The financial community was caught completely asleep. Those few who had paid some attention, like Hambrecht & Quist, were surprised at how well Verbatim did:

> Third-quarter results were above our expectations. [April 20, 1981][17]

> Jointly announced with year-end results was Verbatim's application for listing on the American Stock Exchange. [August 5, 1981][18]

> First-quarter results were above our expectations. . . . We are raising our estimates for revenues . . . and for earnings. . . . We recommend purchase for long-term investors at current levels. [October 21, 1981 with the stock at $35][19]

> Increased expenses in the quarter for new capital equipment and for research and development reduced the sequential quarter-to-quarter margin gains. Nevertheless, even with heavier expenditures planned in the second half of fiscal 1983, further margin expansion is possible. [January 19, 1982][20]

Hambrecht & Quist did a very good job. They provided investment coverage of the stock the whole way through. They were the first firm to recommend its purchase. Still, by the time Hambrecht & Quist recommended Verbatim's stock, it had more than doubled from the bottom (see Illustration 14–7). This rise occurred simply because the stock had become too depressed—like a coiled spring—in the second half of 1980 and the first half of 1981 (see Chapter 2). Sales for fiscal 1981 were only 7.4 percent higher than for fiscal 1980. Earnings, however, were $1,383,000 for the fourth quarter compared to year-earlier losses of $367,000.[21] Sales were much more stable than the earnings (hence the usefulness of PSRs in analyzing the stock).

With the turn-around in hand, Verbatim announced a stock offering—to raise some cash. (If something unexpected should go wrong, cash would be absolutely essential.) There was little financial-community faith in a company which so recently had lost money. The offering was not well received.

In the weeks before the offering (possibly out of fear of the offering and a lack of faith in the company), the stock dropped. On Sep-

---

[17] Hambrecht & Quist update on Verbatim, April 20, 1981.

[18] Hambrecht & Quist update on Verbatim, August 5, 1981.

[19] Hambrecht & Quist update on Verbatim, October 21, 1981.

[20] Hambrecht & Quist update on Verbatim, January 19, 1982.

[21] Verbatim news release, August 5, 1981.

ILLUSTRATION 14–7
Verbatim Corporation

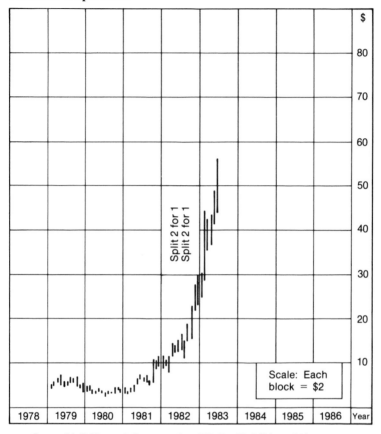

Source: M. C. Horsey & Company, Inc., P.O. Box H, Salisbury, Md. 21801.

tember 3, 1981, Verbatim sold 350,000 new shares at $23⅔ in a public offering. With the offering out of the way and a safe nest egg of cash in hand, the stock immediately recovered back to the mid-30s. From there it soared higher every quarter.

Illustration 14–8 is a copy of quarterly bar charts from Verbatim's first quarter fiscal 1982 shareholder's report. The charts show the relative stability of sales and research expenses compared to other variables in Verbatim's financial statements. Compare these to the charts (Illustration 14–9) that appeared in Verbatim's second quarter fiscal 1983 (ended December 31, 1982) shareholder's statement. The later results show enough steady progress to persuade masses of the financial community to part with money. Verbatim stock continued rising.

ILLUSTRATION 14–8
Quarterly Bar Charts from Verbatim's First Quarter 1981 Shareholder's Report

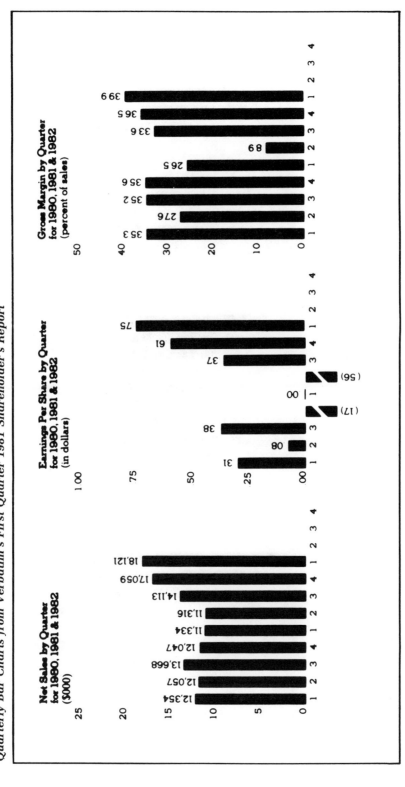

ILLUSTRATION 14–8 (concluded)

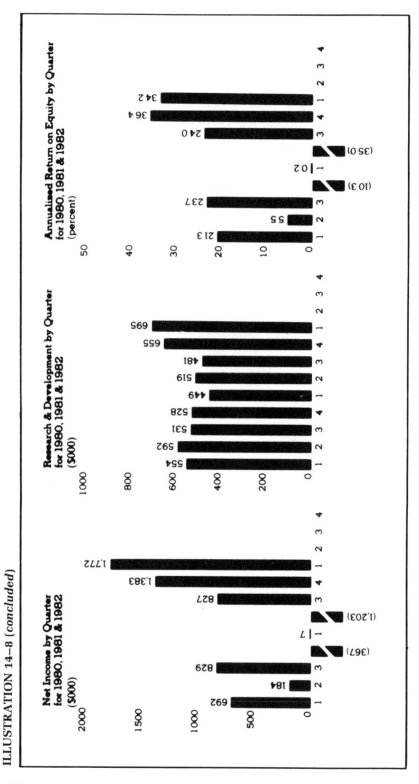

ILLUSTRATION 14–9
Charts from Verbatim's Shareholder's Quarterly Report, Second Quarter Fiscal 1982

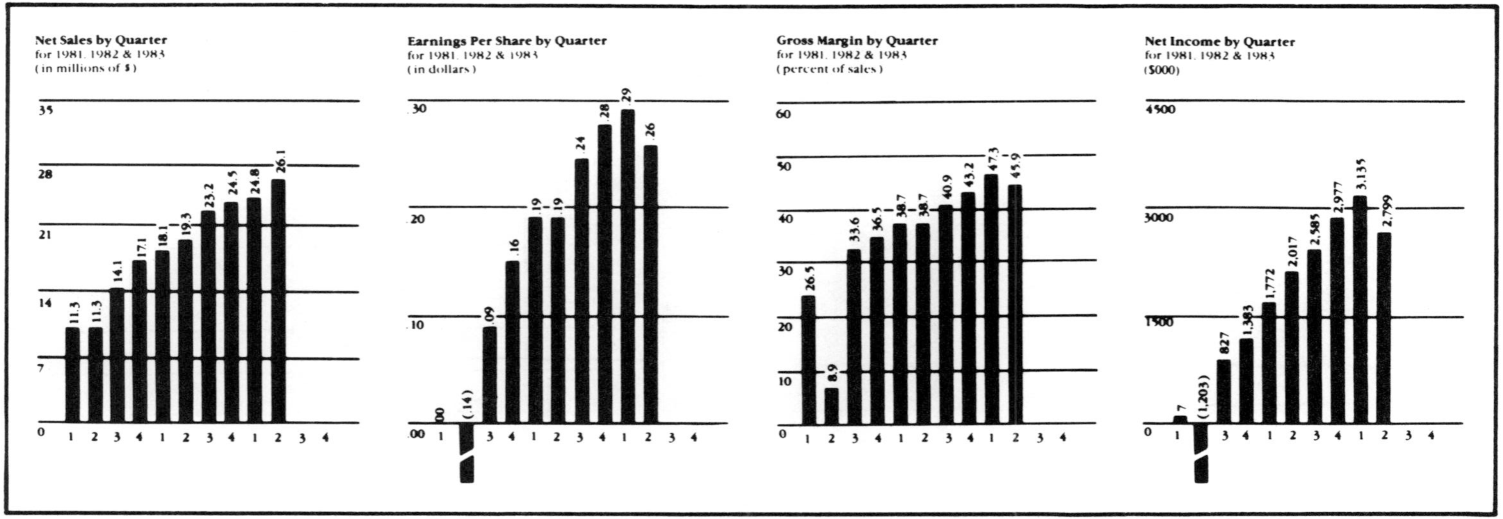

Net Sales by Quarter
for 1981, 1982 & 1983
(in millions of $)

Earnings Per Share by Quarter
for 1981, 1982 & 1983
(in dollars)

Gross Margin by Quarter
for 1981, 1982 & 1983
(percent of sales)

Net Income by Quarter
for 1981, 1982 & 1983
($000)

191

ILLUSTRATION 14–9 (concluded)

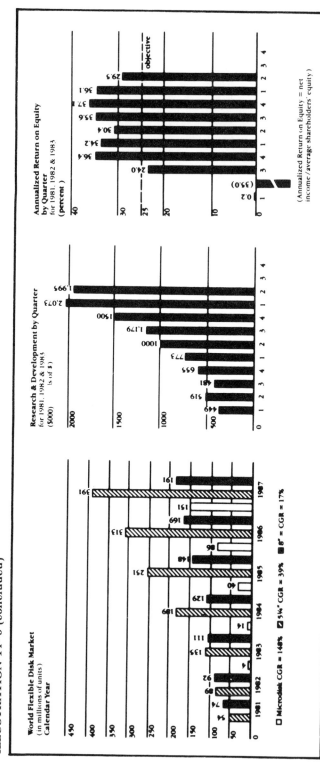

Smiling All the Way to the Bank

Between two stock splits and another offering, Verbatim had 12 million shares of stock outstanding by the spring of 1983. Quarter to quarter, Verbatim reported beautiful operating results. Profit margins exceeded 10 percent. Sales broke through the $100 million annual rate level. With high profit margins, the price-earnings ratio looked merely "high" with the stock between $35 and $55 (remember the stock splits). But the PSR looked astronomical at slightly over 6.0. (Twelve-plus million shares times $55 = $660 million market value divided by $100+ million in sales gives a PSR of 6.)

In 1983, I sold all my stock. One of the only stocks to go public in the low-equity markets of 1979, Verbatim had gone full cycle. It swung from being in favor with a PSR of 2¾ to being out of favor with a PSR of less than 0.5 to being back in favor with a PSR of 6.0. It had all taken just a few years for the stock to go from high to cheap to very high. Verbatim itself, once just a little "disco baby," grew, meanwhile, into a $100 million Super Company with a balance sheet of gold. I think the world of Malcolm Northrup and Wiley Carter, Geoff Bate and Harry Fekkes. I wish them well. They won't need luck. They're very capable men. I appreciate the opportunity to have been able to hitch my financial wagon up with theirs. I also appreciate the free enterprise system that allows me to be gone when a PSR gets too high.

Chapter 15

California Microwave—
Ride the Wave

Early History

California Microwave was founded by Dr. David Leeson in Sunnyvale, California, in 1968. California Microwave designs, makes, and markets microwave technology-based and related electronic equipment.[1]

California Microwave began by pioneering microwave signal-source components to meet specialized relay and airborne radar applications. It then developed signal-source components for radio modernization systems that permit channel capacity to be increased and maintenance costs to be decreased while leaving in place equipment with a useful economic life. With the development of its CM41 microwave generator, California Microwave quickly became the country's largest supplier of microwave-modernization systems.

Today, its products are used in telecommunications and defense applications including terrestrial and satellite transmission of voice and computer data, television and radio network distribution, and radar and military electronic countermeasure systems. Customers include the Bell System, other common carriers, U.S. government departments and agencies, radio-broadcast and wire-service networks, satellite common carriers, and foreign governments.[2]

---

[1] Prospectus to January 1981 stock offering, p. 4.

[2] 1982 SEC Form 10-K pp. 1–6.

The microwave area of electronic technology has expanded rapidly in recent years. FCC decisions throughout the 1970s broadened the potential telecommunications markets.[3] This evolution was enhanced by the parallel evolution of computer technology that required increased data communication capability.

California Microwave made an initial public stock offering in 1972 and has traded over the counter ever since. The company grew rapidly, and its stock was an outstanding performer in the mid-1970s. Below are sales and earnings for the five fiscal years ending June 30, 1979.[4]

	1979	1978	1977	1976	1975
Sales	$40,036	$33,167	$26,061	$18,062	$10,753
Earnings	2,368	1,889	1,496	829	526
Earnings per share	1.17	.96	.78	.46	.29

Note: All numbers in 000s except per-share data. Not adjusted for subsequent stock dividends.

Sales and earnings grew at 30 percent and 35 percent—respectable rates for the late 1970s, a time when many on Wall Street spoke of "stagflation." Throughout most of 1979, the stock traded between 15 and 18, giving the stock a PSR between 0.92 and 1.10—certainly not excessively high. Its price-earnings ratio varied between 15.6 and 18.75—again not outrageously high by most standards. Because the stock was not excessively valued and the company had a consistent record of growth, it received support and recommendation from institutional investors and brokerage firms. Illustration 15–1 on page 188 is the body of a typical "summary form" brokerage-firm report from I.. F. Rothschild, Unterberg, Towbin recommending the stock.

In November 1979, California Microwave announced that earnings in the second fiscal quarter (ending December 31, 1979) would be below the prior year's levels, and earnings for the fiscal year would likely decline as well. The earnings decline was attributed to larger-than-expected production start-up costs in the satellite-communications area coupled with unexpected completion of continuous production of the CM41 microwave-radio-modernization product.[5]

---

[3] Ibid.

[4] 1979 annual report to shareholders, p. 16. Per-share data is accurate in 1979 but does not reflect subsequent changes.

[5] Company announcement, second-quarter shareholder's report, and 1980 annual report to shareholders, p. 2.

ILLUSTRATION 15–1

October 24, 1979

CALIFORNIA MICROWAVE
CMIC (BID 17¼)

California Microwave recently reported 1st quarter earnings for the period ending September 30. Revenues increased 24 percent to $9.9 million, net income increased 25 percent to $608,000, and E.P.S. rose 21 percent to 29 cents versus 24 cents. Of greater importance than this report was the decision by the FCC on October 18 to deregulate a portion of the satellite communications earth terminal market for broadcast and CATV transmission. While the decision was expected, its timing had been somewhat uncertain. The company had received three contracts totaling $9.6 million for single-source procurement for receive-only earth station (small-dish six-foot antennas) from Associated Press, Mutual Broadcasting Systems, and Muzak. The inclusion of these contracts boosts backlog to a record $34.2 million. Additional contracts from these three customers plus other potential contracts in the satellite programming and transmission market are expected over the next year.

We are maintaining our E.P.S. estimate for the current June fiscal year of $1.40 versus $1.17 and are using a preliminary fiscal 1981 estimate of $1.75. We believe the company represents a very attractive small situation in the telecommunications equipment and satellite communications market.

Bruce S. Seltzer

ADDITIONAL INFORMATION AVAILABLE UPON REQUEST

By permission of L. F. Rothschild, Unterberg, Towbin.

The stock "gap-opened" lower—moving from 18 down to 13. The shoe had dropped. With sales up and the price down, the stock had a significantly lower PSR at 0.64 (2.063 million shares times the stock price of $13 = $26.8 million market value: PSR equals $26.8 divided by last 12 months' sales of $41.9 million = 0.64).[6]

This Company Was Worth Further Investigation

California Microwave had been highly regarded for years by the financial community and by engineers. In November, I studied the material I had on file. I sent for and received additional material from

---

[6] Numbers calculated from shareholder's quarterly and annual reports.

the company and initiated my normal library research (see Chapter 12).

I identified and interviewed executives from four microwave companies—Avantek, Frequency Sources, Omni Spectra (not to be confused with the publication by the same name), and Zeta Labs. Omni Spectra was a company with a spotty record for mixed results.[7] Yet I noted that Frequency Sources made a tender offer to buy all of Omni Spectra at a PSR of 0.76 (1.24 million Frequency Sources shares times $16 per share = $19.8 million market value: PSR = $19.8 million divided by sales of $26 million = 0.76). The impression I got when I asked around was that Dave Leeson, California Microwave's founder, president, chairman, and chief executive officer, was a bit of a wild man—single, playboyish, and oriented toward the bizarre hobby of race-car driving. (I later learned most of this was an impassioned impression of the moment only. He was single and did race cars. Wild or a playboy?—No.) I also talked with two suppliers to California Microwave, both of whom saw erratic buying from the company. Volume wasn't down, but the mix of purchases seemed to be shifting (CM41 phasing out, while the CA-42 and satellite business were gearing up).

I also got the impression from these discussions that Leeson was quite competent when he wanted to be. Most of these people thought that Leeson had become complacent—that he was rich enough and was not watching affairs within California Microwave as closely as possible.

On December 7, 1979 (the anniversary of Pearl Harbor Day), I met for the first time with Philip Otto, executive vice president and chief financial officer of California Microwave. Otto explained to me that the announced reduction in earnings resulted from reduced orders for the CM41 radio-modernization product coupled with greater-than-expected start-up costs associated with the satellite earth terminal product. The company expected additional orders for the CM41 but at slower rates than in the past.

There were some 43,000 "sockets" where the CM41 could be used to modernize Bell System TD-2 microwave radios—to date, California Microwave had filled about 30,000 of the sockets. For years, the Bell System had rapidly replaced sockets. Then, suddenly, with only about 13,000 sockets left, orders tapered from a gush to a trickle. The Bell System would replace those other sockets in time—but not in time for California Microwave to continue regular production of CM41s. They expected their troubles to be short-lived, how-

---

[7] Hambrecht & Quist report states: "For some time, Omni Spectra has had mixed results."

ever, and to more than make up for them with the oncoming strength of new products.

I told Otto the concerns that were raised by Dave Leeson's image as a man who was less concerned than he should be about his business. Otto declined to comment on whether Leeson had put in less attention in the past than he should. He was very specific that Leeson was currently very focused on the business. He stressed over and over again that this concern would not be a problem in the future.

I left my meeting pleased with what I had seen. There were another 43,000 sockets where a new product, the CA-42 could go (the same ones the CM41 had gone in, so the company knew the market well), and their satellite earth terminal product line could, in time, be bigger than everything else put together. Regardless of the short term, I was convinced their product lines had a good future. I still wanted to meet Leeson to relieve my concerns about his dedication.

As late as February 1980, management would maintain that third-quarter results (ending March 31, 1980) would be "somewhat below last year's third quarter, but the fourth quarter ending June 30, 1980, is expected to compare favorably with earnings recorded during the same period in fiscal 1979."[8] Within this background, the stock began to recover somewhat, averaging about 16 in January.

I began to become nervous that the stock might get away from me (my first mistake: never, ever rush). On January 11, 1980, I stuck my toe in the water. To get over my nervousness, I bought my first stock at 15¾. It was a mistake. I wasn't ready and the PSR wasn't low enough. (By now, with the information in this case history, you should be able to figure out for yourself what the PSR was.) My nervousness was overcoming my self-discipline. Later in January I bought a little more.

Illustration 15–2 is my very hurried pre-buy valuation—projection from January 1980. With a little stock "under my belt," I thought I would feel content to continue more slowly with my investigation. Instead, I felt just as nervous owning even a small amount of a stock I didn't know enough about and wasn't sure was a Super Company/Super Stock.

Continuing my library work, I learned more about the technology and the commercial costs involved with microwave applications. I sought additional information from knowledgeable individuals in the electronics industry and the financial community. On February 15, 1980, I finally met with Dave Leeson. I was impressed. He was open and honest with me about the company's problems. He had no hesitancy to admit, without any prompting on my part, that he had not focused enough on business. He said he had done some

---

[8] Second-quarter shareholder's report, February 1980.

ILLUSTRATION 15–2

January 11, 1980

CALIFORNIA MICROWAVE PRE-BUY
VALUATION—PROJECTION

Buy Thru:
OTC: H&Q, LFR,

1. CMIC has 2.063 million shares at a price of $15.75. Market value = $32.5 million.
2. Last 12 months' revenue = $41.8 million
   PSR = 0.78—barely o.k.
   Last 12 months' R&D = $2.6 million
   PRR = 12.5—barely o.k.

CONCLUSIONS

1. Stock may drop unless the satellite area and CA-42 overshadows the CM41 in the fourth quarter. Stock may drop if earnings in third quarter are worse than expected.
2. Revenue probably can grow at 25 percent average rate over the next five years????
3. Company ought to be averaging 5 percent net margins after 36 months???

PROJECTION

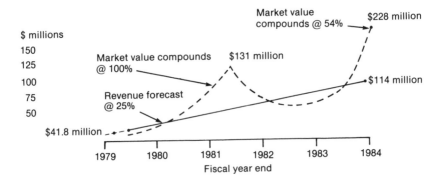

4. Some day CMIC ought to sell at 2.0 times sales. Maybe it happens in 1981–82, or maybe in 1984.
5. If they earn 5 percent margins and sell at a PSR of 2.0, they will have a price-earnings ratio of 40—aggressive, but doable in a Bull Market.
6. Just buy a little—toe in the water. Buy more later—higher or lower.

real soul-searching recently to see if he wanted to spend his life running a business. The answer was that he did.

Leeson is physically unforgettable—short and stocky with unending energy and long hair. What he lacks in physical stature, he makes up for in vitality, sensitivity, and integrity. I felt comfortable that he could listen well and, at the same time, gain the admiration and respect of his followers. His business problems were simple and common to many other businesses with a single-core-product technology. The company had suffered a growth glitch. In the classic manner (see Chapter 2), he had:

Overestimated the product life cycle of the CM41 product.

Underestimated how long it would take to get next-generation products up to speed (particularly the satellite earth terminals and the CA-42—which goes into the same market as the CM41).

While he had overestimated the product life cycle of the CM41, at the time he was unaware how much he had done so. Of course, neither was I. Leaving the meeting, I felt comfortable with Leeson and sure he would overcome his problems. I believed next-quarter's earnings might be poor to almost nonexistent (I had no idea how bad they would be). I thought the stock would hold up under another quarter of bad earnings. After all—he had "telegraphed" a down quarter in his shareholder's quarterly. I had no idea the stock was about to crumble. I bought a little more stock at 15. I still had not fully committed to the stock and perceived myself as still learning about the company.

On March 13, 1980, I had an opportunity to meet Lawrence Thielen, then chairman and chief executive officer of Avantek. Avantek was Wall Street's darling in the microwave area—and perhaps rightfully so. It is an outstanding company—a Super Company. Its stock's PSR was more than 2½, which was very high at the time. (See Chapter 4 on PSRs of technology companies in this time frame.)

Avantek was having an informational luncheon for a planned stock offering. Fortunately for me, the luncheon had unassigned seating except for the company officers. There must have been a half dozen lunch tables or more—each with eight place mats. Mustering up my courage, I quickly introduced myself to Mr. Thielen and asked if I could sit with him at lunch.

During lunch, I listened attentively while he talked about his business and industry. People sitting around the table asked questions. Thielen answered. I was very impressed. He is obviously a very competent man. When asked what he thought of California Microwave, he laughed and indicated that Avantek intended to enter the microwave-radio-modernization market. "If Leeson doesn't pay better attention to his business, he might not have one." Other people around the table snickered. Around this table, there was tremendous confidence in Avantek and no confidence in California Microwave.

Oops! The Other Shoe Drops

On March 19, 1980, California Microwave announced it expected to take an inventory write-down of approximately $1 million associated with the CM41 product line, resulting in a loss for its third fiscal quarter. They indicated earnings for the year would be "substantially lower" than the prior year. They indicated that in the last month, the order rate for CM41s had deteriorated further. From the wording of the announcement, there seemed to be some ambiguity as to the exact size of the write-down.[9]

The other shoe had dropped. The stock "gap-opened" lower, moving from 13 down to 9. It would bottom out at 8½ a few days later. The stock moved between 8½ and 10½ over the next few weeks. Most interested parties seemed nervous as the company indicated they were assessing the magnitude of their problems and didn't yet know exactly how much the write-down would be. (See Chapter 2 for a description of the typical process companies go through at this time.) The $1 million figure had been merely an estimate.

During this same period, management was reshuffled. Two senior officers were encouraged to resign, and two existing vice presidents were given additional responsibilities (a process described in Chapter 2). Gilbert Johnson was named to the new post of executive vice president-operations, and Howard Oringer was named the new president of the Telecommunications Division.[10]

Illustration 15–3 on page 194 is a chart of the stock for several years up until the end of March 1980. It is not a pretty picture.

I was troubled. I don't like it when a stock I've just bought runs right through my buy price—headed lower. It would be easy to blame California Microwave management for all this. Only a month after my recent visit with Dave Leeson, the company was announcing major problems. It would be easy to think, "If they didn't understand the problems earlier, they must be poor managers. Maybe they don't understand their problems now." (See Chapter 2 for a description of this fallacious psychology.) But this is the time, with the

---

[9] *Electronic News*, March 31, 1980, and company news release, March 19, 1980.

[10] Third-quarter shareholder's report, May 1980.

ILLUSTRATION 15–3
California Microwave

Source: Mansfield Stock Chart Service, Jersey City, N.J. 07306.

stock down, to try to forgive management its mistakes (Chapter 2, again).

Most of the next month, I slowly reflected on what I had learned over the past few months. What would I do—buy more stock in a company that might be a Super Company going through a growth glitch or sell out the tiny position I had on the basis the management didn't know what they were doing?

Most of what I had learned indicated that California Microwave was a Super Company. The microwave market was made up of "niches" served by different vendors. Most of these niches were growing quite rapidly. In their niche areas, California Microwave had a high absolute and relative market share. The prospects for long-term above-average future growth at California Microwave appeared quite good.

Top management was very capable. Granted, Leeson had gotten a little off the track in the late 1970s, perhaps affected by so much success, but he was fully back on track now. The recent negative comments of so many people in the industry and the financial community were overshadowed in my mind by their own comments of so many earlier years and my own assessment of Leeson and Otto.

On the critical aspect of profit margins—the company had their long-term history to their credit. They had earned good margins before. This was clearly not a Sleeping Dog. They had the stated intent to earn comparable margins again. With their market share and the prospects for their markets, there was no reason to think they wouldn't get close. Combining margin analysis with a "haircut" on their stated margin goals, I envisioned that in time they could earn 5 percent margins.

California Microwave seemed to pass the test, even if just barely, of meeting the profit-margin hurdle to be a Super Company. Coupled

ILLUSTRATION 15–4

April 23, 1980

CALIFORNIA MICROWAVE PRE-BUY
VALUATION—PROJECTION

Buy thru:
OTC: H&Q, LFR

1. CMIC has 2.063 million shares at a price of $9. Market value = $18.6 million.
2. Last 12 months' revenue = $41.8 million
   PSR = 0.44 o.k.

   Last 12 months' R&D = $2.6 million
   PRR = 7.2 o.k.

CONCLUSIONS

1. Stock may drop unless the satellite area and CA-42 overshadows the CM41 in the fourth quarter. Stock may drop if losses persist in the first two quarters of fiscal 1981.
2. Revenue can easily grow at 25 percent average rate over the next five years.
3. They ought to be averaging 5 percent net margins in 36 months.

PROJECTION

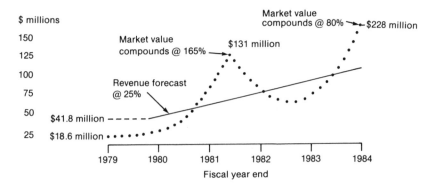

4. Some day CMIC ought to sell at 2.0 times sales. Maybe it happens in 1981–82, or maybe in 1984.
5. If they earn 5 percent margins and sell at a PSR of 2.0, they will have a price-earnings ratio of 40—aggressive, but doable in a Bull Market.
6. If I spend $300,000 and the stock rises to $12 as I'm buying, I will have an average cost of about $10.5. This means I will have bought about 28,500 shares or 1.4 percent of CMIC.

with strong growth prospects and a strong assessment of management, the company seemed to be, in fact, a Super Company which had grown too rapidly for its experience level and suffered from a growth glitch. What about the stock?

At $9, the stock had a PSR of only 0.44 (2.063 million shares × $9 per share = A market value of $18.6 million: PSR = $18.6 ÷ last 12 months' sales of $41.8 million = 0.44). The stock had a Price Research Ratio of 7.2 (Market value of $18.6 million ÷ research as provided from SEC Form 10-K, including third-party-sponsored research, of $2.6 million = 7.2.)[11] It seemed appropriate to commit heavily to the stock, but what about the timing issue?

Taking the Plunge

On April 29, 1980, I was attending a week-long technology conference for investors put on by a San Francisco brokerage firm. Leeson was there to make a presentation on California Microwave. The skepticism among the crowd was so thick you could cut it with a knife. Leeson had a smile on his face as he came to the podium. That didn't stop more than half the crowd from leaving. They just got up and left. The rest mostly sat and stared blankly. Some read newspapers.

I had talked with several individuals earlier. People had received too much bad news in the last six months. One fellow made fun of Leeson's size, saying, "Dave just isn't big enough for the job." Once regarded as a great company with a great management, investors were simply not interested in California Microwave.

This Dave Leeson was the same one I had seen in his office in Sunnyvale—an honest, sincere, and sensitive man. He commented that he was pleased to announce "the nondilutive" acquisition of Satellite Transmission Systems, a New York supplier of turnkey digital satellite earth stations in which they already owned a small minority stake.

As I heard the word *nondilutive*, I knew what I had to do. I left my tape recorder running and got up and walked out myself. I must have looked just like all the others who walked out. I walked across the street to a pay phone and placed an order (with the firm that had put on the conference) to buy California Microwave. With the order working, I returned to the conference. This purchase was not totally spur-of-the-moment. The prior week, I had revised my pre-buy valuation—projection for California Microwave (see Illustration 15–4).

I bought stock over several weeks. On May 8, 1980, California

---

[11] SEC Form 10-K from fiscal 1979 and subsequent quarters' shareholder's quarterly reports.

Microwave announced a loss of $958,000 for the third fiscal quarter accompanied by a $2.1 million write-down of inventory. The announcement indicated backlog and orders were down for the quarter also.[12] The stock continued to trade in the range of $9 to 10½.

By May 31, I had purchased for clients and then myself more than 27,000 shares. This came to a little over 1.3 percent of California Microwave's total outstanding shares. The average cost of this purchase was only about $295,000—it doesn't take a lot of money to buy a good stake in a low-PSR stock. (Over the next several years, I bought several additional pieces of stock whenever it weakened.)

Riding the Wave

From May 1980, the stock rose ever higher, quarter to quarter, nonstop for a year. Operations improved steadily. One year after my last major purchases, the stock was at $32—almost three times my cost. Why did the stock do so well? First, it rose because it had been too low. California Microwave is a great company—a Super Company. Any Super Company selling at PSRs below 0.75 is simply too cheap. Wall Street, which had previously loved the stock, had come to show it no regard. In time, they realized again that the company was not so bad—then they realized it was pretty good. This all took time. What made it happen?

An important swing factor for California Microwave was their backlog of shippable orders. Illustration 15–5 is the backlog at year-end for the five fiscal years ending June 30, 1980, and for the nine months ending March 3, 1981. It is obvious Dave Leeson was again paying attention to his business. The order rate had boomed. Orders and backlog rose steadily quarter to quarter throughout fiscal 1981. Wall Street had come to expect less from California Microwave.

Major increases in backlog were announced on June 4 ($4.9 million), August 29 ($8.2 million), September 12 ($3.1 million), October 15 ($6.6 million), October 16 ($1.5 million), October 20 ($1.3 million), November 7 ($6.9 million), and December 16 ($15.5 million). In less than six months, backlog had risen from $28.3 million to $68 million.[13] This is quite a swing for a company operating at an approximate $40 million annual rate.

With all the unexpected good news, the stock had nowhere to go but up. Sales followed orders with a time lag, and profits followed last of all (see explanation of this process in Chapters 1 and 2). Illustrations 15–6 and 15–7 are charts for sales and profits.

---

[12] Company announcement, May 8, 1980, and shareholder's quarterly report, May 1980.

[13] Miscellaneous company news releases from June to December 1980.

ILLUSTRATION 15–5
California Microwave backlog ($ millions)

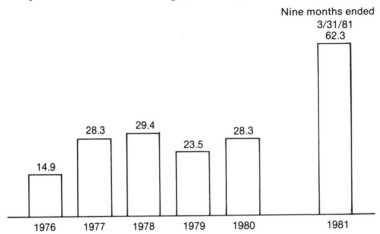

California Microwave backlog ($ millions)

Nine months ended
3/31/81
62.3

28.3   29.4   28.3
              23.5
14.9

1976   1977   1978   1979   1980   1981

California Microwave backlog review ($ millions)

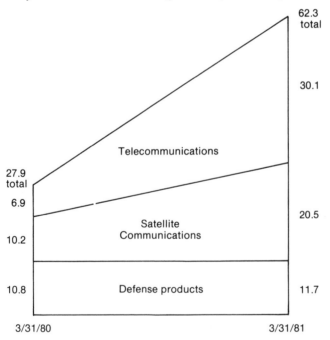

62.3
total

30.1

Telecommunications

27.9
total

6.9

Satellite
Communications   20.5

10.2

10.8   Defense products   11.7

3/31/80   3/31/81

ILLUSTRATION 15–6
California Microwave Sales ($ millions)

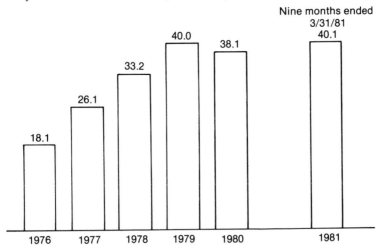

ILLUSTRATION 15–7
California Microwave Net Income ($ millions)

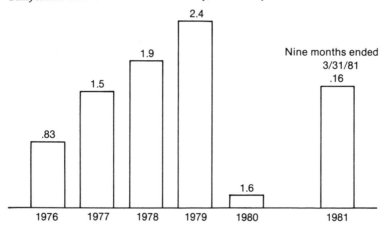

New Blood

During the fall of 1980, California Microwave brought in two additional senior managers: Fred Storke to the new position of vice president-engineering and chief technical officer and George Spillane as the new vice president-finance and chief financial officer.[14] In

---

[14] Second-quarter shareholder's report, February 1981.

George was a new presence with whom investors of the "blame the company for the disappointment" type could relate. As a new man, he could be their contact without concern that he had been part of the process that had "let them down."

Margins in early fiscal 1981 were subnormal for a Super Company. But California Microwave suffered typical low margins on its newer products—the type associated with the early stages of any product life cycle (see Chapters 1 and 2). They suffered these low margins in a number of product lines at once. This was particularly true of the satellite earth stations and the CA-42 product line (which was sold into the same TD-2 radio network of which the CM41 had been a part). The stock reacted strongly, however, because Wall Street hadn't expected earnings at all.

On January 19, 1981, California Microwave sold 440,000 shares of stock at $20.25 in a public offering, raising $8.2 million cash.[15] This process—a stock offering shortly after an earnings glitch—is common among Super Companies. (See the Verbatim case history in Chapter 14 for a comparable example.) Management sees the opportunity to raise cash as a bird in the hand. They know they might be able to get a higher price later (a bird in the bush) but prefer some cash infusion immediately. They still suffer from the insecurity of the long period of problems they have just come out from under. They themselves weren't convinced there might not be more problems still ahead.

Progress was steady over the next several years. Below are sales and earnings for the four fiscal years ending June 30, 1983.[16]

	1983	1982	1981	1980	1979
Sales	$101,209	$88,615	$56,971	$38,066	$40,036
Earnings	5,375	4,154	2,521	158	2,368
Earnings per share	.65	.52	.35	.02	.39

Note: All numbers in 000s except per-share data

The improvement from 1980 is dramatic. Comparing these numbers to the numbers earlier in the chapter for 1975 to 1979, 1980 seems like a typical glitch along the path of California Microwave's growth from a tiny $10 million company to a $100+ million company.

---

[15] Second-quarter shareholder's report, February 1981 and the prospectus to the stock offering, January 19, 1981.

[16] Company news release, August 16, 1983, and 1982 annual report to shareholders.

   While a paucity of brokerage-firm reports existed on the company from December 1979 through September 1980, after that time— with earnings back in hand, the stock received consistently increasing attention from Wall Street. With the normal correction in place, the stock treaded water throughout most of 1982, drifting slightly lower in the face of a major Bear Market. Meanwhile, the company continued to grow.

   In the summer of 1982, with a market value of $66 million— more than three and a half times higher than its value in the spring of 1980, the stock still only had a PSR of 0.74 compared to its then current sales of $90 million. This provided another major buying opportunity.

   When the Bull Market began in August 1982, California Microwave surged ahead. Illustration 15–8 is a chart of the stock in its full rise from $3 (adjusted for subsequent splits) up to $27—an eightfold

ILLUSTRATION 15–8
California Microwave

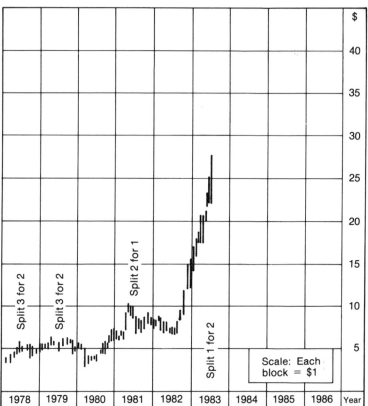

Source: M. C. Horsey & Company, Inc., P.O. Box H, Salisbury, Md. 21801.

ILLUSTRATION 15–9

Future Looking Brighter at California Microwave

After a rocky fiscal 1980, revenues and profits have rebounded and single-sideband radio could become a major new line

Life in the fast lane isn't without its bumps and detours. Since its founding in 1968, California Microwave Inc., based in Sunnyvale, Calif., had set a rapid growth pace, piling up 25 percent compounded annual growth of both sales and earnings. The company seemed likely to continue growing at that rate—until it collided with its 1980 fiscal year.

A pretax inventory writedown of $2 million, accelerated production startup costs in its satellite-communication business, and a drop in sales stemming from completion of continuous production of its CM—41 microwave-radio-modernization product combined to shrink 1980's profits to $158,000 on sales of $38.1 million from the prior year's net income of $2.4 million on $40 million gross.

Those figures forced a period of self-assessment. The problem, the company determined, was strictly internal: What was needed was a tightening of management and operations. CMI bit that bullet, and its finances appear to be improving. For fiscal 1981, sales reached nearly $57 million and net income shot up to $2.5 million.

In fiscal 1981, CMI also booked orders at a record rate, acquired a satellite supplier in which it had been a venture investor, raised through a stock offering $8.2 million used to trim bank debt by $6 million and provide working capital to fund future growth, and distributed a 100 percent stock dividend in the fourth quarter.

Further signs that the recovery is complete come from results midway through fiscal 1982: Earnings jumped 106 percent in the second quarter on an 83 percent gain in sales. For the half, net income increased 92 percent to $1.8 million, net per share advanced 55 percent to 34 cents, and volume was up 65 percent to just under $41 million—greater than total sales for any prior fiscal year.

Keeping a Rein on Expectations

As heartened as he has reason to be, David Leeson, a company founder and CMI's president, chief executive, and chairman since it opened its doors 14 years ago, keeps a tight rein on his enthusiasm, seasoning it with the caution painfully learned through the trials of 1980. "I remember the nasty lesson of letting expectations get out of hand," he says.

Tough as things were in 1980, however, Leeson says the company was not in danger of going under. "Psychologically we were severely dented, but our balance sheet was never at risk" he states. "There never was a point when going down for the third time was an issue. The key issue was stiffening our backbone and turning this thing around."

Because it supplies the same technology to different kinds of customers, CMI is decentralized on

ILLUSTRATION 15–9 (*continued*)

a market basis. Thus "each of our groups was put in a position [of having] less good news to report than we had convinced ourselves was possible, so there was tremendous pressure to look at the most optimistic side," Leeson recalls. "That inevitably gets you into trouble, and that's the bottom line of what we did to ourselves."

He puts no blame on outside influences or factors. "We got ourselves in trouble on our own," he says, "and we got ourselves out of trouble." Analysis of the setback and what caused it prompted creation of an environment in which "everybody could be cheerfully honest, so the bad news and the good news both could come out and we could sort out where we are and go on from there," Leeson says.

One remedy was to separate operational and financial controls, Leeson says, noting that the former tends to be a critical discipline, the latter a nurturing one. "It's difficult for one person to do both, so we separated those functions," he explains. CMI also reduced expenses, made organizational changes to beef up management, and strengthened financial controls, particularly at the division level.

In letting expectations get out of hand, the company made what Leeson calls short-term mistakes "that centered on an eagerness to rush ahead when our markets weren't quite ready to provide us with that kind of business growth."

Nevertheless, he stresses, "our basic strategy was and is very sound. The business we were in,

we're still in. If I had it to do over again, I'd make sure we put less pressure on ourselves so that internally bad news could flow as easily as the good news, and problem areas could be pinpointed to prevent them from being killers when finally brought to light."

At Technology's Forefront

Still small, with sales of less than $100 million expected for the year ending June 30, CMI is "really in the forefront of the technology in the radio-microwave business," says James McCabe, first vice president for research at Dean Witter Reynolds Inc. in New York. The company is working on upgrading the microwave equipment of the Bell System—CMI's biggest customer and for which it also supplies satellite earth terminals. CMI is one of the few outside suppliers to American Telephone & Telegraph Co.'s Long Lines Department.

AT&T has done two major rebuilds of its microwave system over the past five years. For the first rebuild, CMI received 90 percent of the business, with AT&Ts own Western Electric the standby supplier, McCabe notes. "That indicates the degree to which AT&T depends on CMI," he says.

"The next stage will be AT&T putting in single-sideband radio, and my bet is that CMI will end up putting in most of it," McCabe continues. "That's going to drag on for six or seven years, so CMI's outlook is quite good for that part of its business."

Through its defense products, CMI also has a close working rela-

ILLUSTRATION 15–9 (*continued*)

Looking up at California Microwave

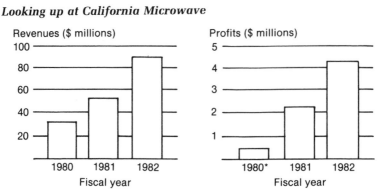

Revenues ($ millions) Profits ($ millions)

Fiscal year Fiscal year

Note: Chart updated to reflect full-year results.
* 1980 profits were affected adversely by a pretax writedown of $2 million and accelerated production startup-costs for a new product line.
Source: California Microwave Inc.

tionship with the U.S. government, another major customer. "CMI's good at what it does, and it's still a small company with a lot of growth ahead," McCabe believes. "It's selling products to those pipelines now, and the trick is to develop new products to sell through existing pipelines and new products for new pipelines."

Analyst Bruce Seltzer of San Francisco investment firm Hambrecht & Quist considers CMI "an important innovator" in microwave-telecommunications equipment for both commercial and defense markets. He emphasizes the company's successful expansion of its capabilities from its core signal-source business into new, related microwave-product areas.

These include analog microwave-radio-modernization systems, commercial and defense satellite communications, digital earth terminals, digital (or T-carrier) telecommunications instrumentation, defense radar instrumentation, and electronic intelligence equipment.

CMI's sales strategy centers on a dedicated marketing approach to customers requiring large volumes in dollars and a close working relationship to develop products for their needs. In CMI's three product areas—telecommunications, satellite communications, and government electronics—that strategy keys on customers such as AT&T and various departments and agencies of the U.S. government, with emphasis on the sale of systems rather than components or subsystems.

Until last year, telecommunications was CMI's largest sales sector. In fiscal 1981, it accounted for 33 percent of CMI's revenues, down from 47 percent the year before and 54 percent in 1979. Seltzer foresees telecommunications bounding back to a 48 percent share of sales in the current year.

Surpassing telecommunications to become CMI's top revenue producer in fiscal 1981 was satellite communications. It accounted for 43 percent of last year's sales, up from 15 percent in 1980 and in

ILLUSTRATION 15–9 (*concluded*)

1979. Behind the segment's performance was CMI's 1980 acquisition of the remaining interest in Satellite Transmission Systems Inc. (STS), a supplier of turnkey digital satellite earth stations, and increased sales of satellite receive-only earth stations and two-way voice terminals. This year, satellite-communications revenue's probably will make up 32 percent of CMI's total.

Government defense communications, CMI's third product area, accounted for 24 percent of 1981 sales, compared with 38 percent the prior year, 31 percent in 1979, and an expected 20 percent this year. In CMI's earlier years, its government business was as much as 60 percent to 80 percent of the total. Leeson would like it to settle at 35 percent. He says CMI stands to gain from the Reagan Administration's proposed major increases in U.S. defense spending: "The parts of the defense budget we relate to are the communications and intelligence sectors, and those aren't subject to the wild variations you see, for example, in weapons systems," Leeson says.

Expanding the Customer Base

Last October, STS was picked by Citibank to supply the major satellite earth stations for its corporate satellite-transmission network. Completion of the first four Citibank earth stations is set for September. Communications services will include voice, message record, data and teleconferencing.

Leeson foresees CMI expanding its business in corporate satellite networks similar to the one being set up for Citibank and for other companies with enough capital to install their own equipment. He also foresees selling to AT&T competitors, such as MCI, and looks to a pickup in business from cable and network TV program originators by supplying satellite terminals. Over the past year, CMI's sales to the cable TV industry were only 5 percent to 10 percent of the total. But the Associated Press is a big customer for small satellite terminals, and Leeson predicts that eventually "just about every newspaper will have one of ours."

McCabe of Dean Witter sees CMI earning around 83 cents a share this year on sales of about $90 million, rising to a net of $1.10 a share and sales of $110 million in fiscal 1983. Leeson doesn't argue with those projections, but he doesn't offer his own forecasts either. The outlook for the communications industry is healthy, and although it's holding its own through economic recession, Leeson is cautious and restrains his optimism. He doesn't intend to let expectations get out of hand again.

Arthur Garcia

Source: Reprinted from *Electronics Business*, August 1982.

increase in value in three and a quarter years—a compound rate of return of 97 percent per year. It is the classic story of a Super Company at a low price—a Super Stock.

Everybody Loves a Happy Ending

The final pages of this case history (Illustration 15–9) show an article from *Electronic Business* depicting California Microwave's shiny bright future. As we've seen—things weren't always so shiny at California Microwave's beachhead. Every kid raised on the California coast knows it takes the right conditions to get surfers into the water. It takes a low PSR to ride the California Microwave wave. But what a ride.

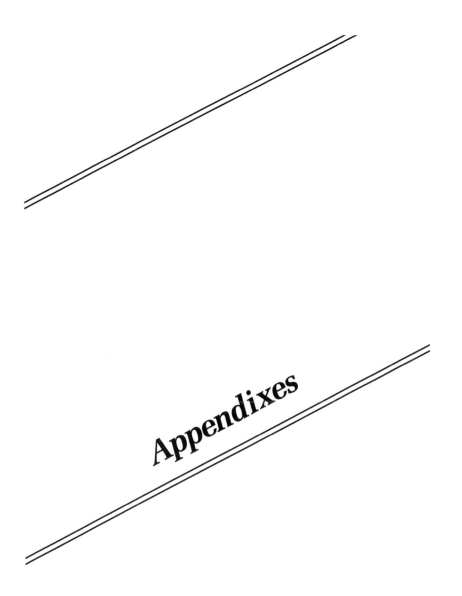

Appendixes

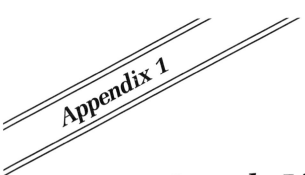

A Sample List of 35 Standard Questions Asked while Interviewing Managements

The following list is not meant to be all-inclusive. These are questions which regularly get asked of management in the course of interviewing them. Other questions more specific to the company almost always need be asked. Still other questions come to mind in the course of the meeting and need be asked at the spur of the moment.

Introductory

1. Who follows your company from the financial community, and what do you see as their attitude toward the company?
2. Please draw a basic organization chart showing how the business is organized and what functional responsibilities report to each key officer.

Marketing

3. Please break down your markets by product type.
4. Why do customers buy your products over those of your competitors?
5. What level of technology exists in your products—what is the technology employed at your company?
6. How is the selling effort conducted—how are the sales made?

7. From the time an initial customer prospect is identified, how long does it take to close the sale?
8. Are there any important sectors of your market which you don't address?
9. What is your market share by product area, and what are the shares of your leading competitor—and who do you view as your strongest competitors?
10. How does your market share compare now with several years ago?
11. Are there any new entrants into your markets in the last two years?
12. How does pricing vary by product—has price cutting been a significant factor in the past?
13. Is there any significant amount of revenues derived from servicing your customer base other than as shown in the income statement?
14. What is the quarterly history of orders and backlog (only asked if not disclosed in publicly available information)?
15. Is there any seasonality to the business other than as reflected in orders and backlog?
16. Please list approximate level of sales in the top five foreign countries in which you do business and among your top five customers.
17. Is the marketing effort conducted any differently overseas?
18. Describe the process at your company through which a product idea passes as it moves from initial inception to initial shipments.
19. How much do your typical salespeople earn, and how much of that is based on sales commission?
20. How long has your typical salesperson been with the firm, and where did he or she come to you from? How did you recruit this person?

Overview/Strategic

21. What is the long-term objective of the company?
22. What are your long-term objectives for profit margins, and how do you intend to achieve those goals?
23. Over the next few years, how would you expect the components of your income statement to change in relation to each other?
24. Should I expect to see major acquisitions or divestitures as part of your plan for the next several years?
25. Do you envision any major functional additions to the senior management staff?

26. Please review each member of senior management indicating what things they are strongest and weakest in. For instance, if Joe Blow, the president, is strongest in marketing, which area is he next strongest in and which area is he weak in.
27. What are your plans for capital expenditures for the next few years, and what specific product areas do you plan to stress?
28. If any of your top officers have left the company in the last few years (check by looking in 10-K), why did they leave and where did they go?
29. Which are your most active members of the board of directors and which are the least active? (While you may think managements would be hesitant to answer this, I have seldom found it to be so.)
30. (This is only asked if not available in public information.) Please review the number of employees by each functional area:

	This Year	Last Year
R&D		
Marketing		
Field sales		
Service		
Production		
Finance		
Other		

Miscellaneous but Important

31. Will research expense as a percentage of sales be greater or less than it currently is in future quarters and years?
32. What areas are you currently spending your money on in R&D?
33. How much of cost of goods sold represents purchases of finished goods and how much represents in-house fabrication and assembly?
34. Is there any crucial part or component with only one or two vendors which could become in short supply?
35. What questions should I have asked that I didn't? (If they can't come up with one or more they are either not bright or not forthright—I've never yet been able to cover all the bases without prompting.)

Appendix 2

TABLE A2–1
Relationships between Price Sales Ratios and Size of Companies Covered in the H&Q Statistical Summary of February 1983

Last 12 Months' Annual Revenue	Number of Companies with Price Sales Ratios between:									Total
	0–.99	1–1.99	2–2.99	3–3.99	4–4.99	5–5.99	6–9.99	10–20	20+	
$0–$50 million	4	4	10	4	0	2	9	3*	1†	37
$50–$100 million	1	6	6	5	1	1	3‡	0	0	23
$100–$200 million	4	6	5	1	3	1§	0	0	0	20
$200–$300 million	1	3	0	0	0	0	0	0	0	4
$300–$400 million	1	1	1	3	0	0	0	0	0	6
$400–$500 million	1	3	1	0	0	0	0	0	0	5
$500–$600 million	1	0	0	0	0	0	0	0	0	3
$600–$1,000 million	1	1	1‖	1#	1**	0	0	0	0	6
Over $1 billion	8	5	2††	1‡‡	0	0	0	0	0	16
Total	22	29	26	15	5	4	12	3	1	120

* Genentech, Home Health Care, and Intecom
† Centocor
‡ Cullinet, Seagate, and Convergent Tech
§ Tandon
‖ Intel
Apple
** MCI
†† HP and AMP
‡‡ Wang

TABLE A2–2
Relationships between Price Sales Ratios and Size of Companies Covered in the H&Q Statistical Summary of May 1983

Last 12 Months' Annual Revenue	Number of Companies with Price Sales Ratios between:									
	0–.99	1–1.99	2–2.99	3–3.99	4–4.99	5–5.99	6–9.99	10–20	20+	Total
$0–$50 million	2	6	9	3	2	2	8	9	2*	43
$50–$100 million	0	8	3	6	1	0	5	1†	0	24
$100–$200 million	2	5	5	4	3	1‡	1§	0	0	21
$200–$300 million	1	3	2	0	0	1‖	0	0	0	7
$300–$400 million	1	3	1	2	0	0	0	0	0	7
$400–$500 million	0	1	2	0	0	0	0	0	0	3
$500–$600 million	1	2	0	0	1**	0	0	0	0	3
$600–$1,000 million	1	2	1#	0	1††	0	1††	0	0	6
Over $1 billion	3	9	2‡‡	1§§	0	0	0	0	0	15
Total	11	39	25	16	7	4	15	10	2	129

* Centocor and Apollo Computer
† Convergent Tech
‡ Intergraph
§ Diasonics
‖ Tandon
Intel
** Apple
†† MCI
‡‡ HP and AMP
§§ Wang

The One that Almost Got Away

By Kathleen K. Wiegner

Verbatim is a classic example of how quickly a promising company can outgrow its founders. Moral: An imaginative scientist can be a lousy executive.

For five years prior to 1979, Reid Anderson's Verbatim Corp. turned in the kind of dazzling performance that makes small, high-technology companies so sexy. Sales grew from $4.3 million to $36 million, earnings from $260,000 to $2.3 million. Return on equity averaged well over 30 percent, with debt a mere 6 percent of total capital. No wonder that when Verbatim went public in 1979 the stock quickly rose from 17 to 29, a hefty 23 times earnings.

But then, suddenly, the magic went away. By 1981 net had dropped to $1 million, return on equity was only 6.6 percent, debt was 45 percent of total capital, and the stock sold for just $12. What went wrong with Verbatim? It's a familiar story. Founder Anderson says success made him complacent.

Verbatim makes flexible computer storage disks, floppies as they are called in the trade. Floppies resemble thin plastic 45 rpm records. Inside a small computer, however, these shiny black "records" play very sophisticated tunes, since a floppy's magnetized surface can be encoded with instructions. While the smaller floppies cannot store as much information as magnetic tape reels, they are cheaper, quicker and easier to use, and thus they make ideal storage units for desk-top computers and word processors.

Some $500 million worth of floppies were sold last year, and that figure is expected to double by 1985. Customers range from small software companies and personal computer makers, like Apple and Tandy, all the way up to big mainframe manufacturers like IBM, Burroughs, and Digital Equipment. Kids even buy floppies to copy a friend's video game, since a blank disk goes for only around $5 at retail, versus, say, $30 for a prerecorded game. Of the more than 20 companies that sell floppies—including 3M, Memorex, Dysan, and, to a limited degree, IBM—Verbatim, with over 23 percent market share, is the largest.

Reid Anderson started Verbatim when he was 51 and had spent 24 years working for others in corporate research laboratories. Seventeen of those years were at Bell Laboratories, the ivoriest of towers, working on electronic switching and storage devices. He also spent two years at NCR and five more at Stanford Research Institute developing new products. His credentials as an electronic engineer were impeccable, but he was an unlikely entrepreneur.

It was at SRI that Anderson then 46, got bitten by the start-your-own-company bug. "We were developing products, essentially starting new businesses for various companies. So I decided to do it myself. I'd thought about it back when I was at Bell Labs and then at NCR, but when you're in a big company like that you kind of get comfortable and don't take risks." Smaller, more entrepreneurial SRI shook him out of his lethargy, however. All of which shows that it's never too late.

An amateur musician who plays the clarinet, Anderson had designed a transistorized metronome/tuner. Inspired by what others had been able to do with the products he developed at SRI, he decided to go into business for himself making metronomes for fellow musicians. After being in business just three years, however, he discovered that he had saturated his tiny market. After that he went into partnership with Ray Jacobson, a business consultant, making acoustic data couplers, devices that permit computer data to be transmitted over dial telephone lines. Meanwhile, Anderson, remembering the work he had done at Bell Labs, decided that magnetized tape in cassettes would replace paper tapes. His partner didn't go along, so Anderson left Anderson-Jacobson. He took out a loan, and with money from several relatives and friends, he started making data cassettes as Information Terminals (later renamed Verbatim).

But Anderson soon discovered that he was in the wrong product. Data cassettes themselves would soon be replaced by faster 8-inch floppy disks, introduced by IBM in 1973, just four years after Verbatim's founding. Anderson asked IBM if he could license the new floppy disk technology. IBM, more interested in selling million-dollar computers than $5 disks, said yes. Verbatim was off and running.

By 1979, at age 62, Anderson was worth $14.7 million on paper.

But then came the almost fatal complacency. By 1981, Anderson was in trouble. Verbatim's problems started with a small oversight. Every floppy disk comes in a black plastic jacket, lined with a soft lubricated cloth-like liner that protects the disk and keeps it flexible. Verbatim changed the liner material for the jackets without doing proper testing. The new liner caused disks to fail after a short period of use because they absorbed too much lubricant, causing the disks to dry out.

Then the mistake was compounded when the company changed the chemical coating on the disks' magnetic surface. That caused Verbatim floppies to wear out even faster. The only solution was a massive recall. In 1980 and 1981, the company was forced to establish a $1.5 million reserve against returns.

Fortunately, the problems were concentrated in Verbatim's slower-growing line of 8-inch floppies. Its newer 5¼-inch line was unaffected. But market share in 8-inch floppies dropped from around 45 percent to 15 percent and has never recovered.

Clearly there was something seriously wrong. Anderson had not installed adequate controls. New designs had been rushed into production without adequate testing. Customers' orders got mixed up. Some delivery schedules were missed altogether. Anderson's penchant for straying off into new technologies had the company heavily committed to an expensive development program. That involved the more costly rigid disk that can store larger amounts of information in equivalent space. Trouble was, the computer makers themselves decided to make rigid disks. So did the Japanese.

In fiscal 1980 (ended June 30) the company took a $2.3 million write-off on rigid disks. Earnings dropped 43 percent for that year alone. Verbatim's board finally acted. They brought in Malcolm Northrup, a seasoned technology manager from Rockwell International's semiconductor division, as chief executive in January 1981. Anderson, who still owns over 20 percent of the stock, was left with only his chairman's title. Says Northrup: "The company needed leadership, new controls, a management structure."

To provide that, Northrup brought in a new vice president of marketing from Memorex, one of Verbatim's competitors. Verbatim's manufacturing and testing procedures were automated. A new high-quality disk brand named Datalife was introduced with a five-year warranty, a first for the industry. The medicine worked. Once known as a low-cost volume producer of disks, Verbatim began to acquire a reputation even among its formerly disenchanted customers as a top-quality producer. Soon Northrup had the company back on track. Verbatim closed out its 1982 fiscal year with sales of $85 million, up from $54 million the previous year, and with income at a healthy $9 million, up from $1 million.

The founder is gone now, and Northrup, at 43, is running the company. His job is no sinecure. Verbatim has its hands full staying on top of fast-changing technology. At the moment, the small computer industry is all abuzz about another downward-size shift—to 3-inch or 3½-inch disks. Northrup thinks that the most serious threat in this potential market will come from the Japanese. Companies like

Hitachi Maxell, TDK, Sony, and Fuji Photo Film, which are all experienced in making magnetic tape, have been talking about getting into the floppy business as a logical extension of their product line. If they were to grab significant market share during the downshift to smaller disks, Verbatim could be stranded with dominance only in older lines.

So Northrup, while keeping a sharp eye on costs, is committing 6 percent of sales this year to R&D, increasing to 9 percent of sales over the next five years, and spending in excess of $10 million for a fully automated plant in North Carolina, which will eventually make these new microdisks. To finance all this, Northrup will have to keep his debt up and may have to make a fresh trip to the equity markets.

And what of Anderson, the man who started it all? He is spending most of his time with several start-up companies he has invested in. "If I saw something really exciting, I might do another company," he says a bit wistfully. But perhaps next time he will be smart enough to let someone else run it for him.

Making Material Progress

My own experiences reinforced my thinking about the relative importance of marketing over research. I had been a significant investor in Material Progress Corporation (MPC, Santa Rosa, California) when it had gone separate ways from its president at a heated board meeting. There was no logical choice from among the existing employees to run the firm. The board of directors, most of whom were not local, chose to seek a permanent president, chairman, and chief executive through a formal executive search. Unfortunately, that would take many months. I was asked to act on a part-time basis as chairman and chief executive officer during the interim.

My first function was to initiate the search for my replacement. During an executive search, you never can know how long it will take or even if you will be able to find a suitable candidate. I had to be prepared for the worst—that I might be responsible for this company's stewardship for a long, long time. My first act was to hire David Powell, Inc., a leading West Coast executive-search firm. Then I began to examine the condition of what I had to work with in the company.

MPC was hemorrhaging profusely. Sales had dropped off, and losses had swelled to more than $80,000 per month. There were no new products to shore up the situation, either. There was absolutely no formal research or engineering function. Engineering was undertaken to an extent—but with no sense of organization. MPC made sophisticated electronic materials. It wanted to expand existing technology into new market areas (some had been defined, some were yet to be conceived). Within existing product lines, technology was good but not great.

My job was much easier due to the presence of an able vice president of technology. By giving him very specific goals and a little coaching in how to deal with certain people, we were able in two months to create a formal engineering function with three major developmental projects. We fairly quickly honed some very elegant technology for our existing markets. Over the ensuing months, we added several more projects. But none had enough potential—our markets were so small. The markets had not been well thought out initially. The company needed more.

The company considered itself a "crystal growth" company, serving sophisticated crystalline electronic materials markets. It produced exotic-sounding products like "Gadolineum Gallium Garnet" and "Yttrium Aluminum Garnet." Crystals were grown in high-temperature furnaces, then fabricated into precise forms required by customers. Fabrication was dominated by a proprietary skill developed at MPC known as "double-sided polishing"—polishing small plates to a very flat parallel plane. They had to have outstanding surface quality. Tolerances were exceptional—measured in microns. While the company did a fine job of growing the crystals, I saw that its reputation was based on and dependent on quality fabrication.

A mediocre crystal with outstanding fabrication was preferable in the customers' eyes to an outstanding crystal with mediocre fabrication qualities. (It was a little like machined steel parts: A tiny variance in the carbon content of the steel is less important than the part fitting perfectly.) I saw that we did outstanding work in fabrication. We shouldn't think in terms of markets for crystal and of ourselves as crystal growers.

We needed, instead, to find markets for products that could be polished. After spreading this message throughout the company, we quickly evolved the idea for polishing 5¼-inch magnetic Winchester memory disks. This market alone was larger than all of the company's other markets put together. And, here, we had something proprietary. I didn't conceive of the idea for disks. I contributed the notion of how to posture ourselves in relation to potential markets. Then the employees did the rest.

From the time the idea was generated, it took only a year or so to come to market—so the technological development obviously was not difficult. Most of that year was spent making sure that the market was well understood. Through customer evaluations—direct feedback, we made sure that our product was really unique. Only through interaction with our potential customers' customers would we be certain that the market was as large as we believed and that we unquestionably understood pricing.

Our recruiters at David Powell, Inc., finally located an ideal president for us, and I was relieved of my responsibilities. Polishing 5¼-inch disks is now the prime business at MPC. All that was necessary was the right perception of ourselves in terms of markets and marketing. We could have spent developmental money forever in our existing crystal markets and never gotten far. By understanding a market opportunity, we were able to leverage our research dollars. Marketing, not technology, was the key.

Appendix 5

A Case History Yet to Come

I've had a vision—a fantasy, maybe even a nightmare. Envision one of the little high-technology, high-PSR wonder stocks. It sells at more than 10 times sales. Maybe it's Convergent Technology. Maybe it's Digital Switch or Intecom. At headquarters sits a chief executive who is impatient for success.

Mr. Big. He dutifully put in his time—years at graduate school earning degrees in both business and electrical engineering. Then he struggled up through the ranks at Integrated Bogus Makers, working in all the different phases of their worldwide empire. Finally, he started his own company. He named it Digicom Conswitchtronics. They make computer software for biogeneticists who want to clone antibodies into networks providing future artificial computer intelligence. The market is very small, but *High Technology* magazine said it's the hottest thing since sliced bread.

The company only did $50 million in sales last year. But the stock market must have read *High Technology* because it values Digicom at $600 million (spelled PSR = 12+). On paper, Mr. Big is worth a lot. In reality, he knows he can't sell much stock without making it crumble. After all, if the president won't own the stock, who will? Mr. Big knows he owns the future. Someday Digicom will be a huge concern. But why should he have to wait? He wants the world and he wants it now.

Back at "biz" school, he was great pals with Mr. Medium. Medium is still at Integrated Bogus Makers. In fact, Mr. Medium is one

230

of their top troubleshooters. When they have problems with a division, they send in Mr. Medium to fix things up faster than you can say "IBM." Mr. Big always thought quite highly of Mr. Medium. In fact, he wishes he could hire Medium just to have him on the Digicom team. He wants the world and he wants it now.

Suddenly an idea comes to Mr. Big. He develops a plan and code names it Operation Blitz. He calls in Medium and offers him a vice presidency and more options than you can stack on a medium-size desk. With Medium committed, he puts Operation Blitz in place. He hires a small West Coast investment-management firm to identify all publicly held industrial manufacturers that:

Are between $50 and $150 million in sales.

Have PSRs between 0.0 and 0.15.

Aren't currently controlled by a plurality shareholder group.

With that list in hand, Mr. Big picks out 10 targets. They each look a little doggy. They are all losing money and each has a significant amount of debt. Together, the 10 make a package that Mr. Big thinks should fit together. He takes the package to his corporate attorney, Mr. Clean, and announces he would like to buy these companies. He wants to take them over completely. Mr. Clean says "fine." Clean asks which he wants to buy first and how he expects to finance the acquisitions. (Mr. Big was always a little concerned about Mr. Clean.) Slowly, but with authority, Big states he wants to buy them all, on the same day, seven days from now, for paper—in a stock swap.

Mr. Clean instantly has a heart attack. After the funeral, Mr. Big hires another attorney. On Tuesday, he moves. At 9 A.M. PST, Digicom announces a joint tender offer for 10 companies—they will form the nucleus of its new industrial division to be run by a new corporate vice president—Mr. Medium (who just announced his resignation from Integrated Bogus Makers).

Together, the 10 companies in the package have revenues of $1 billion. They have a market value of $100 million. Digicom offers to bid them up 50 percent in value with $150 million worth of newly created (just for this event) shares. Many stockholders of these companies never, ever thought they would be able to get out from under these dogs. The tender is warmly received by shareholders—if not by the managers of the 10 companies.

Overnight, Mr. Big has become the chief executive of a billion-dollar empire. Overnight, the chief of enforcement at the Securities and Exchange Commission has his own heart attack and is never heard from again. Mr. Big has hired his old buddy Mr. Medium as he always wished. Mr. Medium has his marching orders—clean up the

Sleeping Dogs. Mr. Big has accomplished all of this while giving away less than 25 percent of Digicom's stock. "Not a bad little maneuver," he thinks to himself. Digicom is immediately a company with $1,050,000,000 in revenues and a market value of $750 million. It has a PSR of 0.75 like a lot of other billion-dollar companies. Mr. Big is quite satisfied.

Two years later, Mr. Medium has cleaned up the industrial division. Forever after, these companies earn 5 percent after-tax margins for Digicom—more than its previous total sales. Forever after, Digicom maintains a PSR of 0.75. Everyone is better off and no one is hurt. Everybody forgets all about those little "antibodies" that Digicom was originally cloned to make. In six years, the name is changed from Digicom Conswitchtronics to DC Industries. Decades later, at his retirement dinner, Mr. Big comments how he managed DC through his founding philosophy of planned growth. After the dinner, everyone rides off into the sunset together and lives happily ever after on the dividends.

It couldn't happen, you say? Similar cases happened over the decades in slightly less-dramatic form. The high-flying conglomerations of the 1960s were large-scale attempts to make a big silk purse from a lot of sows' ears. Among those sows' ears lying in the stock market's garbage dump are future bonanzas just waiting to be picked up. They could be picked up by takeover artists or at the time of rising prices when the financial community decides they weren't all such dogs after all. Either way, wise purchasers will come more and more to view low Price Sales Ratio stocks as fertile fields in which to seek potential opportunities.

Appendix 6

Amendments to the Constitution

Everything in *Super Stocks*, so far, was completed in September 1983. Since then, technology stocks have tumbled. At the same time, PSR research has continued full speed at Fisher Investments—particularly research oriented toward nontechnology issues. This appendix is included to update you on some recent findings. It should further convince you of the merits of PSRs when you see some interesting facts we've uncovered since the book was first written.

The Popularity Monitor

We've found it necessary to focus the bottom end of the PSR scale even lower than referred to in Chapter 6. This is consistent with findings in Chapter 7. Along the way, something interesting popped up. Since PSRs are an almost perfect popularity monitor, we came up with the following table, showing various levels of popularity associated with different levels of PSRs. The table breaks stocks into three categories. First are small technology/growth-oriented companies, like those discussed throughout *Super Stocks*. Then there are big, multibillion-dollar companies coupled with smaller companies in industries without growth attributes—the PSRs of these two groups are lumped together. Finally, responding to suggestion, we have added PSRs of ultra-thin-margin companies—companies whose basic product lines are inherently low-profit-margin activities, such as supermarkets or distributors.

The Popularity Monitor

	Stocks Are:		
	Very Unpopular, with PSRs Less than	Accepted, with PSRs over	Very Popular, with PSRs over
If companies are:			
Small, growth oriented or technology type	0.75	1.50	3.00
Multibillion-dollar-sales sized or without growth attributes	0.20	0.40	0.80
Inherently thin margin, such as supermarkets	0.03	0.06	0.12

These numbers were empirically derived. The interesting thing in each case is that the PSR doubles between steps of popularity. The absolute scale of PSR/popularity seems consistent—two doublings as stocks rise from obscurity to high regard. I have no explanation for this and report it merely as an interesting observation, worthy of further consideration.

The 10 Biggest Winners and Losers of the September 30, 1983 Quarter

On October 4, 1983, the "Heard on the Street" column in *The Wall Street Journal* reported the 10 biggest winners and losers for the quarter ended September 30, 1983. We looked at their PSRs at the beginning of the quarter, July 1, 1983. We calculated PSRs based on reported sales of the last 12 months, with the stock price and number of shares of stock outstanding on July 1, 1983. All information was obtained from either Standard & Poor's or Moody's. The results were fascinating and are shown in Table A6–1.

Note that most companies were losing money at the beginning of the period, so their price-earnings ratios were meaningless. Many others had rather high P/Es. At the same time, the 10 biggest winners started with PSRs ranging from 0.16 to 1.86, with an average of 0.60. The 10 biggest losers ranged in PSRs from 0.88 to 158.01, with an average of 3.61. We looked for a comparable list at year-end, but "Heard on the Street" didn't run one.

The Forbes Study

In January 1984, *Forbes* ran a piece in their statistical spotlight entitled "Who's Where in the Stock Market." From it we culled the top

TABLE A6–1
Third Quarter 1983 Stock Performance

		Percent Change	June 30, 1983 Price	Number of Shares (millions)	June 30, 1983 Market Value ($ millions)	June 30, 1983 Revenues ($ millions)	June 30, 1983 P/S Ratio	June 30, 1983 P/E Ratio
10 biggest winners:								
O	Meridian Bancorporation	89	$32.75	6.679	$ 218.74	$ 381.00	0.57	6.62*
A	Designcraft Jewel Industries	84	6.25	1.149	7.18	13.79	0.52	19.00
O	Shopsmith	68	9.50	1.368	13.00	72.02	0.18	(def)
O	American Diagnostics	67	3.75	1.451	5.44	2.93	1.86	(def)*
N	Kysor Industrial	66	13.13	2.898	38.04	122.52	0.31	(def)
O	Advance circuits	59	4.63	3.008	13.91	22.43	0.62	(def)
O	Louisiana Land Offshore Exploration	59	6.38	9.696	61.81	50.58	1.22	10.00
N	Carrols Development	54	13.00	3.103	40.34	85.17	0.47	16.00
N	G. Heileman Brewing	50	26.50	26.510	702.62	894.80	0.79	14.00
N	Hesston	48	11.38	3.388	38.54	243.65	0.16	(def)
	Total group				$1,139.61	$1,888.89	0.60	
10 biggest losers:								
O	National Data Communications	76	$ 5.75	2.433	$ 13.99	$ 14.88	0.94	24.00
O	Cencor	75	50.25	1.339	67.28	76.40	0.88	27.00
O	Unidata Systems	71	5.25	3.702	19.44	.12	158.01	(def)*
O	Victor Technology	70	14.25	16.270	231.78	116.82	1.98	(def)
O	Computer Devices	70	12.38	2.798	34.63	20.74	1.67	(def)
O	Tocom	69	10.00	7.023	70.23	25.47	2.76	(def)
O	Camseal	67	5.75	9.199	52.89	.44	120.21	(def)*
A	Telesphere International	66	20.75	9.699	201.25	20.49	9.82	182.96*
O	Wicat Systems	64	18.00	20.340	366.19	25.30	14.47	(def)*
A	American Medical Buildings	63	24.50	4.419	108.27	21.95	4.93	(def)
	Total group				$1,165.95	$ 322.60	3.61	

* P/E ratios were calculated from raw data. All others were taken from Standard & Poor's Stock Guide.

20 performing industrial stocks of the five years from 1979 through 1983. We went back and calculated PSRs at January 1979. These companies all had 1978 sales greater than $50 million. Unfortunately, we couldn't get quarterly data in 1979 for many of them. Accordingly, we extrapolated quarterly sales where necessary, assuming annual sales increases or decreases occurred evenly quarter-to-quarter. This would never be strictly true, but it is a good estimate and closer to the fact than anything else available.

For example, consider a company with a January 31 fiscal year. Assume sales of $100 million as of January 31, 1978 and $120 million as of January 31, 1979. We assumed the most current information at year-end would have been their third-quarter results ending October 31, 1978. Not having these actual numbers, we assumed the $20 million year-to-year sales increase occurred equally over the year. Hence we assumed the last 12 months sales ending October 31, 1978 would have been $115 million. Table A6–2 shows the results.

TABLE A6–2

Stock	Five-Year Percentage Increase	January 1979 PSR	December 1983 PSR	Annual 1978 Sales ($ Millions)
Pulte Home	2,885%	0.079	0.829	$ 271
Subaru of America	1,637	0.058	0.536	441
Toys R Us	1,522	0.303	1.981	394
MCI Communications	1,433	0.601	3.044	120
Wal-Mart Stores	1,386	0.292	0.466	1,161
Limited	1,307	0.466	1.715	212
Coleco Industries	1,236	0.167	0.499	129
Zayre	993	0.033	0.373	1,511
Anixter Brothers	881	0.136	0.845	215
Wang Labs	838	1.562	2.910	229
Chicago & Northwestern	830	0.094	0.945	723
Bergen Brunswig	821	0.045	0.243	456
Rose's Stores	800	0.048	0.352	491
Oxford Industries	796	0.112	0.482	238
Stop & Shop	740	0.035	0.243	1,850
Bershire Hathaway	729	0.663	5.786	245
G. Heileman Brewing	728	0.200	0.746	500
Varian Associates	726	0.247	1.646	401
Electronic Data Systems	724	1.090	3.405	224
VF Corporation	697	0.315	1.048	530

Note that 11 of these 20 best performing stocks started 1979 with PSRs of 0.20 or less. Another four started with PSRs between 0.20 and 0.35. Only two started 1979 with PSRs greater than 0.75. The other three spread out rather evenly between 0.35 and 0.75. Eight of these 20, including the top two, had PSR multiple expansions of 700 percent or more. Pulte Home's PSR multiple, for example, expanded 1050 percent, more than tenfold, from 0.079 to 0.829. Twelve of these 20, including the top four, had PSR multiple expansions of 500 percent or more. Some, like Zayre, had PSR multiple expansions greater than their stock price increases. This is because the PSR reflects market capitalization, fully adjusting for dilution from any new shares issued.

Obviously, if a stock's PSR multiple is to expand 500 to 1,000 percent, it has to start quite low or end up quite high. All but two stocks had PSR multiple expansions of 300 percent or more. One of those two was Wang Labs, which started with the list's highest PSR. This demonstrates that stock appreciation usually involves becoming more popular. Becoming more popular seems easier if you start out unpopular. What irony.

DJIA Stocks in 1983

In early 1984, a lot of interest was developing in unpopular stocks. It is becoming common to view low P/Es as synonomous with low popularity. I have nothing against the low P/E school and view low P/Es as a viable way to seek above-average reward at below-average risk. Still, low P/Es are not a strong measure of popularity. P/Es are too elastic. We looked at the Dow Jones Industrial Averages, made up of well-known big companies.

Table A6–3 on page 230 shows the percentage gains for each of the DJIA stocks during 1983. That is to say, International Harvester rose 177 percent between January 1, 1983 and December 31, 1983, and Goodyear Tire fell 14 percent. I also list their January 1983 P/E as taken from *Standard and Poor's Stock Guide*. The sales numbers used in calculating January 1983 PSRs were taken from quarterly data from *Value Line*—again, using then-reported last 12 months' results. Percents are rounded to the nearest whole. U.S. Steel, for instance, slightly outperformed DuPont.

Note when looking over the list:

	Had PSRs Ranging from	Had Average PSRs of
The top:		
5 performing stocks	0.03 to 0.17	0.12
10 performing stocks	0.03 to 0.52	0.21
The worst:		
5 performing stocks	0.29 to 1.39	0.82
10 performing stocks	0.15 to 2.07	0.83

We wanted to compare the low-quartile PSR versus P/E stocks. Unfortunately, there were too many with P/Es of eight to cull the low

TABLE A6–3
1983 Percentage Gains, PSRs, and P/Es of the DJIA

		1983 Percent Gains	January 1, 1983 PSR	January 1, 1983 P/E
1.	International Harvester	177%	0.03*	deficit
2.	Allied Corporation	72	0.17*	5*
3.	American Can	52	0.13*	25
4.	Bethlehem Steel	47	0.14*	deficit
5.	U.S. Steel	45	0.12*	deficit
6.	DuPont (E.I.)	45	0.25	9
7.	Aluminum Co. of America	45	0.52	deficit
8.	Westinghouse	41	0.35	8*
9.	Woolworth	36	0.14*	10
10.	Owens-Illinois	32	0.21	8*
11.	General Foods	30	0.24	8*
12.	American Brands	29	0.39	7*
13.	United Technologies	28	0.23	9
14.	IBM	27	1.79	13
15.	Exxon	26	0.25	6*
16.	Inco	26	0.76	deficit
17.	General Electric	24	0.81	12
18.	Sears Roebuck	23	0.36	13
19.	International Paper	22	0.59	16
20.	General Motors	19	0.31	18
21.	Union Carbide	19	0.40	12
22.	Texaco	16	0.15*	7*
23.	3M	10	1.33	14
24.	Merck	9	2.07	15
25.	SOCAL	9	0.29	8*
26.	AT&T	3	0.81	7*
27.	American Express	1	0.79	11
28.	Procter & Gamble	−4	0.81	12
29.	Eastman Kodak	−11	1.39	12
30.	Goodyear Tire	−14	0.29	11
Average		20	0.54	N/A

* The seven lowest PSR stocks and the nine lowest P/E stocks.

P/E list to only seven stocks. So, we could either compare the low-quartile PSR group of seven stocks to nine low P/Es or the nine lowest P/Es to the nine lowest PSRs. We did both. For your convenience, I placed asterisks (*) by the seven lowest PSR stocks and the nine lowest P/E stocks listed in Table A6–3.

The seven lowest PSR stocks averaged gains of +63.57 percent. The nine lowest PSR stocks averaged gains of +56.11 percent. The nine lowest P/E stocks averaged gains of +28.67 percent. The DJIA averaged a gain of 20.3 percent.

Any way you figure it, the low PSR stocks outperformed the low P/E stocks—by a wide margin. The low P/E stocks did outperform the DJIA as a whole.

Value Line *Composite and PSRs*

As indicated in the text, I am skeptical of attempts to time the overall market. Nevertheless, repeated requests are made for PSR measures for the whole market. We went back 15 years using *Value Line* data and constructed PSRs for the major peaks and bottoms of the market. The PSRs are calculated, as are others herein, on the basis of what would have been the last 12 months' then-reported data, extrapolated from yearly data (see example regarding the *Forbes* study). The table below shows 10 major peaks and troughs in the *Value Line* composite, along with their PSRs.

Peak/Trough	Year	Level of Composite	PSR
Peak	1968	23.4	1.07
Trough	1970	14.3	0.63
Peak	1972	28.7	1.07
Trough	1974	13.2	0.36
Peak	1976	24.5	0.55
Trough	1978	18.7	0.36
Trough	1980	22.5	0.33
Peak	1980	37.0	0.50
Trough	1982	23.1	0.29
Peak	1983	42.0	0.53
First quarter	1984	35.6	0.42

Obviously, looking at the data, something happened differently in the 1968–72 time period than thereafter. Since 1974, the *Value Line* composite peaked at PSRs between 0.50 and 0.55. In that decade it bottomed out at PSRs between 0.29 and 0.36. In early 1984, there was a raging debate as to whether the market had or had not bottomed out in early March. If the 10 prior years are any guide, it did not. But the differences between 1974–1984 as compared to 1968–72 argue for the study of composite PSRs to be carried further back into time.

Updated H&Q List

In both the text and earlier appendixes, I've compiled tables showing relationships between PSRs and size of companies covered in the Hambrecht & Quist *Statistical Summaries*. These relationships are listed again in Table A6–4, updated as of February 1984. It reflects

TABLE A6-4
Relationships between Price Sales Ratios and Size of the Companies Covered in the H&Q Statistical Summary of February 1984

Annual Revenue, Last 12 Months (millions)	Number of Companies with Price Sales Ratios between:									Total
	0–0.99	1–1.99	2–2.99	3–3.99	4–4.99	5–5.99	6–6.99	7–9.99	10+	
$0–50	7	10	11	5	5	2	1	5	9	55
$50–100	3	8	7	3	0	1	1*	1†	1‡	25
$100–200	4	9	3	4	4	1§	0	0	0	25
$200–300	3	2	3	4	0	0	0	0	0	12
$300–400	1	2	2	0	0	0	0	0	0·	5
$400–500	1	1	0	2‖	0	0	0	0	0	4
$500–600	1	3	0	0	0	0	0	0	0	4
$600–1,000	2	4	1	0	0	0	0	0	0	7
Over $1,000	7	8	2	3#	0	0	0	0	0	20
Total	29	47	29	21	9	4	2	6	10	157

* Intecom.
† Network Systems.
‡ Eagle Computer.
§ Micom Systems.
‖ AMD, Tandem.
Wang, Intel, Glaxo.

the 1983–84 market decline when compared to the May 1983 version of the market's peak. On a relative basis, such stocks as Eagle Computer, Network Systems, Intecom, Micom Systems, AMD, Tandem, Wang, Intel, and Glaxo stand out to the right of never-never land, among the stocks most richly valued for their size on a PSR basis. Stocks in similar positions on the May 1983 list later were exceptional disasters.

Conclusions

All of the work done at Fisher Investments since the text of *Super Stocks* was completed argues for the following conclusions:

1. Investors should avoid high PSR stocks.
2. Investors should seek opportunities by looking for good companies among unpopular, low-to-medium PSR stocks.
3. More research should and will be done on PSRs.

Index